Competencies for Leading in Diversity

A Case Study of National Evangelical
Associations in Africa

Aiah Dorkuh Foday-Khabenje

Langham
MONOGRAPHS

© 2016 Aiah Dorkuh Foday-Khabenje

Published 2016 by Langham Monographs
An imprint of Langham Publishing
www.langhampublishing.org

Langham Publishing and its imprints are a ministry of Langham Partnership

Langham Partnership
PO Box 296, Carlisle, Cumbria CA3 9WZ, UK
www.langham.org

ISBNs:
978-1-78368-210-2 Print
978-1-78368-211-9 ePub
978-1-78368-213-3 PDF

Aiah Dorkuh Foday-Khabenje has asserted his right under the Copyright, Designs and Patents Act, 1988 to be identified as the Author of this work.

All rights reserved. No part of this publication may be reproduced, stored in a retrieval system or transmitted, in any form or by any means, electronic, mechanical, photocopying, recording or otherwise, without the prior written permission of the publisher or the Copyright Licensing Agency.

All Scripture quotations, unless otherwise indicated, are taken from the Holy Bible, New International Version®, NIV®. Copyright ©1973, 1978, 1984, 2011 by Biblica, Inc.™ Used by permission of Zondervan.

British Library Cataloguing in Publication Data
A catalogue record for this book is available from the British Library

ISBN: 978-1-78368-210-2

Cover & Book Design: projectluz.com

Langham Partnership actively supports theological dialogue and an author's right to publish but does not necessarily endorse the views and opinions set forth, and works referenced within this publication or guarantee its technical and grammatical correctness. Langham Partnership does not accept any responsibility or liability to persons or property as a consequence of the reading, use or interpretation of its published content.

Contents

Abstract ix
Acknowledgments xi
List of Figures xiii
List of Tables xv
List of Abbreviations xvii
Chapter 1 1
   Introduction
      Purpose 9
      Research Questions 10
         Research Question #1 10
         Research Question #2 10
         Research Question #3 10
      Definition of Terms 10
         Leadership Competencies 10
         Regional President 11
         National Evangelical Association 11
         General Secretary/NEA Leader 11
         Effective NEA 11
         Proficiency Level 12
      Ministry Project 12
      Context 13
      Methodology 16
         Participants 16
         Instrumentation 18
         Data Collection 19
         Data Analysis 20
         Generalizability 20
      Theological and Biblical Foundation 21
      Overview 24
Chapter 2 25
   Literature
      Introduction 25
      Theological and Biblical Foundations 30

    Trinitarian Dimension of Unity in the Church 30
    Mission of God (*Missio Dei*) 32
    Unity and Nature of the Church 34
    Servant Leadership 38
    Biblical Basis for the NEA 42
    Overview of Association as Unique Type of Organization 45
    General Understanding and Definition 45
    History and Nature of Voluntary Associations in Africa 47
Background to Ecumenism 49
    Ancient Ecumenism 52
    Modern Ecumenism 53
Ecumenism in Africa 56
    All Africa Conference of Churches (AACC) 56
    Association of Evangelicals in Africa (AEA) 58
Leading NEA 59
Theories of Leadership 61
    Trait Approach 61
    Behavioral Approach 62
    Power-Influence Approach 62
    Situational Approach 63
    Integrative Approach 63
Styles of Leadership 63
Leadership in the African Context 64
    Need for Paradigm Shift 69
    Leadership Behavior 72
    Leadership Effectiveness 75
Leadership Competencies 78
Association Leadership Best Practice 81
Leadership Dynamics in African NEAs 83
    Structure and Organization 83
    Leadership Challenges and Distortions 84
Design of the Study 86
Summary 87

Chapter 3 91
Methodology
Problem and Purpose 91
Research Questions 92
    Research Question #1 93
    Research Question #2 93
    Research Question #3 93

    Population and Participants 94
        Instrumentation.. 97
        Expert Review... 99
        Reliability and Validity 99
    Data Collection 99
    Data Analysis 101
    Ethical Procedures... 102

Chapter 4 105
Findings
    Problem and Purpose 105
    Participants 107
        Profile of General Secretary of NEA... 110
        NEA Leadership Competencies 115
    Research Question #1 117
        Competencies for the Task of Administrating
            (Self-Described) 117
        Competencies for the Task of Connecting................................ 120
        Competencies for the Task of Representing 124
        Competencies for the Task of Equipping 128
        Core Competencies 132
        Subcompetencies 137
    Research Question #2 139
        Demographic Information of NEA General Secretaries
            in Africa 139
        Educational Qualifications of NEA General Secretaries 143
        Ranking of NEA Leadership Competencies in Order of
            Importance 145
        Comparison of the Ratings of Competencies by the Two
            Sets of Respondents.. 152
    Research Question #3 155
    Summary of Major Findings 164

Chapter 5 165
Discussion
    Major Findings 165
        Profile of the NEA Leader... 167
        The Task of the NEA General Secretary 172
        Perceived Competencies for Leading the NEA 173
        NEA Leadership Competencies in Descending Order of
            Importance 181

      Level of Proficiency in Core Competencies of Current NEA
          General Secretaries 184
    Implications of the Findings 188
    Limitations of the Study 194
    Unexpected Observations 194
    Recommendations 196
    Postscript 197

Appendix A 201
    AEA Regions: Article IX of AEA Constitution

Appendix B 203
    Request for Approval from AEA to Conduct Research

Appendix C... 205
    Consent Form for AEA Regional Presidents' Participation

Appendix D 207
    Consent Form for General Secretaries' Participation

Appendix E 209
    Questionnaire to Be Completed by AEA Regional Presidents

Appendix F 215
    Job Description: Secretary General and Chief Excutive Officer of WEA

Appendix G... 221
    Job Description: General Secretary of AEA

Appendix H 225
    General Secretaries' Ranking and Self-Assessed Proficiency Levels of Competencies Instruments

Bibliography.. 231

Abstract

The church is called as one people from diverse backgrounds to be a witness for God in the world. However, the church is divided into many factions and especially along denominational lines. Ecumenical councils or associations exist to promote collaboration and unity in the church. This research is a case study in the African-based National Evangelical Associations (NEAs), comprising the Association of Evangelicals in Africa (AEA). Although the work of the NEA is important, it was generally not well known and understood. The associations were also in various states of health and many required effective leadership. The purpose of this research was to identify leadership competencies required for leading NEAs as well as leadership development competencies of current NEA leaders in Africa by interviewing current AEA regional presidents and general secretaries.

I used an ethnographic and exploratory, mixed-method approach to gather information from the participating regional presidents and NEA general secretaries, using researcher-designed protocols to interview respondents. Review of literature, which preceded the data collection, highlighted the main tasks of the NEA leader. The various task categories of the NEA leader formed the basis for assessing NEA leadership competencies. The review focused on leadership literature as a discipline, the various elements and factors for leadership effectiveness, and the cultural nuances, especially in the African context. The theological and biblical overview in this study highlights the fact that unity of the church was mandatory and an important strategy for the witness and mission of the church. The overview also made clear the preferred style, type, and nature of leadership expected by Jesus. Exploring the leadership situation in the NEAs as important ecumenical organizations in Africa, discovering what leadership competencies prevail, and discerning how these aspects correlate with servant leadership were all of particular interest for this study.

The research was conducted in two phases; in the first phase, the views of AEA regional presidents were collated using a researcher-designed instrument for regional presidents to highlight perceived leadership competencies for leading NEA and, in phase two, the views of the NEA general secretaries with regard to importance and self-assessed proficiency levels of competency.

The findings revealed a cluster of seventeen core competencies highlighted by the AEA regional presidents. Self-assessment of proficiency levels by the general secretaries revealed a need for improvement in each competency, more so for some of the competencies than others. Applicability and use of research findings by various possible users were highlighted, and recommendations were made for further research.

Acknowledgments

This project, like the work of the national evangelical alliance, required diverse and unique skills from different individuals and groups of individuals. I want to take the opportunity to express my profound gratitude to them all. Thank you Dr Verna Lowe for skillfully facilitating the process of conceptualizing what was a puzzling thought into researchable subject matter. *Asante sana Mbwana Doctari*, Gregg Okesson, for your mentorship, guidance, and encouragement in translating what was then a conceptual framework to a researched doctoral project that would find place on the shelves of the B. L. Fisher Library at Asbury.

The Beeson experience was enriching and indelible in many ways, courtesy of the excellent Beeson Team. I am thankful to the Beeson Team for their invaluable services and support throughout the period. I am eternally grateful for a very generous Beeson Fellowship, without which I would not have been able to do this program.

My profound appreciation to my research reflection team and colleagues at AEA who complemented the support and guidance I received at Asbury. I am thankful to the AEA leadership, both AEA board and member National Alliances, for voluntarily participating in this research.

Finally, thank you my dear sweetheart and friend, Almonda (with Nornie, Ndeana, Nema, and Nafachima) for being there for me. Thank you for your graciousness when I had to be away from home for campus visits and for the time in the upper room instead of being in your company in the living room.

Thank you, God, for your grace – all the provision, people, family, and friends – you brought into my life. "Now to the King eternal, immortal, invisible, the only God, be honor and glory forever and ever. Amen" (1 Tim 1:17).

List of Figures

Figure 1.1 Structure of the Evangelical Alliance at Global, Regional, and National Levels. 15

Figure 4.1. Perceived Subject Areas of Previous Work Experience of NEA General Secretaries. 113

Figure 4.2. Competencies for Task of Administrating for NEA Leader 119

Figure 4.3. Competencies for Task of Connecting for NEA Leader 123

Figure 4.4. Competencies for Task of Representing for NEA Leader..............128

Figure 4.5. Competencies for Task of Equipping for NEA Leader 131

Figure 4.6. NEA Leadership Core Competencies..136

Figure 4.7. Age Range of NEA General Secretaries 142

Figure 4.8. Ranking of Core Competencies by NEA General Secretaries in Order of Importance..148

List of Tables

Table 2.1. Understanding EI's Components at Work 76

Table 4.1. Demographic Information of AEA Regional Presidents.................107

Table 4.2. Profile of General Secretaries of NEA 111

Table 4.3. Competencies of the NEA Leader for Task of Administrating 118

Table 4.4. Competencies of the NEA Leader for Task of Connecting 121

Table 4.5. Competencies of the NEA Leader for Task of Representing 125

Table 4.6. Competencies of NEA Leader for Task of Equipping 129

Table 4.7. Core NEA Leadership Competencies 133

Table 4.8. Subcompetencies for NEA Leadership 138

Table 4.9. Demographic Information of NEA General Secretaries (N=20) 140

Table 4.10. Age Range of NEA General Secretaries in Africa (N=20) 140

Table 4.11. Educational Qualification (Profile) of NEA General Secretaries ..144

Table 4.12. Ranking of Core NEA Leadership Competencies 146

Table 4.13. Ranking of Subcompetencies by NEA General Secretaries in Order of Importance..151

Table 4.14. Comparison between Regional Presidents' and General Secretaries' Ratings of Core NEA Leadership Competencies in Order of Importance 153

Table 4.15. Self-Assessed Proficiency Levels of NEA Leadership Core Competencies..156

Table 4.16. Self-Assessed Proficiency Levels of NEA Leadership Subcompetencies..161

List of Abbreviations

AACC	All Africa Conference of Churches
AEA	Association of Evangelicals in Africa
AEAM	Association of Evangelicals in Africa and Madagascar
ASAE	American Society of Association Executives
AT&T	American Telephone & Telegraph
CEO	Chief Executive Officer
EA	Evangelical Alliance
EFSL	Evangelical Fellowship of Sierra Leone
EI	Emotional Intelligence
IC	International Council
IRB	Institutional Review Board
NAC	North American Council
NEA	National Evangelical Association
OAU	Organization of African Unity
PACLA	Pan-African Christian Leaders Assembly
REA	Regional Evangelical Alliance
WEA	World Evangelical Alliance
WEALI	World Evangelical Alliance Leadership Institute
WCC	World Council of Churches

CHAPTER 1

Introduction

In an era fragmented by division, building and leading healthy and strong National Evangelical Associations and promoting collaboration and partnerships within the body of Christ in a nation is critical to the church's mission. As a community of believers in Jesus Christ, the church possesses unity of purpose in spite of its diversity. Unity of the followers of Christ refers both to the spiritual, invisible church and to the visible church that the world may see and believe (John 17:21). The church, a called-out community of the one God, acts as one people – the body of Christ, and with characteristic cultural and linguistic diversity it reflects God's glory and nature to the whole inhabited world. The unity of the church is consistent with the triune nature and mission of God, since the church acts as the image of God in the world.

God's instrument for evangelizing the world is a united church in which every member is engaged actively in sharing God's love and unique gifts. The early church could change the world forever because its members worked together in harmony to proclaim the gospel. The three thousand believers added to the church on the day of Pentecost were united in fellowship: "They devoted themselves to the apostles' teaching and to fellowship, to the breaking of bread and to prayer" (Acts 2:42, NIV) and "praising God and enjoying the favor of all people. And the Lord added to their number daily those who were being saved" (2:47). Different traditions, denominations, and independent churches can contribute their particular strengths and distinct characteristics to a wholesome witness as the body of Christ in a nation if they, in harmony, partner together in the gospel (Phil 1:5).

Richard J. Foster compares the different ecclesiastical denominations to tributaries flowing into a common stream, giving it strength; as such, the loss of any one tradition would deprive the greater whole of the individual tradition's richness and strength.[1] Every denomination or ecclesiastical tradition has a unique contribution without which the church is poorer. Like the streams with a common source, Christian denominations have their source in Jesus Christ, and the different ecclesiastical traditions all point to the Trinity as the source of their being and the object of their worship. Nonetheless, many of the church's challenges arise from disunity. Separatism and denominationalism, which cause disunity or division, can undermine the church's witness in the world.[2] An emotional topic, the subject of unity in the church can, in itself, cause division in the church.[3] Division and disagreement is a human tendency and develops for all sorts of reasons.

The problem of disunity is important particularly with African Christians even though the African church is experiencing phenomenal growth. Accustomed to communal cultures with strong ethnic or tribal divisions, the African church also experiences disunity emanating from the separatism and denominationalism. Such ethnic division is not complementary to the gospel message of Christ, and the harmful effects of such divisions are manifested in the many ethnic conflicts in Africa. Accordingly, the church's unity is partial and strongly dependent on family ties or tribes.[4] One local church congregation can feature several factions based on ethnicity or blood relationships rather than the bond of unity forged by the Christian creed:

> *There is one body and one Spirit, just as you were called to one hope when you were called; one Lord, one faith, one baptism, one God and Father of all, who is over all and through all and in all. (Eph 4:4–6)*

---

1. Foster, *Streams*, xv–vi.
2. Granberg-Michaelson, *From Times Square*, 27.
3. Rowland-Jones, "Global Christian," 4.
4. Kosse, "Unity of Believers," 1314.

Blood unity tends to conflict with unity of Christian confession. People have a tendency to care more for their siblings or tribal people than for other people outside of their own tribe, even if they share the same Christian faith with the other people of different tribes. For example, people have wondered why a nation that is mostly Christian could go to war and kill one another along tribal lines, as in the Rwandan Genocide in 1994 and post-election conflict in Kenya in 2007. In both these countries, the Christian population is over 90 percent and 80 percent respectively, but the conflict was along tribal or ethnic factions of Hutu and Tutsi in Rwanda and Kikuyu and Kalenjin/Luo in Kenya.

In spite of the transformational potential of the church and the daily cultural realities of African society, Christianity seems not to be impacting African society to a great extent. Jack Chalk views this lack of impact as related to the African worldviews, belief systems, and syncretic practices. According to Chalk, "where the African Christian's beliefs differ from the biblical worldview there is failure in praxis and the Christian religion is rendered ineffectual in the lives of those who claim to be Christian."[5] Alluding to the weakness of the church, Gottfried Osei-Mensah observes, "[T]he African church is a mile long but only an inch deep; swelling numerically rather than growing."[6] An increasing concern exists regarding the lack of impact exerted by a biblical worldview on African society due not only to disunity in the church but also to a dichotomy in the belief system leading to dualism and divided loyalties between Christianity and traditional belief systems.[7] Unlike the received dualistic biblical worldview of African Christians, the cultural worldview is holistic; every aspect of human life is viewed from the belief system. The research is interested in the subject of leadership and how the leader is perceived.

In order for the body of Christ to remain healthy and faithful to its mission and witness to the world, effective leaders must grapple with the problem of disunity. Such an action requires a sustained and courageous commitment by Christian leaders at all levels of the church to find a way toward rediscovering and making visible God's gift of unity. This kind of

---

5. Chalk, *Making Disciples*, 3.
6. Osei-Mensah, "Why PACLA," 21.
7. Chalk, *Making Disciples*, 119.

leadership requires a new eschatological vision for unity based on God's Trinitarian nature. Leadership in the church, as in every aspect of life in a society, is of utmost importance. Byang H. Kato underscores this critical need for the church in Africa: "While it is true that Africa needs help of many kinds, it is in the area of church leadership that evangelicals are most lacking."[8] Chalk asserts this need from a different perspective. He writes, "[T]he most significant factor contributing to syncretism is the lack of leadership at the denominational level."[9] Church documents clearly articulate Christian identity and denominational doctrinal beliefs, but they often remain silent on everyday issues of life. In such instances, local pastors often lack the foundations necessary for a strong stand on doctrinal issues when pressed by the congregation and instead resort to compromise.[10] Chalk's assertion suggests dominance of influence of followers and not the leader, contrary to the popular notion of dominance of the leader in a patriarchal society in Africa.

Ecumenical organizations such as the National Evangelical Association (NEA) symbolize the unified body of Christ within a country. While the function of the NEA varies, it generally includes creating visibility, providing a single voice for the church in the nation and connecting, equipping, and representing various denominations. Accordingly, the solemn call to lead an NEA to promote unity in the body of Christ has import for the mission of the church in a nation. The scriptural imperative for unity in the body of Christ requires obedience. Furthermore, the church needs especially to develop competencies for building and leading evangelical associations addressing concerns of a united body of Christ and contending for the faith without compromise (Jude 3:20–23).

Through its effective witness, the church can be the salt and light in a wounded and dark society. No one tradition or denomination can accomplish the Great Commission, so the collective input of every denomination is necessary in order to make an impact on society. The Lausanne Movement describes this action as "the whole church bringing the whole

---

8. Kato, "Biblical Christianity," 13.
9. Chalk, *Making Disciples*, 3.
10. Ibid., 5.

gospel to the whole world."[11] This kind of action requires a forum such as the NEA to harness and consolidate the individual contributions from various denominations and traditions. Conventional wisdom, human experience, and scriptural admonition all assert strength in unity (Eccl 4:12). The NEA represents an important medium for the expression of unity among different Christian traditions and denominations.

The need for ecumenical associations is a universal phenomenon and long has played a critical role in the work of the church. Ecumenical councils or associations in general have their root in the early church (Acts 15). Early church history is replete with examples of the need and importance of the councils, from the Council of Nicaea in AD 325, to the Second Council of Nicaea in AD 787. Through the centuries, denominational church councils have produced theological and doctrinal statements, but the "ecumenical council is the one that finds broad acceptance as an expression of the mind of the whole body of the faithful both clerical and lay, the *sensus communis* of the church."[12] In the contemporary church, movements such as Lausanne have produced statements that have become creedal, especially for evangelical wings of the global church. Established in 1846, the World Evangelical Alliance (WEA) provides guidance regarding consensus on theological positions related to various pertinent issues. The various NEAs comprise the WEA, and these constitute the *sensus communis* not only at national levels but collectively at the global level.

In Africa, countries with national alliances compose a continent-wide evangelical association – the Association of Evangelicals in Africa (AEA), established in 1966. The AEA is one of seven regional alliances that together compose the WEA. Furthermore, the AEA is represented on the international leadership team of the WEA.[13] The 2013, updated version of the AEA membership directory highlights thirty-six NEAs that exist under the umbrella of AEA.[14] The African-based NEAs in various stages of health and effectiveness need to develop and build capacity and

---

11. Lausanne Movement, *Cape Town Commitment*, 8.

12. Tennent, *World Christianity*, 107.

13. "Introduction," World Evangelical Alliance, n.d. Worldea.org, accessed 19 August 2013.

14. AEA Secretariat, *Membership Directory*, 8–15.

competencies in order to support effective NEA leadership. Accordingly, NEA leadership, like that of any other organization or movement, is critical to the organization's health and effectiveness.

The need for leadership development among NEAs has also been raised in the global church. WEA has articulated this need and led to the establishment of a leadership institute for evangelical association leaders. The WEA Leadership Institute (WEALI) curriculum focuses on six task areas, namely uniting, representing, serving, leading, funding, and partnering.[15] Nonetheless, as a work in progress, the curriculum for WEALI has not been proven and tested. Concerns also exist about contextual relevance regarding content and mode of delivery in the African context.

Few, if any, leadership development programs focus on alliance or association leadership. Available training materials lack adequate focus on building understanding of the nature of voluntary associations such as the NEA, specifically the dynamics of effectively leading the operations of such associations, particularly in the African context. The NEAs are different from church denominations and also from other voluntary and charitable organizations. Accordingly, they have *missional* intent with cultural, societal, and ecclesial implications, which impact the witness of the church in the nation.

The word *missional* is coined from a more familiar word – mission – which involves sending missionaries from one region of the world to another, as a program of the church. According to Darrell L. Guder, the church now realizes that mission is not just a program but what defines the church as people sent by God to the world. The entire work of the church, including clergy and laity, is an exercise in mission rather than mission being a program of the church.[16] The leader's core task or challenge involves understanding the nature and operational dynamics of life in the community of believers with diverse backgrounds and cultural and ecclesial traditions, building commitment and consensus as the body of Christ, demonstrating love for one another, exhibiting fellowship, and deferentially considering the interests of others. Leaders should understand the nature of NEAs, the

---

15. "WEALI." *Worldea.org*. World Evangelical Alliance, n.d. Accessed 21 September 2013.

16. Guder, *Missional Church*, 6.

cultural context of the church, and implications for leading the work of the association in Africa. A leader called to serve the various denominations from a common platform such as the NEA faces the challenge of effectively unifying the various and diverse traditions, ethnicities (tribes), and linguistic barriers for a common Christian voice and witness of the church in the nation. Many people come to this role depending on antecedent and transferable skills from other vocations and their God-given abilities (anointing) to accomplish the task. Currently leadership development programs and curricular materials in seminaries and Bible colleges are lacking, especially in regard to association leadership, the adaptation of these skills to the African situation.

The lack of emphasis in developing leaders for the NEA is not only seen in the lack of training curricula in various institutions but also in the general perception of church denominational leaders in Africa. The leaders perceive the evangelical associations more as community and social development non-governmental organizations with a focus on social work and not evangelism, which is perceived as the mission of the church. While I served as the leader of the NEA for ten years in my home country of Sierra Leone, my call to a *missional* vocation in the same manner as those persons in pastoral leadership roles proved a subject of contention in both my denomination and the Annual Convention of the Evangelical Fellowship of Sierra Leone (EFSL), the NEA. Many denominational leaders believed that as the CEO of EFSL, I should be an ordained minister or clergyperson. The head of my denomination viewed the role of local pastor as the *missional* call, more in line with the mandate and mission of the church. Leading the EFSL was viewed as a parachurch role, which could be accomplished by non-clergy persons of various backgrounds. This view, in effect, downplayed the *missional* intent and the value of the EFSL's contribution to the mission of the church in the nation.

During this time the EFSL represented the church in peace negotiations and conflict-resolution activities as part of the wider religious community and civil society, which led to cessation of war in the country. In addition, the EFSL was active in many local and international forums for international support in recovery efforts and law and institutional reforms in the country. These efforts constituted part of my work as the chief executive of

EFSL and also as the chair of the humanitarian community, Sierra Leone Association of Non-Governmental Organizations, a position to which I had been elected to serve the country. These efforts appeared to lend both credibility and opportunities to impact society from the Christian point of view.

Church leaders' concerns with their own respective denominations contributes to paying less attention to the need for developing personnel for leading movements to serve all denominations in the manner of the NEA. This lack of concern for work outside the particular denomination also seems to question the public mandate of the church in society. The challenge of leadership also includes sociocultural and religious antecedents. The resulting African worldview represents a challenge in public leadership, both in the church and in secular society. The way followers and the wider community view the leader can affect leadership style and effectiveness. For example, Tokunboh Adeyemo highlights some common leadership flaws:

> [M]ystical explanation of events that excuses taking personal responsibility for failures, or looks for scapegoats, tribal or ethnic ties that promotes [sic] nepotism, ritual attachment to land that dampened pioneering spirit, exclusion of youth, and retaining positions of leadership for life.[17]

These statements do not represent an outright condemnation of culture; however, since most of Africa's problems are attributable to their worldview and belief systems, they need a paradigm shift in their worldview in dealing with their problems.

Africa appears to be looking for different leadership outcomes, but the search for the desired leadership outcomes will not happen if leaders continue in the same direction. As a result, a need exists for African leaders to assess leadership practices to identify desirable outcomes and areas consistent with best practice and then ceaseless liberating and less empowering practices. God's call and endowment always include periods of preparation and training, so the church has emphasized excellent discipleship and training institutions and programs to nurture and equip God's people for all kinds of work. The church often limits this training to theological

---

17. Adeyemo, *Africa's Enigma*, 18–19.

training in Bible colleges and seminaries, but the task of the NEA leader is multifaceted and requires various skills in order to carry out this role effectively. The training programs of the church should seek to align training with competencies required for carrying out the various roles in the mission of the church.

Jesus emphasized the importance of training when he devoted much of his earthly ministry to prepare the twelve disciples to ensure the building and sustenance of the church on earth. Scholastic schools, monasteries, and modern-day universities and seminaries emerged from the need to equip the church. In spite of the growing need for partnerships and collaboration, the church does not seem to give as much effort to developing leaders with an intentional and strategic focus for effective leadership in the NEA as it does in developing pastoral leadership for teaching or other ministry areas. The orientation for denominational leaders seems focused inward rather than outward and public, which suggests a tendency to privilege the self rather than the more diverse, trans-denominational others.

Jesus modeled Christian leadership and clearly taught his followers that church leaders should not be like secular or worldly leaders (Matt 20:25–28). As a result, fundamental differences exist between the church's views on leadership and the world's views on leadership. Jesus' leadership is based on selfless and loving service to the needs of others (John 13:1–20). Therefore, NEA leadership should be missional and based on the principles of Jesus Christ. The nature of this study is exploratory and attempts to discern understandings of leadership competencies perceived as essential for effective leading of the NEA in the African context.

Purpose

The purpose of the research was to identify leadership competencies required for leading an NEA as well as needed leadership development competencies of current general secretaries or NEA leaders in Africa by interviewing current regional presidents and national leaders in the Association of Evangelicals in Africa.

Research Questions

Through this exploratory and qualitative research, I sought to identify the specific leadership competencies deemed essential by AEA regional presidents for effective NEA leadership and to assess proficiency levels of current general secretaries/NEA leaders in these competencies.

Research Question #1
What leadership competencies did current AEA regional presidents identify as necessary for leading an NEA?

Research Question #2
How did current NEA leaders or general secretaries in Africa rate competencies in order of importance for effective NEA leadership?

Research Question #3
What levels of proficiency did African NEA leaders or general secretaries attribute to themselves in each specific leadership competency for leading an NEA?

Definition of Terms

A few phrases in the purpose statement and some words used in the research require some definition or explanation in order to clarify the meaning and context of the study.

Leadership Competencies
Leadership competencies refer to the various factors participants said contributed to the success of NEA leaders in the activities and programs related to the objectives of their organization. These areas of competency included a combination of knowledge, skills, behavior, and relational and context-related factors.[18] Joel A. Caperig defines competency "as an ability to do something, especially measured against a standard."[19] Caperig further writes that competent leaders are those who clearly understand God's

---

18. Haruna, "Leadership Paradigm," 942; Hyatt and Williams, "21st Century Competencies," 58.

19. Caperig, "Enhancing," 5.

call for their particular ministry as taught in the Bible and who develop skills fitted for the work.[20] This research is about the NEA leadership competencies.

Regional President

The president of an NEA in one of seven regions within the AEA, elected by peers in the region and with responsibility to advance AEA vision and mission and to promote the establishment and strengthening of NEAs in the region. The regional president also sits on the Board and Council of AEA.[21]

National Evangelical Association

The NEA is a membership-based voluntary national association composed of church denominations, individuals, and parachurch and other Christian organizations adhering to common fundamental beliefs attributed to evangelical Christian orthodoxy and meeting basic criteria for membership in the AEA and WEA. NEA membership requires a process of application, vetting, and admission into membership in the AEA and WEA. Individual denominations and other Christian organizations seeking membership in a nation's NEA follow a similar membership process and adhere to similar criteria. The NEA is the representative voice for its members.

General Secretary/NEA Leader

The NEA leader or chief executive officer is designated as general secretary, but some variation of this designation exists, such as Executive Director. The general secretary provides strategic direction to carry out the mission and achieve the objectives of the NEA. In addition, the NEA leader is responsible for the daily running of the NEA and is accountable to the NEA chairperson and board.

Effective NEA

An effective NEA demonstrates well-balanced spiritual health and organizational/financial health; provides helpful programs, products, and services for members; focuses on a global orientation; mentors other national alliances; and, is led by an experienced leader and an engaged governing

---

20. Ibid.
21. AEA Secretariat, *Constitution*, 8.

board. The WEA Secretary General, Geoff Tunnicliffe describes an effective alliance by their function: "[T]he four primary functional areas have been identified as essential to national alliance effectiveness – association management, sustainable funding, strategic partnerships and public engagement."[22] A healthy NEA is also deemed to be viable, visible, and vibrant. The typical NEA in Africa is struggling in all of these areas, but lack of finances is often cited as the main cause of weakness.

Proficiency Level

Merriam-Webster defines proficiency as "advancement in knowledge or skills; quality or state of being proficient."[23] Proficiency level refers to the measure of dexterity or ease with which leaders carry out a particular task or demonstrate competency.

Ministry Project

The ministry project was a preintervention study seeking to identify specific leadership competencies required for effective leadership and to assess competency levels of leaders for leadership development in African NEAs. Two groups of participants were involved with the research, including current AEA regional presidents of the seven regions in Africa (see appendix A) and current leaders or general secretaries responsible for leading the NEA in each one of the thirty-six AEA member countries. In this study I sought to gather information from participants regarding perceived competencies based on their respective experiences in governing, leading, and sustaining an NEA within the African context.

The design of the project was ethnographic and exploratory and involved persons responsible for governing and leading the NEA. I identified competencies AEA regional presidents perceived as essential for leading NEAs based on their experiences in recruiting NEA leaders. Furthermore, the current NEA leaders in Africa rated the competencies in order of importance for effectiveness. The NEA leaders completed self-assessments

---

22. Geoff Tunnicliffe, "WEA International Director Report for International Council," Nairobi, November 2007, 9.

23. *Merriam-webster.com*. n.d.

regarding their proficiency levels in each specific area of competency in order to explore possible needs for future intervention.

I utilized a cross-sectional survey design in order to elicit participant response, and I conducted the research in two phases in order to obtain information to provide answers for the research questions. The first part of the research sought to identify NEA leadership competencies by administering a researcher-designed questionnaire and sending an email to AEA regional presidents involved with governance and recruitment of NEA leaders. Next, I collated and analyzed the data collected from participants' responses and then generated a list of competencies. During the second phase of the research, this list served as the basis for the researcher-designed instruments for ranking the competencies and self-assessing competency levels by the general secretaries. Finally, I analyzed, reported, and integrated the results with existing knowledge from the literature review. Then I made conclusions and developed recommendations from the project.

Context

This study focused on African NEAs, which brought together the different denominations and parachurch organizations within the nation. While the individual organizations composing the membership of the NEA have common objectives, they are independent. Sometimes, the unique differences and organizational cultures tend to serve as the dominant factors in the relationships between the denominations and organizations. The unique organizational cultural differences rather than the greater Christian worldview tend to shape people's individual worldviews and generally impact the church's influence on African society.

The NEA has the challenge of overcoming these barriers and promoting unity within the body of Christ in the nation based on biblical and scriptural principles. Accordingly, the NEA differs from the denominations that combine to compose it. As such, the NEA leader is more likely recruited from one of the member organizations. Furthermore, as a member of a particular ethnic community in a nation of multiple ethnicities, the leader needs to demonstrate the spirit of unity as envisioned by Jesus and consistent with God's Trinitarian nature and the community of God's people.

The context of the associations differs from other independent organizations, such as church denominations, and has unique challenges for effective leadership. This need prompted my research, which sought to discern the competencies essential for leading a healthy NEA in Africa. The findings may be useful for denominational leaders as well, since some aspects of the denominations' work compare with those of the NEAs. To that end, some denominations serve their various local congregations as separate and independent units in the denomination. The experience in one nation also can benefit other nations in the region. Similarities and dissimilarities, as well as obvious needs for learning and adaptation across the continent, exist. The African NEA experience also can prove valuable for other regions, the global church, and the relatively under-researched field of association administration.

With a common platform, the NEAs come together to form the AEA. During this research, at least thirty-six nations combined their efforts as full members of the continental association. The individual and collective experiences of AEA member nations provide invaluable opportunities for learning and building. The NEAs composing the AEA were in various states of health and effectiveness. Accordingly, some of the thirty-six NEAs were strong. The same people had been leading some of them for a relatively longer period. Others were struggling to build the association, and still more had relatively new or inexperienced leaders. The AEA platform provides opportunities for mutual enrichment, which underscores the importance of this study, namely, the enrichment of NEA leaders.

The AEA is one of seven regional evangelical associations around the world that constitute the WEA, but the individual NEAs also hold membership in the WEA. During this research, the WEA membership consisted of 129 NEAs from all over the world and the seven regional evangelical associations.[24] The WEA offers its members the WEA Leadership Institute (WEALI), developed in California in recognition of the movement's critical need for developing NEA leaders. Nonetheless, a casual perusal of the curricular content and its delivery suggested the need for assessing relevance and adaptation within the African context. Thus, this project

---

24. "Introduction," World Evangelical Alliance, n.d. Worldea.org, accessed 19 August 2013.

contributed to the work of the WEALI and the WEA in general. Valuable lessons from the African experience can be of use to WEALI and other regions of the world. This study enhanced greater understanding of the nature of ecumenical movements and the global church. Africa has important gifts needed by the rest of the world for the good of the global church, the body of Christ.

The Evangelical Alliance (EA) family is inherently a collaborative network of relationships at global (i.e. WEA), regional (i.e. REA), and national (i.e. NEA) levels. The structure is polarized between a *top-down hierarchical* structure and a *bottom-up service* structure, depending on situation and issue as depicted in figure 1.1. The top-down hierarchical model is desired when the issue is a large challenge and needs a multilevel intervention. The representative voice at the regional and/or global level(s) is required.

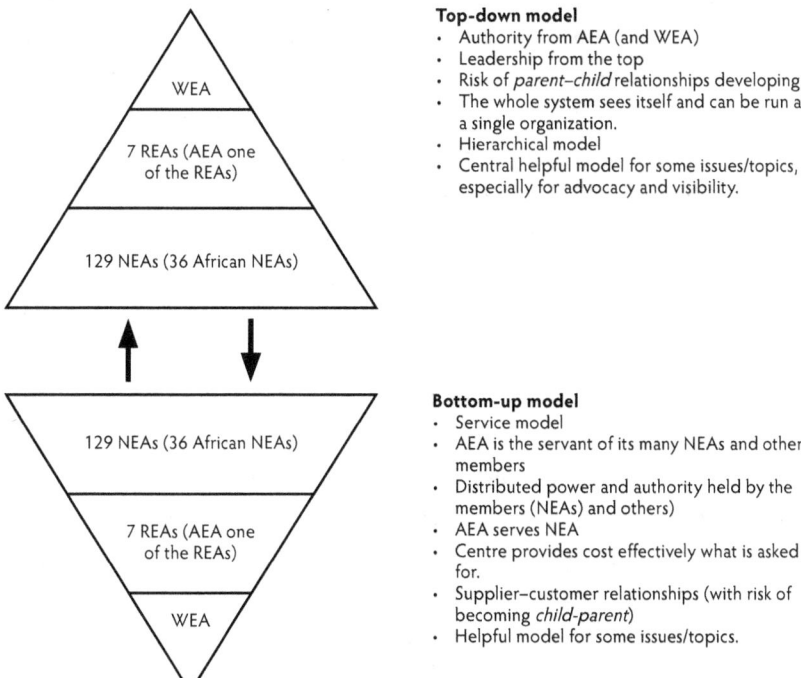

Source: Tricordant 8: "WEAILF2015" PowerPoint presentation (adapted).

Figure 1.1 Structure of the Evangelical Alliance at Global, Regional, and National Levels

This structure is leveraged for advocacy and a representative voice of evangelicals. Internally, the structure is reversed as an inverted pyramid with the WEA and REA at the bottom of the pyramid to service members (i.e. NEAs) at the top. The NEA is the basic unit of the WEA because it represents the national evangelical churches and the structure supports the NEA. The goal is consensual; service, accountability, shared responsibilities, mutuality, communication, and ownership form the bedrock of the relationship not conciliar authority. However, the two models do not capture fully the working relationship and structure, which tends to resemble independent networks with a web of relationships.

Methodology

I developed this project from my underlying assumption that NEAs differ from other organizations. Furthermore, I discerned a need to understand how the associations operate, especially in the complex and diverse African environment. The opportunity existed to learn from leaders with firsthand experience in building and sustaining the NEA in Africa. I also assumed that unique leadership competencies, essential for African NEA leadership development resided in contemporary and serving leaders. Through this project, I hoped to contribute to the work of the WEA from an African perspective and enrich the global church. Thus, the project sought to discover leadership competencies perceived by African-based NEA leaders and their governors.

I used appropriate survey design to collect the views of two sets of purposive populations of regional presidents at the governance level and at the level of the NEA leader in order to identify leadership competencies perceived by the regional presidents familiar with and engaged in the task of building and sustaining NEAs. The study made use of an ethnographic and exploratory, mixed-method approach to gather information from the participating regional presidents and NEA. I collated and analyzed the data, and then drew conclusions and made recommendations.

Participants

Two sets of targeted populations participated in the research. The first population included the seven regional presidents of the AEA. As board chair of his or her particular NEA with some limited governing responsibility for the other NEAs in the region, each of these presidents was responsible for recruiting and selecting the general secretary or leader. For the purposes of the work of the AEA, the continent is divided into seven regions, with each region comprised of an average of seven countries (see appendix A). The second group of participants represented African NEA leaders or general secretaries from thirty-six nations with full AEA membership.

Given the entire population of evangelicals constituting NEA membership, the targeted populations could be seen as purposive samples. The specific group of participants in each case was representative of the larger evangelical population. Therefore, since each group targeted included everyone in the group, these groups were considered purposive populations, and the criterion for their selection was based on experience, suitability to respond to research questions, and familiarity with the context. These groups were best situated to provide the information required for this study.[25] The experiences of the current regional presidents and the NEA leaders are invaluable for NEA leadership development.

I am an insider and relate to the respondents at different levels. My role is general secretary of the AEA, which has a dotted-line accountability relationship between me and the NEAs' general secretaries. The relationship is a collaborative one, polarized between a *top-down hierarchical* structure and a *bottom-up service* structure. Depending on the issue and situation, the NEA general secretaries report to me at the top, but in terms of service delivery and accountability for stewardship of my office, I am accountable to them. The regional presidents comprise the board of directors who are my employers. I report to them at all times (see appendix G for job description).

Before coming to this role, I was general secretary of an NEA for ten years after previously serving for six years in the NEA in another role. I have continuously served the evangelical alliance family at both national and regional levels for the past twenty-two years. I have experienced many of the challenges the NEA general secretaries endure. My first role in the

---

25. Creswell, *Educational Research*, 143, 145–146.

NEA was based on some administrative experience, but my training and qualifications were in oceanography/zoology.

However, my interest and strong link with the church began with my conversion to Christianity as a teen in secondary school. I heard the gospel of Christ in Scripture Union and was discipled in that movement for several years through my time at university. My experience and training in Scripture Union shaped my theological and biblical views. I relied on that experience mostly for my service in the church.

As general secretary of the NEA, I was in the caucus of top church and religious leaders in the country. I felt the need to understand the world of the clergy and the demands for a theological and biblical position by evangelicals. During the ten-year period as NEA general secretary, I strived to attain two postgraduate degrees in theology and administration in addition to attendance at numerous seminars and short training programs in a variety of areas, including development, advocacy, leadership, project management, and computer studies. In the meantime, ministry responsibilities continued to grow, especially in terms of representation of the church in government circles and non-governmental and civil society organizations. I have a burden for the general secretaries who are in similar roles and wonder how they can use their positions to enhance the church's impact on society. I really think NEA leadership is an important aspect of the mission of the church and needs to be supported and strengthened.

Instrumentation

The nature of the study was mostly qualitative with limited numerical quantitative descriptions. I used a researcher-designed survey that sought to generate a list of competencies contributing to success in leading NEAs and to assess proficiency levels of current NEA leaders. Furthermore, I collated and organized a list of competencies according to theme and then had the general secretaries ranked them in order of importance for effective NEA leadership.

Three instruments proved essential for this research. The first researcher-designed instrument surveyed AEA regional presidents' perceptions of necessary competencies for leading an NEA. The second was a researcher-designed instrument ranking perceived leadership competencies and the third instrument self-assessed proficiency levels of competency of the general secretaries in the competencies identified by the regional presidents. I administered these questionnaires via email in each phase of the research and asked respondents to return them to me via email within a given period of four weeks. This length of time was estimated to be adequate to have all the respondents fill out the questionnaires and return them to me. In the first phase of the research, I collated the respondents' data and identified a list of competencies regional presidents perceived to be essential for leading an NEA. Following the analysis of the data collected in the first phase, I developed the second instrument and asked the general secretaries to rate the NEA leadership competencies in order of importance for effectiveness. The third instrument required the general secretaries to self-assess their level of proficiency in each competency. The second group of participants was also given a timeframe of four weeks for completing the questionnaire.

Data Collection

For this study, I utilized three instruments for data collection. The first instrument was a researcher-designed protocol for identifying leadership competencies AEA regional presidents deemed necessary for leading an NEA. The second instrument was designed to collect general secretaries' ratings of AEA regional presidents' perceived leadership competencies and the third instrument was general secretaries' self-assessed proficiency levels of competencies. After completing the literature review, I designed the research instruments. Next, I pilot-tested the instruments by administering them to an expert review team consisting of members of the research reflection team in order to assess the instruments for validity, reliability, and user friendliness. I used the pretest feedback to review the instrument and improve the design of the questionnaire for increased reliability and validity.

Next, I distributed the questionnaire via email to the respondents and the seven AEA regional presidents whose consent and voluntary participation in the research I previously had obtained. To that end, along with the research instrument, I sent a letter in which I outlined the confidentiality of the exercise, as well as the purpose and significance of the study. In the letter, I also gave clear guidance to participants regarding questionnaire completion and the timeframe in which I needed them to return the completed questionnaire to me.

In the second part of the research, the participating general secretaries ranked the competencies identified in the first phase of the research in order of importance. In addition, I asked participants to engage in self-assessment regarding their levels of proficiency in each of the competencies. I accomplished this task with the second and third researcher-designed instruments, following the analysis of the first phase of the research. I administered the instruments and requested participants to return them via email within four weeks following the completion of the first phase of the research.

Data Analysis

After collecting the data, I organized the responses and presented them in an accessible, readable, and easy-to-understand format. Accordingly, I organized, coded, tabulated, and analyzed the information collated in the first phase of the research. The survey resulted in a list of leadership competencies AEA regional presidents deemed necessary for leading the NEA. This list served as the basis to design the second and third instruments, which were combined on one protocol, for the second phase of the research. I asked participants in the second phase, namely the African NEA leaders or general secretaries, to rate the competencies in order of importance and to assess their own respective levels of proficiency in each specific area of competency.

Generalizability

This study focused specifically on African NEAs. I conducted the study in two phases and limited participants to the AEA regional presidents and NEA general secretaries. I also focused my research on competencies the regional presidents identified as necessary for NEA leadership. Participants engaged in self-assessment regarding the importance of the competencies and their proficiency levels.

As a result, this project was limited in scope. Nonetheless, the findings of the project could be of interest to other ecumenical movements such as the Council of Churches and Pentecostal fellowships that exist alongside the NEAs in many nations and have similar objectives to the African NEAs. The findings also could be of interest to denominational and conference leaders and could contribute to current conversation on the subject of leadership development within the WEA, especially in regard to ways in which other regions of the world might learn from the African experience. Other leadership research also could benefit from the findings regarding unique African leadership competencies.

Theological and Biblical Foundation

An NEA seeks to create a common platform for unity, a scriptural strategy for missions, in the body of Christ. To this end, Christ prayed that his followers might be one, "that all of them may be one, Father, just as you are in me and I am in you. May they also be in us so that the world may believe that you sent me" (John 17:21). Accordingly, the work of the NEA, like that of the individual denominations, is *missional* and consistent with the *missio Dei*. Like any other ministry of the church, solid theological foundation exists for the NEA and God's calling and equipping people to serve in this area of ministry. NEA leadership, like leadership of any Christian ministry, is primarily the work of God and is seen in the nature and work of the Godhead – Father, Son, and Holy Spirit. Stephen Seamands articulates the theological implications for unity and ministry:

> Christian ministry is shaped by a Trinitarian understanding, and the church was created in the image of the Triune God for relationship, thus characterizing the inner life of the Father, Son, and Holy Spirit. Like the Trinity, relatedness is characterized by full equality, glad submission, joyful intimacy and mutual deference.[26]

Unity is not forced; members of the community derive fulfillment from voluntarily being present and serving others.

How God is perceived has implication for the work of the NEA especially in the African context. The vision and mission of the NEA issues a call to live out the life of God. Jesus Christ modeled service to the world and the church. The work of the church is Christ centered, and the source of all Christ's power is derived from fellowship with the Father. This fellowship is the source of his wisdom, power, and abilities (John 5:19–20;

---

26. Seamands, *Image of God*, 18.

8:16; Acts 10:38). Without the triune God, Christians can do nothing on their own. Jesus was concerned about the unity of the early apostles as well as that of believers after them for all time. He prayed in John 17 that the church would be one just as the Father and Son are one (v. 21), through the Holy Spirit.

In the diversity of Christians, Jesus envisioned unity – the many being one, and the one representing many (Rom 12:4–8). The priesthood of all believers exists when Christians are all united as one community (2 Pet 2:9). Therefore, all ministries should be under the lordship and headship of the one body: Jesus Christ. Christians celebrate their oneness in the Eucharist (John 6:56–57). Christians are commanded to serve one another, to honor, forgive, and submit to one another. In addition, Christians should bear each other's burdens as well as carry out many other mutual tasks. The *one another* exhortations are important because they confront Christians with their own biases and help them move together as one body. Paul's admonitions in Ephesians 2 and 3 serve as a critical foundation for this unique kind of unity and have implications for being part of the body of Christ.

An exegetical study of Ephesians 4:1–16 demonstrates the unity of the church as a given, and the passage exhorts Christians to "make every effort to keep the unity of the Spirit through the bond of peace" (Eph 4:3). The text further reveals God's gracious act of equipping every believer with diverse spiritual gifts and the exercise of these gifts among believers for nurturing the church to maturity. Unity of believers reflects God's identity and glory and issues an authentic proclamation of the gospel (Phil 2:1–2; Gal 3:26; Eph 2:14–16). The visible manifestation of the unity and love of the church is the direct fruit of sound theology and high respect for Scripture. AEA, in encouraging its members to work towards unity of the church, states, "True evangelicalism implies eagerness to break down walls of hostility in the household of faith between church denominations as a service to the wider community (Col 1:17; Eph 2:14–15) because of Christ's work."[27] The Great Commission and Creation commandments were given to the church as a whole and not to individual denominations, and the collective

---

27. "Afroscope." *AEA Newsletter* 1, no. 4 (Apr–June 2010): 5.

effort of all in the church is required to fulfill the commandments. Not only must followers of Christ seek cooperation with others in witnessing to the gospel, but they must also stand together to contend for their faith (Jude 3–4). Scripture clearly asserts that Christians must work together in unity of purpose:

> Two are better than one, because they have a good return for their work: if one falls down, his friend can help him up. But pity the man who falls and has no one to help him up! Also, if two lie down together, they will keep warm. But how can one keep warm alone? Though one may be overpowered, two can defend themselves. A cord of three strands is not quickly broken. (Eccl 4:9–12)

Jesus' commission and mandate to the apostles was collective; Jesus did not single out individuals and expects the church to be one in purpose. Individual endeavors should be seen in the context of the whole body of Christ and as a contribution to what others are doing. The desired impact and outcome is realistically achieved from the synergy of collective effort.

In Scripture God often chose a people or a community for his revelation. God frequently chose individuals in the context of the community they represented:

> In the Old Testament, the community refers to Israel, God's chosen people. In the New Testament, the first evangelical group can be identified as composed of 120 people including the eleven apostles, Mary the mother of Jesus, and others. These persons witnessed the death, bodily resurrection, and ascension of Jesus Christ.[28]

Furthermore, "all the believers were together and had everything in common" (Acts 2:44). The early community of Christians set the precedence for community life and their work of taking the gospel message to other ethnicities.

The Christian life, in general and Christian leadership, in particular, comes from fellowship with God (1 John 1:3). Christ demonstrated to

---

28. Ibid., 4.

his followers how to be in fellowship with the Father and serve others. Christian leadership is a call to God's workmanship (Eph 2:10; 4:1–16) and service to others. The call is servant leadership, and good stewardship of God's call requires excellence in service. David, a great leader and king, is an example of good Christian leadership: "And David shepherded them with integrity of heart; with skillful hands he led them" (Ps 78:72). Servant leadership represents a heart issue and requires preparation for appropriate and excellent skills. The label *servant leader* is experiencing much coverage in popular culture; however, it needs to be understood from its biblical intent. Christians are called to serve the needs of others not by their own choice or according to leaders' respective agendas but driven by others' needs.[29] The needs of the followers dictate a timely response from the servant leader.

If a need exists for spiritual, mental, social, emotional, and physical preparation for pastoral leadership, then leading denominations in an association requires no less leadership preparation and training. The message of the church offers hope and holistic redemption for overcoming the challenges Africa faces, and the collective effort of the church on the NEA platform has tremendous potential.

Overview

The next four chapters provide a detailed account of how the project was executed and concluded. Chapter 2 gives an overview of the related research and literature on the subject of association leadership, particularly as related to ecclesiastical ecumenism and leadership competencies. Chapter 3 details the design of the project, including a description of the research method, the ministry context and participants involved, the evaluation instrumentation, procedures for data collection, and analysis of the collected data. Chapter 4 reports the findings of the project. Finally, Chapter 5 integrates the review of literature with the findings of the project. It also presents a summary of the project results, conclusions, and reflections for application in this area of ministry, specifically in the African context.

---

29. Dickson, *Biblical Research*, 898.

CHAPTER 2

Literature

Introduction

The overall objective of this research was to explore leadership competencies for leadership development and strengthening African NEAs. This chapter presents a review of literature in order to build an understanding of ecumenical and evangelical associations as types of organizations. Furthermore, this review of literature also seeks to explore leadership effectiveness and competencies and biblical and theological foundations for this area of ministry. The import of this study hinged on the fundamental doctrine of the Trinity, the nature of God represented by his church in the world. God's Trinitarian communion and the subsequent doctrine of unity in the church as the body of Christ also are foundational to an understanding of Christian unity as espoused in the work of NEAs.

Fellowship with God and fellowship with one another is one of God's purposes for his church and every believer:

> Christians are called to belong, not just to believe. They were not meant to live lone-ranger lives; instead, they belonged to Christ's family and were members of his body. Baptism was not only a symbol of salvation; it was a symbol of fellowship.[1]

The call for unity among followers of Christ does not apply only to members of a particular local congregation, denomination, or communion but instead is a call to Christians everywhere and all times to oneness in spirit

---

1. Warren, *Purpose Driven Church*, 58.

and purpose.² The call for unity is important especially for followers of Christ within the same nation, as exemplified by the NEA.

The NEA emphasizes essential unity as the invisible bond existing among all believers, especially within the same nation. These believers create visible unity through their national association.³ Jesus Christ was earnest in his prayer for unity among the apostles and all his followers for all time:

> My prayer is not for them [apostles] alone, I pray also for those who will believe in me through their message, that all of them be one, Father, just as you are in me and I am in you. May they also be in us so that the world may believe that you have sent me. (John 17:20–21)

The purpose for unity of believers is missional and mandatory. The leadership of the church in a nation needs to be developed and strengthened in making "every effort to maintain the unity" forged by God himself (Eph 4:3). The unity of the church in general is creedal and affirmed by believers in Christ as the basis of their faith.

The community of believers and the people of God did not start with the birth of the church on the day of Pentecost. Instead, the church stands in continuity with the people of God beginning with the call of Abraham to be the foundation of a community of God's people in Genesis 12, fashioned in the image of the Trinitarian God. The New Testament church stood in continuity with that larger community. Unity as an end in itself is sterile; it can be sought for the wrong reasons, as demonstrated in the story of the Tower of Babel (Gen 11:1–9). Such a quest for unity can lead to compromise in order to achieve artificial oneness. When societies establish different conceptions of unity, Christians must test and examine these ideas on God's foundation. Often African societies feature much discussion of unity or togetherness, sometimes for very good reasons. Nonetheless, these discussions require critique in order to determine their theological roots. An African view of community based upon the Trinity likely would prove

---

2. Palau, "Foreword," xi.
3. Breman, "Association of Evangelicals," 316.

compelling for the rest of the world. W. Harold Fuller describes the kind of unity Christians seek:

> A cemetery has unity, of a sort; it has harmony, in a sense but it is dead. When Jesus spoke of unity, he used the example of a living organism – his body. That kind of unity comes from life within, the unity of the Spirit of God; it is a body that has purpose and a mission, the mandate given by God.[4]

The call for unity is an imperative for Christians and demands obedience by faithful followers of Christ. According to Tunnicliffe, the WEA envisions the church "joined together in every community around the world, effectively living out and proclaiming the good news of Jesus. These allied churches seek transformation, holiness and justice for individuals, families, communities, peoples and nations."[5] Unity of the church is missional.

The church's need for common expression and unity of purpose and spirit has been a clarion call for church leaders in Africa. In the post-independent era, the African church has held two major assemblies – the Pan-African Christian Leadership Assembly (PACLA) 1 and PACLA 2 in 1967 and 1976, respectively. These assemblies focused on the theme of unity, "living out the unity of truth and love that exclusively belonged to the body of Christ."[6] These assemblies brought together church leaders from all the major Protestant traditions and from all regions of the continent to deliberate on the factors fragmenting the church in Africa and isolating Christians from one another. In the welcome address at PACLA 2, Michael Cassidy offered a succinct proclamation:

> We want to see Africa crisscrossed from Cape to Cairo by a great new network of relationship based on our one-ness and fellowship together in Christ. Such fellowship could heal the wounds of Africa, bring new stability and peace, forward the cause of the evangelization of Africa in our time and help

---

4. Fuller, *People*, xiv.
5. WEA website, http://www.worldea.org/news/504/WEA-Welcomes-Dr-Joel-Hunter-to-the-North-American-Council, 1.
6. Osei-Mensah, "Why PACLA," 22.

prepare Africa for its destiny in world mission in the twenty first century.[7]

The church can do more together than when it is divided into different denominations. In a region that is faced with all kinds of ethnic division, the witness of the church is crucial in proclaiming the message of Christ, a message of peace and hope.

The growth of the church in Africa also has resulted in a large number of independent churches with no denominational affiliation. These churches likely could achieve much more if they work together. To that end, the NEA endeavors to bring the various churches under one cover. Various biblical, theological, and practical reasons make compelling argument and appeal for unity. Ecclesiastes 4:9–12 asserts that more can be accomplished in Christian mission if Christians work together. The different church denominations and church organizations are called for partnership in all aspects of human endeavor. Strong theological reasons exist for such a perspective, one in which Christians give their gifts to one another for the sake of growing into the full likeness of Jesus Christ. As a result, Christians somehow must deal with differences in regard to unity.

In spite of the compelling call for unity and need for collaboration, the church is divided. Cassidy observes, "[F]ellowship or unity is not easy to achieve or maintain due to the diverse nature of people and people groups. After all there are people, from different nations, tribes, races, sexes, denominations, age groups and different theological viewpoints."[8] In short, unity includes diversity.

The mission of the NEA offers a corrective and an important effort to unite the church in the nation.[9] However, concern exists regarding the health and effective functioning of the NEA. One of the goals of the global and regional associations is strengthening the NEA.[10] Many NEAs operate in a fledgling state of effectiveness. The effectiveness of the NEA in achieving its objectives, like any other organization, depends on leadership. Accordingly, leadership effectiveness depends to a large extent on the

---

7. Cassidy, "Problems and Possibilities," 73–74.
8. Ibid., 74.
9. Fuller, *People*, 8.
10. Showell-Rogers, "Regional Alliance," 3.

competency of the leader and how he or she interacts with followers and the environment.

George Barna observes that the church is dying and losing its influence because of a lack of strong leadership. Leaders are needed to facilitate the well-being of the society or organization. The church needs leaders to guide God's people spiritually and in Christian formation.[11] Barna writes, "[N]othing was more important for the future of the church than leadership."[12] Godly leadership is needed to overcome challenges in the church, community, and the society. Every problem in society points to the lack of leadership God intended for his people and creation.

The subject of leadership is complex and difficult to define. Leadership is more of an art than science, and as many definitions as experts exist.[13] Leadership is a process, not a position; as such, leadership is an interaction among the leader, follower, and the environment. The interaction and complex nature of these three elements informs understanding of the subject.[14] The complex nature of the NEA as an association of voluntary, independent, and different church denominations and other Christian organizations makes the leadership task even more complex. Barna writes, "A Christian leader is one who is called by God to lead; lead through Christlike character; and demonstrates the functional competencies that permit effective leadership to take place."[15] Jesus demonstrated this model of leadership and demands it of his followers.

This study sought to engage and obtain the perspective of the African AEA regional presidents and NEA leaders regarding leadership competencies contributing to success in their work. To that end, the purpose of the research was to identify leadership competencies required for leading an NEA as well as needed leadership development competencies of current general secretaries or NEA leaders in Africa by interviewing current regional presidents and national leaders in the AEA.

---

11. Barna, "Nothing," 18–19.
12. Ibid., 20.
13. Ibid., 21.
14. Hughes, Ginnett, and Curphy, *Leadership*, 1–2.
15. Barna, "Nothing," 25.

Theological and Biblical Foundations

The NEA offers strategic means to accomplish the mission of the church in the nation. The theological reason for unity emerges from the will of Christ, and to do otherwise contradicts the very nature and purpose of the church. Unity of the church also is based on the Trinity. The church represents communion in Christ.[16] Church unity emerges from God's completed work of uniting believers with Christ when they come to faith in Christ through repentance. To that end, church unity rests upon fundamental Christian doctrines such as the Trinity, the mission of God (i.e. *missio Dei*), unity and nature of the church (i.e. ecclesiology) and servant leadership. The understanding of these doctrines forms the basis for appreciating the ministry of the NEA, its missional intent, biblical mandate, and leadership implications.

Trinitarian Dimension of Unity in the Church

The sovereign God is revealed to Christians as triune – the Father, the Son and the Holy Spirit. Thomas C. Oden writes, "This is the ancient ecumenical faith into which all Christians of all times and places were baptized and affirmed in the Apostles' Creed, the most common confession of Christians."[17] The biblical purpose of unity or community is grounded in the divine Godhead; from eternity God is community as Father, Son (Word), and Holy Spirit (Gen 1:1–3; John 1:1, 14). God's very nature is community, and the community in the Godhead is the perfect pattern and basis for relational harmony taught in the Scriptures. The members of the divine community do not exist for themselves but for one another, totally dependent on one another to perform their distinct roles. No one person of the Trinity can accomplish his distinct role without the support and empowerment of the other two persons; as such, the Trinity features both distinct persons and integrated oneness.

God always has enjoyed community in the Godhead. Accordingly, when he created humans, he did so that people might share in the fellowship of the divine Trinity. Humans are created in the image and likeness of

---

16. Zizioulas, *Communion*, 15.
17. Oden, Living God, 11.

the triune God and created to live in community with God and with one another (Gen 1:26; 2:18). God created people with the need for fellowship. His original plan was damaged, and, as a result, society struggles with loneliness, alienation, and selfishness – a far cry from the loving community God intended. Every human being has an ingrained longing for fellowship because God created humans first to live in communion with him and then to reflect this relationship with one another. The Trinity represents a mystery beyond human comprehension. Nonetheless, the doctrine of the Trinity is critical to understanding fellowship because true fellowship is based upon the unity modeled by the Trinity.

The Old Testament concept of fellowship is grounded in God's covenant with Israel and his promise to them – one nation and one people and under one king; "you will be my people, and I will be your God" (Ezek 36:28; Deut 7:6–12); and, "I will be with you" (Exod 3:12, 16). Israel enjoyed a unique relationship with Yahweh as the people of God. Symbolic of God's presence with them were the cloud and the pillar of fire (Exod 14:24; 40:34–38; Num 9:15–23), the Ark of the Covenant (Num 10:35–36), and the tabernacle and temple (Ps 11:4; Ezek 37:27). The presence of God today exists in the indwelling of the Holy Spirit in the believer (Rom 8: 9–11). The spiritual unity of the church has expression in the physical realm, and the NEA embodies that unity.

In Genesis 1–3, the Bible reveals how Adam and Eve enjoyed the gift of community with God and with each other until sin broke the fellowship with the divine community with the consequent effect on fellowship between people. Since that time human beings lost the capacity to enjoy fellowship with God or one another at the level God originally intended. Sin separated humans from God and one another. Humans also are at odds with the created world as a consequence of their sin.

Salvation and the mission of God address the restoration of that relationship. The Old Testament text of Ezekiel 37:15–28 illustrates the people of God as one nation under one king in spite of the division or diversity. Following the reign of Solomon, the people of God were divided into two kingdoms – the Northern Kingdom (Israel or Ephraim) and the Southern Kingdom (Judah). In this passage Ezekiel demonstrates how God brought together the divided nation and described God's covenant promise, steadfast love, and commitment to his people.

The New Testament clearly attributes the unity of Christians in the sharing of the common meal of the sacrament or Holy Communion. The Eucharistic formula underscores the oneness of believers:

> For I received from the Lord what I passed on to you: The Lord Jesus, on the night he was betrayed, took bread, and when he had given thanks, he broke it and said, "This is my body, which is for you; do this in remembrance of me." In the same way, after super he took the cup, saying, "This cup is the new covenant in my blood; do this, whenever you drink it, in remembrance of me." (1 Cor 11:23–25)

In the early church, the believers ate the remembrance meal of communion when they gathered. The common meal was a way of bonding with Christ and to one another. The bond, based on their common belief in Christ, was stronger than their earthly family bond. Jesus also demonstrated the importance of brotherly fellowship when his earthly family wanted to see him: "He replied, 'My mother and brothers are those who hear God's word and put it into practice'" (Luke 8:21). The dominance of ethnocentricity can be attributed only to the fallen nature of humanity, characterized by persons acting according to their own desires and commands rather than God's. When people follow this pattern, they sin against God, against others, and even against themselves.

Mission of God (*Missio Dei*)

The doctrine of Trinity not only serves as a theological construct but also requires practical application in the way Christians do ministry.[18] God is revealed in his activity and mission to be triune in nature. God's mission is seen in the work of the Father, the Son, and the Holy Spirit.[19] Accordingly, J. Paul Stevens asserts that since ministry derives from God, a Trinitarian dimension exists regarding the church's ministry. Furthermore, implications of the Trinitarian character and nature of Christian service or ministry exist

---

18. Seamands, *Image of God*, 20.
19. Stevens, *Six Days*, 56–57; Wright, *Mission*, 62.

particularly in the ministry of the NEA. Consequently, all God's people minister to each other and receive ministry from one another according to each person's unique gifting, place of service, and context (call). Through love, the Holy Spirit oriented the whole life of Jesus toward the Father in fulfillment of the Father's will. The Father sent his Son (Gal 4:4) through the operation of the Holy Spirit, and only through the Holy Spirit was Jesus Christ able to fulfill his mission.

The same could be said of the leaders of the apostolic church. Jesus asked them to wait for the infilling of the Holy Spirit before they launched out for ministry (Acts 1:8). Such infilling is the requirement for all Christians called to do the work of Christ. Ministry is self-sacrifice and enabled by the Trinity. The objective of Christian ministry is love for God and neighbor. Unity is the divine strategy for participating in God's mission, and for that reason unity is required of all persons desiring to obey and serve the purposes of God. Working together in unity as a body of Christ, each person has a unique and distinct role committed to work within and outside of the self. Taking the Trinity as the example, equality is characterized by collaborative work – treating one another with respect, seeing the good in one another, and valuing diversity as each person complements the other for completeness or wholeness. No plays for power exist in the Trinity, since interactions occur among persons of equal worth. Every genuine mission work is about God, and all God's people are only coworkers with God in God's mission.[20] God takes the lead in all the work of the church and is trusted to take care of the challenges the church faces.

The prerequisite for doing God's work or serving as coworkers with God is through the agency of the Holy Spirit. Without the power of the Spirit of God, Christians cannot do the work God has called them to do. Jesus' work was empowered by the Holy Spirit (Acts 10:38), the first community of Christians – the 120 disciples gathered in the upper room on the day of Pentecost (Acts 2:4), Peter (Acts 4:8), Stephen (Acts 6:3, 5; 7:55), and Paul (Acts 9:17; 13:9) and Barnabas (Acts 11:24). Ministry workers need to be filled and under the influence of the Holy Spirit (Eph 1:13; 5:18). The Lord Jesus, the apostles, and first generations of Christians could do

---

20. Wright, *Mission*, 533.

nothing on their own without the help and infilling of the Holy Spirit. Being filled with the Holy Spirit is not always an emotional experience identified with an external manifestation or action. Rather, being filled with the Spirit involves a relationship with the person of the Holy Spirit characterized by radical abandonment and surrender to the Holy Spirit.

The Bible commands that believers should "be filled with the Spirit" (Eph 5:18). This imperative represents not an option but instead a necessity. Accordingly, only in the Spirit do Christians have life and live and bear fruit (Rom 8:11; Gal 5:22). The Holy Spirit is intended for, needed by, and available to all believers. Without the Holy Spirit, believers can do nothing on their own. Jesus said, "As the Father has sent me, I am sending you . . ." (John 20:21; 17:18). Jesus also breathed on them and said, "[R]eceive the Holy Spirit" (John 20:22). The persons of the Trinity operate and connect to one another in complementarity.

God's purpose for creation is for relationship. God wants fellowship with humans, unlike any other creature, and humans were created to reflect God. Seamands writes, "It is in our relatedness to others that our being human consists. Like the Trinity such human relatedness is characterized by full equality, glad submission, joyful intimacy and mutual deference."[21] Ministry not predicated by such relatedness exists at a counter purpose to God's mission. Solitary religion is unbiblical; so is solitary service for God. Christians either must find companions or make them in order to do the work of God. Christians can faithfully image God only together with other diverse image bearers.

Unity and Nature of the Church

Christ wants all believers to be one in Spirit (Eph 4:3). Unity in the body of Christ is a fundamental doctrine at the heart of this study. As such, believers are all parts of the one body, serving the same master. Regardless of social status or background Christians were one people in Christ: "For he himself is our peace, who has made the groups one and has destroyed the barrier, the dividing wall of hostility" (Eph 2:14). Unity of believers is a witness to the world for their salvation. Christians cannot mount walls of hostility and proclaim the gospel of reconciliation.

---

21. Seamands, *Image of God*, 51.

Unity in diversity is a central theme in the Bible. The history of Israel is God's story in his revelation through the one nation and one covenant people of God. God's redemption and call of his people began with Abraham and continued through Abraham's line of Isaac, Jacob, and Ephraim, through which all peoples of the earth would be blessed (Gen 12:3; 15:18–21; 17:7; 48:3–6, 12–16, 19). This calling serves as the foundation of the oneness of all God's people.

Generally, Christians also share a common humanity; they are created in God's image (Gen 1:27). The values and doctrines of faith that unite humans and believers are much more eternal than the temporary barriers and walls mounted to divide people. The following statement from the church in the Asian region supports the position core thesis of this research and calls for unity in the church in Africa. In a communiqué, following a theological consultation, Sang Bok David Kim, Yung Han Kim and Richard Howell described and called for unity of the church:

> The members of the church unite in Christ like vines in the root, with unity that must overcome all that divides us, whether gender, race, language or social differences. God calls us to demonstrate this unity for the sake of Trinitarian God's mission (John 17:21, 23). Because this is a major challenge in Christianity, we commit ourselves afresh to maintain the unity of the Spirit.[22]

Believers in Christ have a bond of unity forged by Christ, and that bond is stronger than any other relationship. Believers can celebrate rather than emphasize their differences because Christians are complete in Christ, in whom they can find other image bearers.

Exegetical hermeneutics of God's covenant with his people in both the Old and New Testaments reveal a demonstration of the doctrines of unity and ecclesiology. Hermeneutical reading of Ephesians 2 through 4 describes unity in the church. Ephesians 4:1–16 particularly illustrates the biblical foundation of the doctrine of Christian unity and equipping for service in the church. Unity of the church is forged by God and modeled after God's nature. The church is depicted in Ephesians 4:7–12 as the "body of

---

22. Sang Bok David Kim, Yung Han Kim, and Richard Howell, "The Triune God."

Christ." From among the Jews and Gentiles, God has chosen a people for himself who are united into one body – the church. Unity includes people of God in all ages, namely, those persons who believe in Christ then, now, and in the future (John 17:20–21). Christ reconciles all peoples from different backgrounds with himself, and all believers are baptized into Christ.

Diversity exists in the unity of the church, and God gives the gift of grace to every member. All members have gifts for mutual care and the building up of the body (the church) for its growth. God ordains diverse gifts for individual members of the body by his own grace, so no one can boast. Francis Foulkes writes, "[N]o member of the body of Christ is endowed with such perfection as to be able without the assistance of others, to supply his own necessities."[23] While all Christians have gifts, no one Christian has all the gifts. This giftedness is as true for the leader as for the followers.

Christ the exalted and victorious king makes a public showing of his victory and triumph as he distributes his power and authority to his followers, for his glory (Eph 4:11). God has not only given individual gifts but also gives gifts to the church as a whole. The individual gifts in fact exist for public benefit. He gave the church apostles and prophets (Eph 2:20; 4:11) to lay the foundation for his church, evangelists to carry the message of the gospel of Christ, and pastors and teachers for the local church. This cluster of five gifts is often described as the fivefold ministry of the church.[24] Nonetheless, ministry in the church is not limited to these five offices. The Bible mentions a number of callings other than the fivefold ministry and many others perhaps not mentioned at all but nonetheless useful for God's work and building his church.

Acts 8:1–8 demonstrates the life of covenant community or the body of Christ with dynamism, mutual care with exercise of a variety of gifts for common good and God's glory: "Each member contributes to persons in adversity, which helps build a rich social unity, like the loving unity through diversity found in the triune God in whose image the church, the people of God (*laos tou theou*) was created."[25] The purpose of equipping the

---

23. Foulkes, *Ephesians*, 122.
24. Turaki, *Ephesians*, 1432.
25. Stevens, *Six Days*, 53.

church with diverse spiritual gifts and peoples is for building the church and further equipping each individual for works of service until the church is mature and complete in Christ.

Not given for the benefit of the recipient only, spiritual gifts are intended for the benefit of the church, to help it grow physically and spiritually. This ongoing task should occupy the church until Christ returns. Lack of maturity leads to stunted growth with believers remaining like infants, dependent on others, open to every influence (Eph 4:14), and vulnerable to the influence of false teachers, which results in a fragmented church. Ultimately, the goal is to be found complete in Christ, which requires the diversity of others. Mature Christians grow in faith and knowledge of Christ and ultimately see all things from the perspective of Christ. They become more Christlike and speak the truth in love. Christ is the head of the church and connects all parts of the body, helps the body grow, helps it build itself up in love, and enables each part of the body do its work through the agency of the Spirit. The core of biblical history is the calling of the community and God's revelation of himself in their encounter with God.

Every community has some structure to facilitate the function of the community. The vision and mission of the NEA is to encourage unity and cooperation among the different denominations and church organizations for a common witness as one community, the body of Christ. The coming of the messianic king, the Lord Jesus Christ, fulfills this unity. Through Christ the walls of hostility and barriers are broken down. Samuel Kamaleson outlines four dominant images used in Scripture to describe the united community:

1) Flock – Matt 15:24; 18:12–14; Luke 15:3–7; John 10:11–18; Heb 13:20;
2) Building – 1 Cor 15:9; Matt 7:25; 1 Pet 2:5;
3) Bride and groom – Eph 5:24; Rev 19:16f; 21:2; and
4) Body of Christ and relationship to head – Eph 1:22–23; 4:15–16; 1 Cor 12.[26]

---

26. Kamaleson, "Discovering Our Gifts," 84–91.

The metaphors or images of flock, building, bride and groom, and body of Christ are all very different, but each one of them in their unique way demonstrates elements of united community.

In the structure of the flock and shepherd relationship, the accent is on mutual sensitivity. The building metaphor focuses on stability: the relationship of the superstructure to the foundation. The bride and groom relationship focuses on loyalty to each other. The dominant image of the body of Christ has accent on relationship.[27] These metaphors give a visual picture of the characteristics of a community united as one people but also of diverse nature.

The head of the church is Christ, and the church on earth needs leadership structures that reflect the leadership of Christ. Christ modeled leadership for the Christian community. Paul exemplified leadership in the church and appointed leaders and expounded on pastoral leadership of the church. Paul spells out the qualifications or profile of the leader in the church in the pastoral letters (e.g. 1 Tim 3:2–10; Titus 1:6–9). Like the local church, the NEA needs good leadership in order to carry out effectively its role at the national level. The model for Christian leadership is servant leadership, which Jesus demonstrated and demands of his followers.

Servant Leadership

Jesus modeled the kind of leadership needed in the church, as did Paul, one of the most outstanding leaders among the apostles of Christ.[28] In the quest for leadership in the church, leaders who model how to follow after Christ and live under Christ's rule are needed.[29] In 1 Corinthians 4, Paul envisions four models of church leadership also applicable to contemporary Christian leaders: "Leaders are underlings of Christ, stewards of God's revelation, and fathers of the church family, all in humility."[30] These leadership images call for Christlike leadership – servant leadership.

Secular studies in leadership have also recognized the importance of servant leadership. Robert Greenleaf's servant leadership theory was developed

---

27. Ibid., 86.
28. Stott, *Basic Christian Leadership*, 11.
29. Dodd, *Empowered*, 33.
30. Stott, *Basic Christian Leadership*, 114.

when he worked at AT&T and later taught at Harvard Business.[31] Both Christians and non-Christians share the word *leadership*, but these two groups hold to different understandings of the word.

Jesus told his disciples the style of leadership he expected from them and that he modeled: servant leadership (Mark 10:42–44). When Jesus spoke about leadership, he emphasized that while worldly leaders lord and rule over their subjects, his followers should not follow such a pattern when struggling with leadership rivalries due to cultural or worldly perspectives (Mark 9:33–34; 10:35–37; Luke 22:24). Jesus brought to the attention of the disciples a behavioral pattern of leadership completely different from the world in which the disciples lived. Even more than a behavioral pattern, Christ showed the disciples an inner identity, a way of thinking about themselves. He made clear his principle of leadership, namely that the leader who wants to be great should serve others. When Christians serve others, God exalts them; Jesus' life and ministry exemplified this principle (Phil 2:1–10). He demonstrated servant leadership not only in washing the disciples' feet but also in laying down his life for all people.

Servanthood, like many other symbols Jesus used in his teaching, was a cultural reality with which his audience could relate. The Palestinian homes in Jesus' day had servants in the house to care for the needs of the family; the family needs were the responsibility of the *diakonos*.[32] Jesus taught that the church should reflect this same reality. Furthermore, the needs of the members should be the responsibility of servant leaders. In their service to others, leaders are able to lead those persons they serve. Jesus moved out of the home and into the public arena or cultural fields of Palestine in shaping his disciples' understandings about the leadership principle he wanted among them. The leader is not only servant as in the household but a slave as well, with implications for public service. He said, "[A]nd whoever wants to be first must be slave of all" (Mark 10:44). The Greek word used here for slave is *doulos*.

The imagery has moved from *diakonos* (servant) to *doulos* (slave). Roger E. Dickson writes, "Slaves have no rights of command, no rights

---

31. Greenleaf, "Servant Leadership," 454.
32. Dickson, *Biblical Research*, 897.

to determine how, when or what to do."[33] People often know how to offer service, but they attempt to do so on their own terms by choosing to volunteer their service, time, and other resources and choose where and when to do so. However, slaves do not have the privilege of choice; they simply serve others without the benefit of choice. Servant leaders, as slaves, do not have the privilege of choice; they serve in response to the needs of others, whether or not they feel like serving. Their very identity is caught up in that of the master; they have no identity of their own.

Unfortunately, the kind of leadership observed in many churches today often tends to be influenced by society rather than by Christ. Christian leaders live in cultures that affect their thinking and behavioral patterns.[34] Cultural and biblical values in the life of the Christian, influences the kind of leadership exercised in the church. Alluding to the tension between the two values, Stott describes the struggle Christians face:

> [T]he church is a paradox between the "divine" ideal and the "human reality"; what it "claims" to be and what it "seems" to be; between the romantic talk about the "bride of Christ" and the very unromantic, ugly unholy and quarrelsome Christian community we know ourselves to be.[35]

Living the Christian life is a struggle, and it is unattainable without Christ (Gal 2:20). The struggle for the leader is to model the style of leadership Jesus expects of believers, which is often in conflict with the way society or culture views leadership. John Stott highlights the characteristics and dominance of the style of leadership in the different cultures and regions of the world:

> In Africa it is the tribal chief, in Latin America the machismo (exaggerated masculinity) of the Spanish male, in South Asia the religious guru fawned on by his disciples, in East Asia the Confucian legacy of the teacher's unchallengeable authority.[36]

---

33. Ibid., 898.
34. Ibid., 891.
35. Stott, *Basic Christian Leadership*, 17.
36. Ibid., 113.

These styles of leadership are based on cultural worldviews that are different from the Christian worldview, and the Christian leader cannot serve the purposes of God by adopting these models.

The need for the right kind of leaders, servant leadership modeled by Christ, exists not only at local congregational and denominational levels but also at the level of the NEA. Many denominational leaders within the national association are looking for material benefits from their position, and when such benefits are not forthcoming, they show little or no commitment to the fellowship or association. In building the association, leaders should reflect on the Trinitarian dimension of practice of unity. Unity in the body of Christ is never about benefiting the self. Instead, this unity involves self-giving and mutual deference for the other. Rather than asking about the personal benefits, leadership instead should ask how their service benefits others in the union and how together they can exalt Christ through their service to others.

African NEA leaders need to heed the biblical call for unity in the body of Christ. Believers cannot share the gospel while mounting a barricade. The many walls of division in Africa related to ethnicity, gender, religious tradition, political affiliation, and economic and social status have to be removed through the ministry of the persons of the Trinity. African theologians seek an authentic African voice and identity, and Kato observes, "[T]he advocates exalt African culture, religion, and philosophy beyond proportion."[37] Furthermore, Kato writes of "the funeral march of the biblical Christianity and heralding syncretism and universalism."[38] This theological view has the tendency to make African culture sanctified above everything else. Paul Gifford expresses a similar concern when he discusses "romanizing what is cultural"[39] and what works. Furthermore, he writes, "[W]hat is often rejected as Western may not be after all Western, and Africa does not need to reinvent the wheel – struggling to find 'cultural' ways of what works and rejecting proven ways of doing the same effectively."[40] Biblical orthodoxy cannot be exclusive to the West, to Africa,

---

37. Kato, *Theological Pitfalls*, 51.
38. Ibid., 55.
39. Gifford, "Africa's Inculturation," 18.
40. Ibid., 25.

or to any other region of the world. God's principles and demands of followers are the same, just as they are one people even in their diverse and uniquely different personalities, communities, and societies.

The kind of leadership espoused can also be described as spiritual. As a result, much of what is required of Christian leaders depend on their relationship with God and God's enablement. Spiritual disciplines, training, and development of leaders are not mutually exclusive. The church needs to be intentional about training and leadership development, especially in the area of ecumenism and promoting unity in the body of Christ. Paul's admonition to Timothy, urging the young spiritual leader to train in godliness, is insightful (1 Tim 4:7). Godliness requires training, and spiritual endowment is not an excuse to neglect training. Spiritual endowment and the exercise of spiritual gifts must take into consideration various dimensions of spirituality. In Scripture, at least two dimensions exist – the relational or love for God and neighbor (1 John 4:20) and the communal or ecclesial, as believers were created or re-created to function in community. Thus, they need to learn and grow to maturity in faith and service.[41] Leaders should be willing and eager to learn for their personal growth and development.

A perceptive reading of Scripture reveals the Lord Jesus as a master teacher with a definite teaching strategy, content, and trainees. The same can be said of the disciples and early apostles. Jesus grew from childhood "in wisdom and stature, and in favor with God and man" (Luke 2:52). Thus, training, skills acquisition, and competency building are not at counter purposes with the spiritual endowment of God. Often these gifts must be exercised and groomed in order to support and enable effective ministry.

Biblical Basis for the NEA

The NEA is a symbol of unity for the church in a nation. As such, this association functions as a church organization with distinctive features that require understanding for effective leadership. The church is both an organism (i.e. life) and an organization (i.e. structures and systems). Furthermore, the church is an organism in that it unites around the Trinity – the creation work of the Father, the saving work of Christ, and the indwelling of the Holy Spirit – no matter where individual members

---

41. Cole, "Sharing the Opportunity," 175.

are located (Eph 4:4–6). In addition, the church is an organization in that it gathers around a common purpose and doctrine and acknowledges particular systems and modes of operation, officers, and leaders. Christian understandings often emphasize the church as an organism, a spiritual being with life, but the organizational aspects, a necessary and vital means for proper functioning, require leadership competencies traditionally outside the realm of competencies for the traditional fivefold ministry leadership offices of apostle, prophet, evangelist, pastor, and teacher (Eph 4:11–13) in the church.[42] Leaders tend to focus on seemingly spiritual matters and perform poorly in running institutions or organizations. Even less often are they prepared to engage the political realm.

The organism dimension of the church needs to influence the organizational dimensions with marketplace navigation skills. The latter were perceived as worldly human techniques without which the church can do well, as opposed to spiritual gifts.[43] In the first place, God's gifts are not limited to these five offices (1 Cor 12:28). All types of gifts are given to the church in order to grow to maturity. Naturally endowed gifts would need training and skills development to use them well. Experience and leadership studies have demonstrated that natural, God-given endowments or attributes need exercise and training to develop to appropriate maximal potential.

Nonetheless, whether the local congregation, or a denomination, or an association such as the NEA, the church is primarily *missional* with God as the head. The church is different from business, social or other worldly organizations or associations; therefore, biblical and theological foundations exist to justify the NEA as a church organization that informs its leadership. According to J. Robert Clinton, Christian leaders' knowledge of the Word of God enhances their effectiveness:

> There is only one guarantee for an effective life time experience of leadership. Leaders must be people of the Word or Bible centered; one whose leadership was informed by the Bible, who had been personally shaped by biblical values, had grasped the intent of scriptural books and their content in

---

42. Ngewa, "What Is the Church," 1457.
43. Cole, "Sharing the Opportunity," 172.

such a way as to apply them to current situations and who used the Bible in ministry so as to impact followers.[44]

Further, Clinton writes, "[T]he various types of training institutions, seminaries, institutes, workshops, seminars and conferences are good and helpful in leadership development but they do not guarantee equipping."[45] God guarantees the equipping.

Isaiah 40:8 states, "The grass withers, the flower fades; but the word of our God will stand forever." Regarding this Scripture, Clinton reminds his readers, "God ensures that this unfading word, which will stand forever, can equip them."[46] Christians need to know God's Word and to discover which portion of Scripture they need to master for effectiveness.[47] Christian leaders need to be knowledgeable about God's Word and what the word says about the subject of leadership, especially for leading NEA as a *missional* organization.

Not only do biblical and historical precedents support the importance of the NEA but so do fundamental Christian theological doctrines, as had been previously demonstrated. The biblical basis for unity is perhaps best seen in Paul's comments as a Jew to Gentile believers at Ephesus (Eph 2:11–22). Cassidy observes how Paul reminded the Gentile Christians "how they were separated from Christ (v. 12a), excluded from citizenship in Israel (v. 12b), foreigners to the covenants of the promise (v. 12c), without hope (v. 12d) and without God in the world (v. 12e)."[48] Paul contrasts the past or previous situation of division with a new situation of unity in Christ because he made the believers one (Eph 2:14). Christians are part of a ministry, the diverse body of Christ, through the Holy Spirit. Ministry that seeks to unite the church in a nation, therefore, honors God and is *missional*.

---

44. Clinton, *Ministry That Lasts*, 17.
45. Ibid., x.
46. Ibid.
47. Ibid., x–xii.
48. Cassidy, "Problems and Possibilities," 72–74.

Overview of Association as Unique Type of Organization

An NEA is a voluntary organization, and like other types of associations or societies such as nonprofit organizations, they are unique and complex. The nature of associations, in particular the NEA not only as an association but also as a *missional* organization different from other associations, needs to be understood. The nature of the NEA as an organization and role of the leader seem the least understood constructs. This section seeks to highlight the essential features of organizations, particularly ecumenical organizations, in order to appreciate complex leadership challenges.

General Understanding and Definition

An association is a type of organization with a goal, structure, systems, and staff. The following definition highlights different elements of what an organization entails:

> A social unit of people that is structured and managed to meet a need or to pursue collective goals. All organizations have a management structure that determines relationships between the different activities and the members, and subdivides and assigns roles, responsibilities, and authority to carry out different tasks. Organizations are open systems-they affect and are affected by their environment.[49]

This definition is true of business organizations as well as for nonprofits, societies, charities, and evangelical associations or church councils. However, each type of organization is different and has its own unique culture that requires understanding.

Association management expert John W. Pearson writes, "[T]he profession of association management is not well understood by the average person. Even less understood was what an association executive does. Now add 'Christian' to 'association management' and the meaning was even fuzzier."[50] NEA leaders face the challenge of people understanding and supporting the work they do. In addition, the larger population of Christians

---

49. "Organization." *Businessdictionary.com*. Business Dictionary.com, n.d. Accesssed 10 February 2014.

50. Pearson, *Management Buckets*, 2.

whom the NEA represents often does not know the role and rationale of NEA as an organization. All types of associations exist across the world, but these organizations are called various names. For example, evangelical associations mostly are referred to as evangelical fellowships in contrast to councils of churches, which are mostly associations of the historic churches affiliated with the World Council of Churches (WCC). The differences between these types of organizations lie primarily in the theological and doctrinal beliefs of the council churches and the evangelicals who belong to the global counterpart of the WCC, the World Evangelical Alliance. These two main Protestant umbrella organizations as well as the Roman Catholic Church constitute the global church, although many smaller types of councils likely exist than just these three.

In every country and culture, words have unique meanings. *Alliance* or *association* may not fit within some cultural contexts. Some other more common names for associations include society, coalition, confederation, council, federation, fellowship, institute, league, network, outreach, partnership, or union. Nonetheless, the missions of such organizations are relatively the same. The church councils and evangelical fellowships exist alongside each other in many countries. Nonetheless, this coexistence adds to the misunderstanding of NEAs and church associations in general.

Definitions of associations and alliances are as varied as their names. According to the American Society of Association Executives (ASAE), the US government defines an association as "a group of persons banded together for a specific purpose."[51] This definition implies associations formed for all kinds of purposes and allows for different interpretations of associations. The different associations provide some value, services, or projects for their members and the larger community. Like other organizations, they have a goal. They reach out primarily to their members, but they also often try to meet needs of "the general public, needs that the government would otherwise have to meet."[52] For this reason, associations are often tax-exempt, such as the 501c or nonprofit organizations in America.

---

51. "Association FAQ." *Asaecenter.org*. ASAE Center for Association Leadership, n.d. Accessed 10 February 2014.

52. Ibid.

Associations have their roots in guilds of artisans who controlled the practice of their craft. Associations are formed for all kinds of purposes and objectives. Associations enhance a sense of community.[53] Individual and community objectives are better achieved with collaborative effort than doing the same alone.

The church is not the only institution coming together as one community. Community is a deeply social need of humans, and people unite for all kinds of purposes: "People voluntarily join associations because they want to work together on a common cause or interest. Associations in Europe and America contributed to the development of democratic institutions."[54] The members of associations expect some benefits in return for their membership. The benefits can come in the form of training, professional development, recognition, and opportunity for networking with people of similar professional backgrounds or social needs. The scope of what associations do and competencies needed to do the work of the association is vast and depends on the nature and objective of the association.

Ecumenical associations and NEAs in Africa require unique skills in unifying, such as those skills related to theological insights: "Believing in the mission of an organization is a powerful incentive and a great reason to go to work every day, and many people volunteer to offer their services for the work of the association."[55] However, if any community should be committed to unity, the church should exhibit such a commitment. The church does not exist for itself; instead, it exists for others, serving and reaching out to others with the love of Jesus Christ for their eternal salvation.

History and Nature of Voluntary Associations in Africa

Most of the indigenous peoples of Africa live in units or clusters commonly referred to as tribes. Each tribe has own distinct language and social and political organizations.[56] Geographical region also often differentiates one people group from another. In addition, a common culture is another characteristic of each people group. Members of a group share a common

---

53. Ibid.
54. Ibid.
55. Ibid.
56. Mbiti, *African Religions*, 100–101.

history, which traces at least mythologically either to the first human created by God or national figures responsible for establishing a particular structure of the society.[57] A person is born a member of a tribe. Community is the way of life for Africans in general marked by a spirit of sharing among ethnic groups through intermarriage, trade, and other interactions.

Family life, as in other societies, is the primary unit of the community. People live in a village as a community; children grow up conscious of being almost as much a part of the neighborhood association in which they live as of their immediate family. Various community associations include fishing parties, bush cutting, tree felling, self-help groups, or sowing and harvesting teams of men and women. Young people get together in sports clubs, study groups, peer groups, and other groups.[58] These communal groups or associations ensure each person in the association gets help from others in the group and overcomes problems and challenges together. Separate male and female secret societies are typical of traditional African culture as means of education and development of the adolescent in society. Nonetheless, these groups tend to be ethnically homogeneous, and every tribe or people group tends to have its own version of the secret society to the exclusion of other tribes.

Tribal associations exist in urban areas as well, in which village people come to the city to find better jobs and stay in contact as a community. In many cities or urban settlements, descendant unions or associations group people from each of the smaller geographical subdivisions of the country, provinces, counties, districts, or even clans and tribes. Africans come together especially when faced with common challenges as a way of dealing with the challenges. For example, in Sierra Leone, women groups come together regularly, collect money from each member, and pool these funds to provide capital for investment for one member of the group at a time. This process is repeated until every member of the group gets her turn to collect the total sum put together each time. This way, they mitigate the challenge of their inability to access loans from banks. This process works differently for communities across Africa. In Sierra Leone, this process is called *osusu,*

---

57. Ibid., 102.
58. Traub, "Community," 106–107.

but *harambe* in Kenya occurs when community members raise funds for a community member's medical bill, school fees, funeral expenses, or other financial challenges.

The challenge of the problem of colonialism drove African leaders to the conclusion that they needed to band together and cooperate for their mutual benefit. The African Union (formerly the Organization of African Unity or OAU) and various subregional groupings formed in response to the aforementioned challenges.[59] African society is a collectivist culture. People in different cultures tend to organize themselves in patterned ways that give life a distinctive look and feel in achieving personal and group goals. During colonial occupation, smaller self-help groups formed all over Africa.

Marriage, kingship, and descent (mostly patrilineal) continue to function, structure relationships, form groups, and define society in Africa. These patterned ways of life function to establish identity, determine access to resources, and prepare people for engaging larger political, economic, and religious structures.[60] Traditionally, African communities gather for discussion when faced with a serious challenge or issue. Hearing everyone, exploring solutions, and reaching agreement can take time. This process strengthens relationships, values, and common identity. Such gatherings are called *indaba, Ubuntu, Harambe,* and *Osusu,* and they all represent common features of some form of association. The different forms of associations or gatherings to find consensus show the importance of leadership as a collective process in Africa.

Background to Ecumenism

Ecumenism is the Anglo-Saxon transliteration of the Greek word *oikumene,* meaning the "inhabited earth."[61] The ecumenical movement became known as the movement aimed at recovering the unity of the church in spite of the diversity, differences, and divisions that exist in the church, shedding off their identities as Lutherans, Roman Catholics, Anglicans,

---

59. Ibid., 108.
60. Rynkiewich, *Soul, Self, and Society*, 99; Mbiti, *African Religions*, 35.
61. Kato, *Theological Pitfalls*, 29; Githiga, *Bulwark*, 186.

Orthodox, or members of independent churches in order to put on the full image of united Christendom rather than mere interdenominational cooperation in mission.[62] The Protestants call separately organized groups of churches *denominations,* meaning specific associations of congregations with distinct beliefs and governance. This term makes no ecclesiological sense to Orthodox or Catholic traditions, which conceive of the church as one entity unified in doctrine and a structure of authority.[63] These two traditions preceded the Reformation, but schism exists between them, even if they do not regard their schism in the same sense as the Protestants regard denominations.

The genesis of denominations in the church is the Reformation; Christians in Europe began organizing themselves into separate and distinct groups. Wesley Granberg-Michaelson observes that in the democratic, cultural, and religious soil of the United States, along with the missionary movement, such division flourished. As Christianity spread to other parts of the world, it did so with "separate and separating identities; denominated" from one another.[64] The pitfall of this separation is the spirit of *denominationalism.* Denominationalism is the tendency to divide the church into different groups or denominations and advocate for such separations. Merriam-Webster defines denominationalism as "devotion to denominational principles or interest; the emphasizing of denominational difference to the point of being narrowly exclusive."[65] Denominationalism is a disposition or inclination to criticize opposing opinions and an attitude of mind that favors one denomination over others.

Even though sufficient theological and biblical foundations exist for unity in the body of Christ, sections of the church also find theological basis for local church autonomy or *separatism.* Separatism is "a belief in, movement for, or state of separation – as schism, secession, or segregation."[66] Separatism is a sectarian attitude and tendency to stop the church from being united, as one body of Christ, in spite of the denominational differences,

---

62. Mbiti, *African Religions,* 266.
63. Granberg-Michaelson, *From Times Square,* 13.
64. Ibid.
65. "Denominationalism," *Merriam-Webster Online.* Accessed 14 February 2014.
66. "Separatism." Ibid.

as espoused by certain denominations. Europe experienced some devastating years of ecclesiastical wars in which people killed each other over doctrinal differences. Paige Patterson alludes to the tension between the two views – unity and local church autonomy:

> The New Testament church demonstrates congregational sensitivity and respect for congregational cooperation (Acts 15; Acts 13: 2–3; 15:22; 1 Cor 5:2–5; 2 Cor 2:6, 10; 1 Tim 5:19–20); the practice of the Apostles and the commands of Jesus Christ upon which the practices were based (e.g. Matt 18:15–20; John 20:19–23), have not held the same authority by all Christians; the Roman Catholic and the Protestant innovations beyond scripture provided the historical wedge that required the free churches to remain separate.[67]

As Scripture asserts, the causes of denominational division are motivated by less honorable goals. Accordingly, James asks, "What causes fights and quarrels among you? Don't they come from your desires that battle within you?" (4:1). Divisions often result from judgment of fellow Christians and convictions that separation is required for purity of practice and fidelity of doctrine, even in its most minute specifics. Granberg-Michaelson posits tens of thousands of ideas of such purity exist, even within the same denomination.[68] The reasons for division may be very trivial, ignoring the far weightier reasons that unite the church. When Christians assert these divisions, they seem to say that Jesus needs to be crucified again (Rom 2).

To illustrate some of the reasons for division, a proponent for *separatism* states, "[S]o long as 'sacramentalism' and 'sacerdotalism' and 'infant baptism' prevail in a great part of the Christian world, and so long as centralized 'ecclesiasticisms' ruled over the 'spiritual lives' of men the Baptist will have a mission."[69] These words seem to allude that traditions other than Baptist are not saved or at least practice the wrong doctrines. Biblical orthodoxy does not support such a position.

---

67. Patterson, "Baptists," 1.
68. Granberg-Michaelson, *From Times Square*, 30.
69. Scarborough, "What We Have to Expect," 8.

Unlike that of early ecumenical councils, many evangelical denominations hold the opinion that contemporary ecumenism minimizes doctrinal issues and that ecumenists believe "doctrine divides, but service (social action) and common humanity unite; and unity, almost at any cost, is the greatest thing that can happen to the Christian church."[70] Biblical orthodoxy affirms a high view of Scripture as the final authority of opinion and interpretation. Those matters of truth fundamental to salvation are clear and simple and need no interpretation. They come from God through his word, the Holy Scriptures, as imperative commands to obey or reject with free will to choose. Choice has consequences; obedience gains eternal salvation and rejection peril of eternal damnation.

Ancient Ecumenism

Early church councils such as the Councils of Nicaea (325), Constantinople I (381), Ephesus (431), Chalcedon (451), and Constantinople II (553) are commonly called ecumenical councils.[71] The early ecumenical councils were concerned with issues of doctrine. In fact, for the first millennium of the Christian era, every council condemned a major heresy. Although ecclesiastical politics played a part in some of the struggles, the primary concern of the Orthodox church was purity of doctrine. The five councils were decisive for the development of orthodox Christian doctrine, which has had huge influence upon the church throughout its history.[72] Like the Pharisees in the Old Testament, religious leaders or teachers may be inclined to conflate some doctrines with tradition or personal preferences; therefore, a forum such as the NEA, is used to build consensus on the fundamentals that unite the church.

While the whole church seems to agree on the subject of unity, it does not agree on what such unity looks like. The default assumption sees differences not as opportunities for experiencing the diversity of the Holy Spirit's gifts but instead as excuses for division and separating from one another.[73] Furthermore, the nature and perception of unity by the different

---

70. Kato, *Theological Pitfalls*, 130.
71. Ibid., 129.
72. Tanner, "African Church," 204.
73. Ibid., 215.

factions is also a point of disagreement. Various efforts attempt to forge unity, whether ecumenism or approaches such as alliances, associations, unions, or communions – groups generally preferred by evangelicals. The form, shape, structure, and expression of the attempts to create unity can cause disunity. As a result, the problem of disunity emerges not from differences or diversity but instead from the ways diverse groups position themselves in juxtaposition to other groups.

Some sections of the church believe unity is spiritual and invisible, while others wonder how Jesus and the apostles could require and command unity so the world may believe and conclude unity as inapplicable to the divided physical church. Nonetheless, the invisible church is united. Granberg-Michaelson writes, "[T]his pilgrimage of Christian unity has to be a spiritual, mystical journey, woven into practical steps to be taken; and that the practical way and the mystical way have to be constantly held together."[74] Christians need a stronger, more organic and more Trinitarian understanding of unity to combat false senses of unity that give the appearance of being together but, in fact, fundamentally oppose each other. If indeed Christians are united spiritually, this unity should find visible and even structural expression.

Modern Ecumenism

Founded in 1948, the WCC institutionalizes modern-day ecumenism and envisions bringing together all churches, including the Roman Catholic Church, under one tent.[75] Nonetheless, ecumenism is a child of the evangelical mission field. As missionaries went out to the various mission fields, a need existed for cooperation among them and their supporters that led to a call for various missionary conferences. The four major landmark conferences that preceded the formation of the WCC were Edinburgh 1910, Jerusalem 1928, Madras 1938, and Whitby in 1947.[76] The Edinburgh 1910 was most influential because of its global nature.

---

74. Granberg-Michaelson, *From Times Square*, 45.
75. Lowell, *Ecumenical Mirage*, 11.
76. Kato, *Theological Pitfalls*, 130.

The Edinburgh 1910 World Mission Conference is noted for purposively barring doctrinal issues in its discussion at the outset of the conference.[77] Kato describes downplaying doctrinal issues as a weakness, one of the features that today's ecumenism justifiably can claim for its heritage.[78] Apart from the weaknesses of the Edinburgh 1910 Conference, Kato claims that Edinburgh 1910 was a conference of evangelicals, rebuffing claims of ecumenist enthusiasts as the only champions of unity. Kato criticizes the ecumenical movement; he says ecumenism portrays the general idea of a brotherhood and is symbolized institutionally by the National Council of Churches. Its forte is brotherhood, based on the feeling that doctrinal differences do not matter as long as all can come together to eat together and talk together.[79] As a result, the key issue involves striving for unity without discounting the importance of doctrinal differences.

Another aspect of ecumenism, from the liberal viewpoint, is to unite the Roman Catholic Church with the Protestant church, including the different denominations, and create one ecclesiastical institution.[80] Kato is concerned particularly that the WCC is making a large investment in the third world to peddle what he calls poisonous elements or liberal theology that does not accept the absolute nature of the Bible.[81] Kato posits, "[W]hile the evangelicals believe that 'the Bible is the word' of God, liberals advocate that the Bible 'contains' the word of God."[82] The difference in opinion is not simply semantics but the way the Bible is interpreted and how Christians come to and live out their faith.

The evangelical association or fellowship represents an alternate conception of ecumenism especially when it emphasizes spiritual unity and doctrine of the Bible, the person and work of Christ in salvation, and life and conduct. The premier symbol of global evangelical unity is the WEA, which traces its founding to 1846 in London, when it was called the International Evangelical Alliance, nearly a century earlier than the

---

77. Van Beek, *Revisioning*, xiv; Kato, *Theological Pitfalls*, 132.
78. Kato, *Theological Pitfalls*, 32.
79. Ibid., 130.
80. Ibid.
81. Ibid., 140.
82. Ibid., 140–141.

WCC.[83] The WEA structure has tended to be mercurial since its beginning. It prides itself as being a movement rather than an organization. Many leaders blame this self-assessment on its pietistic disposition, which tends to focus on personal piety rather than on ritual and church government. This tendency to shy away from building a structure is probably a reaction to the conciliar nature of the Vatican and the WCC. While likely rooted in its theological leaning, Christina Breman asserts that the problem was "slave-holding," which nearly killed the WEA at its very start. The fledgling WEA was a loose organization of mainly individual Christians rather than their denominations, and they were very wary of taking responsibility for one another's actions, especially with regard to owning slaves.[84] Elements of this fragile nature still exist in the WEA today.

Between the First and Second World Wars, the WEA diminished in influence because of tensions and controversies and a lack of a good program of action.[85] At a meeting in Woudschoten, Netherlands, in 1951 the evangelical leaders from twenty-one nations decided to revitalize the WEA. The World Evangelical Fellowship was then born[86] in 1951. However, the fledgling structure or lack thereof continues as the heritage of the WEA and proves rather problematic for the movement. As a global body with over 600 million individual Christians in 129 countries, the WEA does not have a physical location of its own.

However, the WEA in many ways continues to be a dynamic movement with seven regional alliances (one of which is the AEA), 129 national alliances (associations), and over 150 organizations. WEA's mission is "to speak as a trusted voice, to equip members and leaders for global impact, and connect its members and others for common action in the furtherance of God's reign."[87] The WEA plays an important role in global Christianity and the mission of the church.

---

83. Breman, *Association of Evangelicals*, 316.
84. Ibid.
85. Ibid., 317.
86. Ibid.; Fuller, *People*, 25–28.
87. "Introduction." *Worldea.org*. World Evangelical Alliance, n.d. Accessed 19 August 2013.

Despite the WCC's stated commitment to deepen ecumenical relationships with churches and widen the ecumenical movement at the same time, new sources of division both within and among churches continue to happen. The multiplicity and complexity of churches, Christian bodies, and interchurch organizations constitute a great challenge to ecumenism.[88] Recognizing that ecumenism as fully understood went beyond the WCC, since the 1990s, efforts for new initiatives aimed at achieving the WCC's vision.[89] Through a series of regional consultations on five continents, the Global Christian Forum was birthed. Thus, the WCC seems to be getting closer to achieving its vision in the Global Christian Forum, although the Forum is more flexible and non-conciliar by nature.

Ecumenism in Africa

The schisms and divisions of the church in the West and other regions of the world did not spare Africa. The doctrinal battles and other courses of divisions in Europe and America, in particular, played out on the continent of Africa at the same time as the church was planted across the continent. Such division was part of the heritage of the African church. Both the WCC and WEA have their affiliate (branches) organizations on the continent.

All Africa Conference of Churches (AACC)

The split of the church at the global level plays out on the continent of Africa as part of the package of the Christian faith. Several national councils and evangelical fellowships have been formed in many countries. These organizations preceded the formation of the All Africa Conference of Churches (AACC), an affiliate of WCC, in Kampala in 1963. The AACC criteria for membership are very basic and accommodate churches that would be considered by other traditions as sects. They affirm the lordship of Jesus Christ as God and the only Savior and the Trinity according to the Scriptures. Membership is open to denominations and individual churches. Kato criticizes the AACC regarding its minimal membership criteria

---

88. Miller and Tveit, *GCF Committee*, 3.
89. Rowland-Jones, "Global Christian," 3–38.

such as that of its affiliate, the WCC. In addition, some of their theologians question Scripture as the final authority. Many AACC theologians subscribe to the liberal theological concept of evangelism and salvation.[90] Political independence from colonialism and Africanization was the message preached. The conception of sin is not clear; therefore, they have no urge to call people to repentance.

Silent on its theological beliefs and confessional statements, the AACC says very little compared to the basis of faith and criteria for membership in the evangelical associations. Particularly, the statement is mute on the virgin birth, vicarious death, resurrection, and second coming. It also remains silent about the authenticity, inspiration, and inerrancy of Scripture.[91] The doctrinal lapses in the message of salvation were the fundamental differences between the conciliar types of ecumenical movements in the WCC affiliate national councils and the evangelical fellowships. The WEA and the regional and national affiliates must not just react to liberal and neo-orthodoxy beliefs of the ecumenical councils and the WCC affiliates but must live out their own values and build bridges with the ecumenists as vital members of the body of Christ in a true and proactive manner. The ecumenical tradition is reputed for its stance on and work in social justice. The *Word-centered* life of evangelicals can be enriched by discovering the compassionate life of the social justice tradition in the ecumenist, recognizing that Christ lived a Word-centered life that also was compassionate and, indeed, virtuous, prayer filled, Spirit empowered, and sacramental as the various other traditions emphasize one or the other of these streams of the Christian life.[92] The leaders who have led the different traditions in history can trace their allegiance to the lordship of Christ.

Nonetheless, efforts toward church union or cooperation at the continental level could not come to a common consensus. The evangelicals advocated for unity based on God's Word, namely that belief and practice of believers seeking unity should be in accordance with what the Bible says. Realizing that unity was desirable and that Jesus prayed for both spiritual and visible unity (John 17:21), evangelicals pulled together to have

---

90. Kato, *Theological Pitfalls*, 148.
91. Ibid., 149.
92. Foster, *Streams*, 137.

an association of their own.[93] This effort led to the founding of the AEA. African Christians probably would have addressed the differences differently. However, Western missionaries still dominated much of the leadership of the church in the 1960s and divisions in Europe and America were inevitably bound to unfold in Africa. Without healing the divisions in the church in Europe and America, missionaries arriving in Africa somehow were insulated from one another and planted churches in separate parts of the same country. These churches remained separate entities from one another, with much emphasis on doctrinal distinctive and differences rather than on the elements uniting different groups as the one body of Christ.

Association of Evangelicals in Africa (AEA)

The Association of Evangelicals in Africa and Madagascar (AEAM), currently the AEA, was founded in Limuru in 1966. The NEAs comprise the AEA membership and has much more elaborate criteria for membership based on accepting the entire affirmation of faith.[94] A fundamental difference between the Council of Churches and the evangelical association is that the latter is less conciliar, advocates for partnership in the gospel with little emphasis on organizational structure and more emphasis on spiritual life, and fellowship. The evangelicals focus more on evangelism rather than on social action.

Thirty-six national associations constitute the Africa-wide association, the AEA. The NEAs are in various states of health in terms of effectiveness in achieving their objectives. The NEA, like any organization, depends very much on leadership competency and other leadership factors for effectiveness. In the available leadership development programs in the church and seminaries, few prepare people for leading a church association such as an NEA. The men and women who bear the responsibility of leading the NEAs come from diverse backgrounds and have built a wealth of experience while carrying out the responsibilities of their respective jobs over the years. The NEAs can benefit from these experiences for future development of leaders in enhancing NEA leadership as a *missional* vocation.

---

93. Kato, *Theological Pitfalls*, 170.
94. AEA Secretariat, *Constitution: Amended* (Nairobi: AEA, 2010), 1–2.

This project assumed that the experiences and perspectives of participants – AEA regional presidents and the general secretaries of the NEAs in Africa – would reveal a list of competencies essential for effectiveness in leading the NEA. The purpose of the research was to identify leadership competencies required for leading an NEA as well as needed leadership development competencies of current general secretaries or NEA leaders in Africa by interviewing current regional presidents and national leaders in the AEA.

Leading NEA

NEA leaders need to understand the concept of leadership as well as the theological and biblical perceptions of unity in order to build commitment in unifying the body of Christ composed of churches from various backgrounds, denominations, and traditions. This section attempts to provide an overview of discourse on the subject of leadership. The goal is to build understanding of the nature of leadership, cultural practices and impact, and leadership effectiveness and how these aspects apply to the subject of leading African NEAs.

Leading and leadership in associations and, specifically in NEAs, is complex. The cultural milieu in which leadership is exercised contributes to its complexity. According to Richard L. Hughes, Robert C. Ginnett, and Gordon J. Curphy, "leadership is a process, not a position and viewed as an interaction between the leader, follower and the environment."[95] The three elements of follower, environment, and leader interact, and the complex nature of that interaction informs the understanding of the word *leadership*.

The leader is the most important or influential of the three elements in the leadership process; therefore, the behavior, influence, and attributes the leader brings to the equation can offset the balance for better or worse.[96] Leaders influence the outcome by the way they interact with their followers in the environment. The leader facilitates the crafting of the organization's identity and shaping of culture rather than creating or primarily controlling

---

95. Hughes, Ginnett, and Curphy, *Leadership*, 4.
96. Ibid., 16.

it.[97] Peter. G. Northouse similarly highlights the complex nature of the concept of leadership: "[F]our central components to the concept of leadership. First, leadership is a process. Second, leadership involves influence. Third, leadership occurs within a group context. Finally and fourthly, leadership involves goal attainment."[98] The leader's role is to harmonize the different elements to achieve a single goal.

Leadership can be understood according to the leader's action. Thus, the leader's task is to set direction to bring about change, resulting in vision and strategies for realizing the vision. The leader's task also includes "looking for the right fit between people and the vision and motivating them to overcome barriers to change toward the desired future."[99] Accordingly, leadership simply involves coping with change. However, sometimes leadership takes place when the leader is absent, which presents another dimension to the complex process of leadership.

The definition for leadership varies from one scholar to another. James G. Clawson defines leadership as "managing energy first of yourself and those around you and that the quality of leadership can be assessed by the level of energy exuded by the leader and followers alike."[100] Low energy means low leadership, and high energy means good leadership. Furthermore, Clawson describes leadership as human behavior that occurs at three levels: "visible behavior, conscious thought and semiconscious or preconscious basic values and assumptions."[101] At the first level, others can see and describe what the leaders do; level two is the conscious and subconscious thoughts and may or may not reveal these. At level three, are "values, assumptions, beliefs and expectations – VABEs – about the world."[102] As such, a person's point of view can characterize him or her as a follower or a leader and even can identify one's type and style of leadership.

---

97. Dockery, *Christian Leadership*, 2.
98. Northouse, *Leadership*, 158.
99. Kotter, "What Leaders Really Do," 40.
100. Clawson, *Level Three*, 3.
101. Ibid., 25.
102. Ibid., 26.

No universally accepted definition exists for leadership; nevertheless, the various perspectives provide some understanding of the concept of leadership. Barna suggests a fairly inclusive and descriptive definition:

> [A] leader is one who mobilizes, one whose focus is influencing people, a person who is goal driven, someone who has an orientation in common with those who rely upon him for leadership, and someone who has people willing to follow him.[103]

The goal of leadership is to bring about outcomes that benefit followers and the community. Many leaders have used their influence for debilitating ends for their followers and their community. Leadership that cannot benefit followers is poor leadership, and it is non-Christian.

Theories of Leadership

Various leadership theories have been postulated to enhance its understanding. These theories represent outcomes of considerable empirical research over the years, and even though they help promote various understandings of leadership, none is very conclusive.[104] This lack of a conclusive definition underscores the complexity of the subject of leadership. The following overview explains five major leadership approaches or theories, including trait, contingency, power, influence, behavioral, situational, and approach.[105] New theories are always propounded when the old ones lose their effectiveness or when the new one tends to complement existing ones for effectiveness.

Trait Approach

The trait approach points to attributes such as motives, values, and skills, as the key factors for leadership effectiveness. The trait theory assumes "leaders possess certain traits other people do not possess."[106] Nonetheless, no definitive list of traits has proven to account for leadership effectiveness. The theory is also based on the assumption that leaders are born rather than

---

103. Barna, "Nothing," 23.
104. Moore, *Leadership*, 17–21; Hughes, Ginnett, and Curphy, *Leadership*, 520.
105. Moore, *Leadership*, 17–21.
106. Ibid., 19.

made. Whereas attributes or traits of the leader may contribute to leadership effectiveness, they are limited in scope. Trait is only a single variable and does not adequately explain the complex process of leadership.

Behavioral Approach

The behavioral approach focuses on leaders' actions and how they spend their time. Furthermore, this approach also studies the patterns of activities, functions, and responsibilities of the job and behavior of effective leaders. Like the trait approach, the behavioral approach focuses on one variable and does not take into consideration other leadership factors or variables. As a result, the behavioral theory too provides only a "simplistic understanding of the complex process of leadership."[107]

Power-Influence Approach

The power-influence approach involves the study of the leader's influence on other people and relates to the power possessed and exercised by a leader. Lori L. Moore writes, "Power and influence are of concern to researchers as influence is the essence of leadership and power is important not only for influencing followers, but also for influencing peers and superiors, as well as individuals outside of an organization."[108] The power-influence approach tends to be manipulative and hardly transformative. Jesus does not recommend this style of leadership for his followers, and it may not lead to effectiveness in the context of the church. Jesus used a different nature and ethic of power in his earthly ministry.

Nonetheless, power can be useful if conceived properly. Hughes, Ginnett, and Curphy write, "Although we usually think of power as belonging to the leader, it is actually a function of the leader, the followers and the situation."[109] Transformational leaders use power to empower others. Power can be redemptive or abused. Worldly people use power to lord over their followers, but Christ's model of leadership empowers others.

---

107. Ibid., 21.
108. Ibid., 19.
109. Hughes, Ginnett, and Curphy, *Leadership*, 118.

Situational Approach

The leadership outcome depends on the context and the situation. It emphasizes the chemistry among the leaders' and followers' behavior and the prevailing circumstances. In the choice of leadership in an organization, consideration for the relationship among leaders and followers and the prevailing situation plays a critical role in the decision. To that end, Moore writes, "[E]ffective leadership depends on finding balance between individuals and the organization such that both can obtain maximum satisfaction."[110] The organizational and personal goals of people should have a confluence.

Integrative Approach

The integrative approach takes into consideration more than one type of leadership variable and is dependent on other types of leadership variables. Because of the complex nature of leadership, it can be expressed in an integrative and overlapping process. Leadership flows out of aspects of the leader-follower-situation interaction.[111] The leader alone does not influence the outcome.

Styles of Leadership

Styles of leadership are personal; as a result, classifying leadership styles into broad categories can prove vague. Nonetheless, early categorization spelled out these categories as autocratic, democratic, and laissez-faire.[112] The characteristic style of the different types of leaders is mostly based on their attitude and use of power or authority. Sanghan Choi maintains, "[A]utocratic leadership style implies a high degree of control by the leaders without much freedom or participation of members in group decisions. Both democratic and laissez-faire leadership imply a low degree of control by the leader."[113] The democratic leader encourages participation of group members to develop methods or procedures used to set goals. The

---

110. Moore, *Leadership*, 20.
111. Hughes, Ginnett, and Curphy, *Leadership*, 520.
112. Moore, *Leadership*, 21.
113. Choi, "Democratic Leadership," 245.

laissez-faire leader neither maintains a high degree of control nor motivates the group towards achieving its goals.

Understanding of leadership continues to build on new ideas based on research on leadership behavior and leadership effectiveness. A new understanding of leadership effectiveness is the transformational style of leadership.[114] Transformational leadership is a shift from traditional or transactional styles. Transactional leadership is based on contingent rewards for others in return for compliance, and the team does not necessary possess shared values. Transactional leadership is task oriented and stresses obedience and loyalty, as autocratic leadership does.[115] A transformational leader recognizes followers' potential and helps them to achieve full potential. This type of leadership resembles that of the servant leader, the kind of leadership style commanded by Jesus.

Leadership in the African Context

A fluid relationship exists between the secular and sacred in the African context.[116] Understanding of the African worldview is necessary in order to grasp the issue of leadership, like many other issues, in Africa. Adeyemo defines worldview as "basic presuppositions that serve as a grid through which people see their world."[117] According to Adeyemo, the African lives in a religious world and perceives, analyzes, and interprets reality or events through his or her religious grid. In illustration, Adeyemo cites an example of how two leaders dealt with national disasters in their various countries concurrently:

> In 1979, Britain experienced an excessive snowstorm and the then Prime Minister had to appoint a minister of Snow to handle the situation. In the same year, Kenya experienced a severe drought and the then President Moi, called a day of

---

114. Moore, *Leadership*, 22.
115. Giltinane, "Leadership Styles," 36.
116. Okesson, "Are Pastors," 133.
117. Adeyemo, *Is Africa*, 82.

national prayer and fasting and as was his practice, went to church that day.[118]

According to Adeyemo, the two examples make a sharp contrast between a mechanistic Western and a mystical African worldview.[119] Africans believe that the visible, tangible, material world of humans is influenced, impacted upon, and even controlled by forces of the spirit world. The laws of physics, which explain natural occurrences, are a foreign concept to the African mind. The difference in worldview illumines not only strengths in African leadership but also the weaknesses and dangers associated with making leadership sacred.

The African believes that the invisible world of spirits, including ancestors, has great influence upon the visible world.[120] Consequently, those persons with access to the invisible world are believed able to manipulate the spirit forces. As such, religious leaders, witch doctors, and *jujumen* are respected, venerated, and feared in the society. Where this African worldview dominates, the following socioeconomic and political or leadership implications are evident:

1) Leadership in society is conferred either by possessing mystical or magical power, military might, inheritance, by being wealthy and generous, or a combination of these. Leadership is also viewed as hereditary, associated with ancestors. Appointment to public office is by selection rather than election, and the process is sacred. This sacredness is both a gift and a concern when dealing with the subject because it posits the leader as higher than others (superhuman) and not able to be touched, which makes the leaders sacred.
2) Positions and powers are usually retained for life unless the leader falls out of favor with the ancestors.
3) Governments in traditional society have no opposition parties, and those opposed to the authorities are treated as rebels.
4) Bloodlines running through extended family, clan, and tribe

---

118. Ibid.
119. Ibid.
120. Ibid., 82–83.

are very strong, giving rise to nepotism, tribal favoritism, and patrimony.[121]

Making leaders accountable and critically assessing leadership in dealing with community challenges is difficult with the kind of belief system described.

Peter Fuseini Haruna describes a poverty of leadership in Africa. To that end, he writes, "Leadership is personalized and this personalization leads to idolization of the leader to such an extent that people are made to believe that their rights come from generosity of the leader."[122] The people have no rights of their own and are not able to hold the leader accountable for anything. Accordingly, Henry Okullu writes, "Every leader becomes an ungazetted king; sitting in an unimpeachable position and ruling supreme for life."[123] Leaders have a tendency to stay in office until they die without thinking of another person succeeding them.

In order to understand the issues surrounding leadership or the poverty of leadership in the African context, exploring the sociocultural and theological antecedents contributing to the kind of leadership practiced in the church is necessary. Gregg A. Okesson discusses the deification of the leader and coins the word *sacralization*:

> There are many possible meanings to this concept. As implied by the word, an extra endowment of sacred power becomes associated with a person or thing, whether: (1) intended for a particular purpose over a specific period; (2) inculcated within a person as a permanent aspect of their being; or, (3) perceived as self-evident by the masses. Sacralisation elevates a person (or thing) in terms of being or essence; creating tiers of importance (or, personhood).[124]

Followers perceive a sacralized leader as being transcendent, possessing sacred power, and being closer to God than other ordinary humans. The association of power with nearness to the divine in order to stifle opposition

---

121. Ibid., 83–84.
122. Haruna, "Leadership Paradigm," 940.
123. Okullu, "African Context," 30.
124. Okesson, "Are Pastors," 111.

and defend autocratic rule represent some of the defining characteristics of sacralization. Accordingly, neo-patrimonial systems of authority in which power resides with the person rather than with the office often feature sacralization held together by kinship ties. The concept of sacralization explains the problem of tribalism, corruption, and nepotism. Power becomes an attribute of the person, and leadership succession is problematic. Leaders think they become lesser persons when they step down.

While patrimony is not all bad, and while some benefits exist in this system, it creates certain problems in governance. One leader staying in office for a long time can provide peace, stability, and socioeconomic well-being for the community, especially under a benevolent and transformational leader. However, the people will suffer under the yoke of a dictator interested only in his personal security and comfort and who ruthlessly crushes any dissenting voices among his or her subjects.

Sacralization requires a sociocultural understanding of traditional African society. In the context of this research, leadership in the church, distortions of the Christian faith enforce the problem of deification with further alterations from the history of Western evangelicalism. The Judeo-Christian faith long has suffered tendencies to elevate humans as godlike. Sin is rooted in humans' devaluing of their humanity and image bearing of God when instead they strive to be like God. Ultimately wanting to be more, they became less. Such striving is true of all human cultures, but it may manifest and impact the cultures differently. Okesson writes, "Leaders are continually enticed to deny their own humanity over and against the alluring promise of being more than human, 'Godlike' or imbibing some special form of deity with their person."[125] The cultural perceptions of the leader pose a challenge to Christian leaders who are commanded to live out Jesus' style of leadership – as a servant.

Western evangelicalism faces a trend to elevate supernatural elements of the Christian faith, often at the expense of the natural, along an emphasis upon the rise of the enlightenment, shifting from ecclesiastical powers to a focus upon the natural world inclusive of industrialization, the scientific method, and elevated importance of human reason. Evangelicals

---

125. Ibid., 117–118.

reacted against many of these secularizing currents by overemphasizing the supernatural as a defense against the modernistic influences taking place within their Western societies. Hence, they defended the divine origins of Scripture, emphasized Jesus' deity, and promoted the supernatural calling of pastors, leaders, and missionaries. Such theology indicates God, and thus divine power, as always primary, total, monopolistic, omnipotent, and ultimate.[126] This mode of thinking about divinity, which seems to be the norm in many traditions, often fails to help because it conjures a magical sense of divine power that frequently ignores the gentle, suffering, and loving nature of God, which Easter and its surrounding symbols reflect.

The power and providence of God for the well-being of people does not exclude pain and suffering. Humans struggle with a theology of Christ's humanity and his particularity because of their own humanity. This image of the suffering and loving God is important because it gives a holistic understanding of the mystery of divine power and holds promise in any attempt to recover human power that has been subjected to the whims and caprices of certain individuals and their violent acts.[127] For these reasons, Christians must ground their understandings of leadership in the Trinitarian nature, which resists all of these tendencies within the self-giving of the community.

Okesson's observations exist in tandem with the rise of the all-male Afrikaner secret society *Broederbond* (Brotherhood) in South Africa, which uses neo-Calvinist philosophical views developed by Abraham Kuyper. The Afrikaners see themselves as God's special breed of people chosen to fulfill a "messianic destiny" through the apartheid system and practices in that country.[128] They used the Bible, even if with wrong interpretations, to justify their beliefs.

The leader is the sole individual that tends to dominate discussion on leadership in Africa. According to Haruna, "much of the discourse on leadership in sub-Saharan Africa emphasizes leader characteristics, skills, styles, and behaviors, while ignoring the relationships, interactions, practical judgments, and unique contexts that constitute leadership in everyday

---

126. Ibid., 119.
127. Bongmba, "Rethinking Power," 108; Okesson, "Are Pastors," 126.
128. Bloomberg, and Dubow, "Christian-Nationalism," 5.

cultural community life."[129] The emphasis on the leader characteristics and behavior has the tendency to make leaders appear to be more human than their followers, with a blotted ego.[130] History is replete with heroic stories of individuals whose exploits brought positive transformation for their community and society. However, Haruna argues that these stories and leadership accomplishments have not had the same success in every leadership situation. As a result, Haruna asserts that in Africa's quest for good leadership and capacity for governance the time has come to rethink the approach to leadership in Africa and look at leadership in the context of not just the leader but of the community as a whole to bring about the needed sociocultural change.[131] This view is consistent with the African worldview in which African people act collectively to find solutions to common challenges.

Need for Paradigm Shift

Africa needs a paradigm shift, a careful revising of leadership perspectives in a manner that is in consonant with the community's way of life.[132] The leader-follower perspective has advantages, but it also has "a limited circumscription, definition, and operationalization of leadership."[133] The location of power, whether open to all or limited to certain people, is debatable. Power does not have to be oppressive in the hands of the individual, especially when viewed as generative from theological perspective.

The family and wider community and networks have a role in decision making and finding solutions to community problems collectively. This kind of collective leadership has greater chance of success than giving the responsibility exclusively to the leader. Evidence in contemporary leadership literature suggests that emphasis is shifting from priority of the leader to community-focused leadership.[134] This shift appears to occur from a sociological perspective, which needs a critique from a theological perspective. Elias K. Bongmba posits that "a theological perspective on power,

---

129. Haruna, "Leadership Paradigm," 941.
130. Ibid., 943.
131. Ibid., 944.
132. Ibid., 941–942.
133. Ibid., 941.
134. Ibid., 946.

taught that power must enrich an 'intersubjective' mode of existence; 'intersubjective' meant the convergence of two or more subjectivities."[135] The object of good leadership is human and societal advancement, and a moral imperative to engage the entire community and not just an individual.

Referring to changes in power that make capturing and confining power difficult for one person, Bongmba writes, "[P]ower in institutions and that of individuals is fluid and temporary in nature – this is either permanent or out of reach."[136] Although institutions and certain individuals within them have power, such power cannot be considered permanent or out of reach. The nature of power is transient, dynamic, and difficult for one person to capture and confine.[137] Ultimately power is God's and people are entrusted with it to the extent of its faithful use to build others up rather than tear them down.

The leadership structure in the church is also changing where the trend is moving toward ecumenism and a global church. One important indication that this change is taking place concerns the provision of leaders from Southern and Eastern Christianity rather than the European and American domination of leadership characterized by previous times.[138] The scenario in the church poses a challenge to have the church respond to societal issues holistically.[139] The church should not only have mission as a program, but the very reason and all of what it does is mission – it is *missional*.

Birgit Meyer asserts that extroversion or patriarchy does have both its advantages and disadvantages; nevertheless, she highlights the critical role the church in Africa has to play in the global church and the need to promote peace and social cohesion in a region that is also divided by ethnicity.[140] People are incurably ethnic; the gospel has not touched that part of their identity. For these and more reasons, this study was important because it addressed the issue of unity within associations and how to remove some of these barriers.

---

135. Bongmba, "Rethinking Power," 131.
136. Ibid., 126.
137. Ibid.
138. Carpenter, "Christian Scholar," 1–14.
139. Ibid., 3.
140. Meyer, "Christianity in Africa," 463.

In Mikael Karlström's critique of Mbembe's portrayal of African leadership, he asserts that much of what Mbembe highlights is negative and familiar in leadership literature on Africa: "His depictions of presidential grandiosity, political sycophancy, ostentatious corruption, flamboyant violence, and coercive ceremonialism are depressing commonplaces in literature on postcolonial African politics."[141] Karlström gives a more optimistic view of these practices, citing an example of how patriarchal leadership unfolds in the community in Southern Uganda, as elements of mutual reciprocity. The ritualized dialogism between state and people are not necessarily pathological and inherent in the African political imagination. The tendency is to imitate what is practiced at the various local community levels to the national level that is more elaborate and visible. The relationship between the leader and the community is rooted in ethnic solidarity and patron clientage, which is uncritically viewed as exploitative and disempowering of the subjects by their political leaders.[142] Karlström observes that followers spur on seemingly unhelpful leadership practices:

> Africans criticize and ridicule the excesses and grandiosity of their rulers, using lewd humor to deflate their pretensions. But the very same Africans also expect and even demand such grandiosity, seeming to positively relish rulers who indulge in excesses, amass illicit fortunes, and gorge themselves on scarce resources. Vacillating incoherently between these extremes, African subjects systematically disempower both themselves and their leaders.[143]

The cliché that the community deserves the kind of leader they have is a truism. The subject can contribute to the making and shaping of the leader.

The contribution of followers to the process of leadership and the way the community or society is governed is critical. The role of the followers is important for the NEA as the voice of the church in the nation. The NEA leaders have to hear the voice of the people they represent, in political governance and actions, which hugely determines the well-being and levels

---

141. Karlström, "Aesthetics," 58.
142. Ibid., 57–58.
143. Ibid., 61.

of peace in a society. The church's prophetic voice and advocacy for godly influence is critical not only for the economic and social well-being of the people but also in order to guarantee religious liberties in an increasingly and aggressively secularized society.

Leadership Behavior

Leadership is described as both an art and a science. As such, leadership involves "affecting human behavior, which can be thought of as occurring at three levels: visible behavior, conscious thought, and semiconscious or preconscious basic values and assumptions."[144] Visible behavior constitutes level one leadership – peoples' actions that can be seen by others or captured on video. The next level describes what goes on in the minds of people and what alerts them but not others. Leadership is exercised at another level based on the person's "values, assumptions, beliefs, and expectations ('VABEs') about the way the world is or should be."[145] These values systems are learned and developmental.

Many would-be leaders influence others at the first level. This type of leadership is easier than that occurring at deeper levels. Nonetheless, effective leadership will not happen unless the potential leader can get below the surface to level three. The implication for the leader is to know his or her own VABEs and those of others. Techniques are required to discern these VABEs for all three levels. At the organizational level, the implications include leadership tasks such as "strategic thinking, self-leadership, influencing others, organizational design, and managing change."[146] This level of understanding implied leadership has to do with body, head, and heart issues. Leaders do more than tell followers what to do; instead, they participate in shaping the culture, informing the implicit dimensions, and generating healthy power relations in the community.

Another proponent of hierarchical levels of leadership competency, Jim Collins, postulates five levels of leadership for effectiveness. He cites the turnaround of Kimberly-Clark by its CEO, Darwin Smith, as "one of the best examples in the twentieth century of a leader taking a company from

---

144. Clawson, *Level Three*, 25.
145. Ibid., 26.
146. Ibid., 26–28.

merely good to truly great."[147] He describes Smith as little known, but he cites him as one who best demonstrates level 5 leadership – "an individual who blends extreme personal humility with intense professional will."[148] According to Collins, the level 5 leader has the capabilities to turn around an organization from being merely a good organization to a great one.[149] Leadership at various levels has different strengths but level 5 surpasses all. The fifth-level leader principle supports servant leadership. Humility is one of the characteristics of a servant leader.

People do not have to climb the ladder of leadership hierarchy one step at a time to achieve level 5; however, at the zenith, the leader has the attributes of all the previous levels.[150] Each of the levels has specific characteristics:

1) Level 5 – Executive: Builds enduring greatness through a paradoxical combination of personal humility plus professional will.
2) Level 4 – Effective leader: Catalyzes commitment to and vigorous pursuit of a clear and compelling vision; stimulates the group to high performance standards.
3) Level 3 – Competent manager: Organizes people and resources toward the effective and efficient pursuit of predetermined objective.
4) Level 2 – Contributing team member: Contributes to the achievement of group objectives; works effectively with others in a group setting.
5) Level 1 – Makes productive contributions through talent, knowledge, skills, and good work habits.[151]

While other factors exist for transformative leadership, level 5 leadership is essential and indispensable for transformative leadership.[152] Level 5 leaders boost leadership effectiveness from average or good to great.

Level 5 leaders give credit to other factors and people for success but accept blame for any poor performance of the organization. Level 5 leaders

---

147. Collins, "Level 5 Leadership," 115.
148. Ibid., 115–116.
149. Ibid., 116.
150. Ibid.
151. Clawson, *Level Three*, 117.
152. Ibid.

also act with quiet, calm determination, guided by set principles and standards and not personality to achieve their task and are very averse to underperformance and mindful of succession planning.[153] For level 5 leaders, work is not for personal gains – wealth, fame, power, and glory; work is about what they build, create, and contribute.

Paul D. Houston and Stephen L. Sokolow highlight another perspective about leadership. According to these authors, leaders hardly talk about the motivators for their difficult work: "Values, beliefs, and principles guide and inform their work and sustain them in difficult times. Many of the values, beliefs, and principles that guide and sustain the leader have underlying spiritual roots."[154] Their work occurs in a secular context, and the authors are not necessarily Christians. Nonetheless, the authors posit that when a leader is connected with his or her spiritual roots, his or her leadership becomes more enlightened and more effective. Enlightened leadership knows the right things to do and how and when to do them; in addition, these leaders do these things for the right reasons.[155] This assertion affirms biblical principles, and Christian leaders should not do any less.

Houston and Sokolow postulate eight principles for enlightened leadership, including "intention, attention, unique gifts and talents, gratitude, unique life lessons, a holistic perspective, openness, and trust."[156] These spiritual principles resonate with Clawson's VABEs for effective leadership. According to Houston and Sokolow, friends, family, feelings and faith, and busyness do not propel leaders to neglect their inner guidance system. Accordingly, organizations have great importance and are composed of people and charged with leading people. Furthermore, leaders must remain connected with basic constants, and they must connect leadership to head, hand, and heart, similar to Clawson's body-mind-heart analogy. Interconnectedness of life at all levels portrays leadership as transcendental. Houston and Sokolow write, "Spirituality is an unseen force which is both part of humankind, and at the same time is greater than humankind."[157]

---

153. Collins, "Level 5 Leadership," 118.
154. Houston and Sokolow, *Spiritual Dimension*, xiv.
155. Ibid.
156. Ibid., xvii.
157. Ibid., xxiv.

However, great variance can exist in how people understand spirituality and how it connects with other facets of life. The Christian should understand this interconnectedness better; thus, the Christian leader must rely on God for effectiveness in carrying out the leadership role.

Leadership Effectiveness

Leadership is not just about position or power; instead, leadership orients itself toward goals that are beneficial to followers and the organizations or institutions they serve. Leadership effectiveness connects with efficient goal achievement. John C. Maxwell writes, "[L]eadership ability is the lid that determines a person's level of effectiveness. The lower an individual's ability to lead the lower the lid on his or her potential and the higher the leadership the greater the effectiveness."[158] This truism is correct in that leaders can limit or aspire for much greater levels of performance given their full human potential. However, for the Christian, this principle is understood in the context of the leader's God-given potential and the possibilities available to him or her in the Lord.

Daniel Goleman, in a seminal work on the subject of leadership effectiveness postulates that emotional intelligence (EI) rather than IQ is the common factor for leadership effectiveness.[159] Skills and IQ are basic leadership requirements, but EI is what puts the leader on the cutting edge. Emotional intelligence is "a group of five skills that enable the best leaders to maximize their own and their followers' performance."[160] However, like leadership itself, these factors of EI as outlined by Goleman are deep heart issues rather than superficial ones. Accordingly, understanding how these issues can lead to beneficial outcomes without God's redemption through the Holy Spirit can prove difficult. With the ethnocentricity and self-centeredness of humans, Christian leaders will do well to remain faithful in trying to understand and apply Christ's thoughts about these EI factors.

According to Goleman, "scientific enquiry strongly suggests that there is genetic component to EI; also, psychological and developmental research

---

158. Maxwell, *Twenty-One*, 1.
159. Goleman, "What Makes a Leader," 1–2.
160. Ibid., 3.

indicates that nurture, plays a role as well."[161] Each person is born with some level of EI skills. Nonetheless, the EI abilities, as outlined in table 2.1, are skills that can be acquired by learning. EI also increases with age or maturity. Even with maturity, Goleman asserts the need for training to enhance EI through motivation, extended practice, and feedback. EI also proves more effective with an individualized approach and takes time.[162] The elements and characteristics of EI are self-discipline as is expected of Christian leaders, and Goleman's findings affirm of Christian leadership principles.

Table 2.1 illustrates and builds understanding of the EI concept. It highlights the various attributes that constitute EI, the definition of each of these five components, the distinguishing characteristics of the components, and examples of them.

Table 2.1. Understanding EI's Components at Work

EI Component	Definition	Hallmarks	Example
Self-Awareness	Knowing one's emotions, strengths, weaknesses, drives, values, and goals and their impact on others. The ability to recognize one's moods, emotions, and drives, as well as their effect on others.	• Self-confidence • Realistic self-assessment • Self-deprecating sense of humor • Thirst for constructive criticism	Managers know tight deadlines bring out the worst in them, so they plan their time to get work done well in advance.
Self-Regulation	Controlling or redirecting disruptive emotions and impulses. Propensity to suspend judgment; to think before acting.	• Trustworthiness • Integrity • Comfort with ambiguity and openness to change	When a team botches a presentation, its leader resists the urge to scream; instead, he or she considers reasons for the failure, explains the consequences to the team, and explores solutions with them.

---

161. Ibid., 8.
162. Ibid., 3, 8; Drucker, "Effective Executive," 36.

Motivation	Being driven to achieve for the sake of achievement; a passion to work for reasons that go beyond money or status. A propensity to pursue goals with energy and persistence.	• A passion for the work itself and for new challenges • Unflagging energy to improve • Optimism in the face of failure; strong drive to achieve; organizational commitment	A portfolio manager at an investment company sees the company's fund tumble for three consecutive quarters. Major clients defect. Instead of blaming external circumstances, the manager decides to learn from the experience and engineers a turnaround.
Empathy	Considering others' feelings, especially when making decisions. The ability to understand the emotional makeup of other people. Skill in treating people according to their emotional reactions.	• Expertise in attracting and retaining talent • Ability to develop others • Sensitivity to cross-cultural differences; service to clients and customers	An American consultant and team pitch a project to a potential client in Japan. The team interprets the client's silence as disapproval and prepares to leave. The consultant reads the client's body language, senses interest, and continues the meeting. The team gets the job.
Social skill	Managing relationships to move people in desired directions; proficiency in managing relationships and building networks. An ability to find common ground and build rapport.	• Effectiveness in leading change • Persuasiveness • Extensive networking • Expertise in building and leading teams	A manager wants the company to adopt a better Internet strategy. With kindred spirits they assemble a de facto team to create a prototype web site. The manager persuades allies in other divisions to fund the company's participation in a relevant convention. They then form an Internet division and puts the manager in charge of it.

Source: Goleman 4-6

These personal capabilities contribute to outstanding performance within organizations. Organizations need to invest time and other resources to develop the EI of their leaders as a sure means of production and profitability. Self-leadership is a disciplined style that can be effective and beneficial to leader and followers.

Peter F. Drucker postulates another practice effective leaders share in common. According to Drucker, effective leaders follow the same eight practices:

    i. They asked, "What needs to be done?"
    ii. They asked, "What is right for the enterprise?"
    iii. They developed action plans.
    iv. They took responsibility for decisions.
    v. They took responsibility for communicating.
    vi. They were focused on opportunities rather than problems.
    vii. They ran productive meetings.
    viii. They thought and said, "We" rather than "I."[163]

Effective leaders are knowledgeable about the need of their organization and the leadership tasks to meet the needs. Effective leaders realize their need to work in teams and endeavor to create a conducive and accountable work environment: "Using discipline to apply these rules, the leader gains knowledge needed to make smart decisions, convert knowledge into effective action, and ensure accountability throughout the organization."[164] Associations such as the NEA demand greater accountability and understanding about the needs of members and robust action for effectiveness.

Leadership Competencies

Within an organization, humans are the most prized assets. To that end, people are employed to make the right fit, identifying competencies required to perform particular tasks effectively. Effective leadership requires particular competencies in every situation. Therefore, identifying the leadership competencies for effective leading of NEAs is necessary.[165] The role and required competencies for any position in an organization should be in line with the mission, values, and purpose and strategy of the organization. The information describing a job vacancy is framed in what is known as a job profile: "The job profile usually consists of two parts – a job description

---

163. Drucker, "Effective Executive," 23.
164. Ibid., 24.
165. Pernick, "Creating," 435.

and a person specification."[166] The job description spells out roles and responsibilities. The goal of this project was to establish the person specification that makes a good fit for leading an NEA.

However, "it makes no sense to try to identify essential leadership capabilities unless one knew the business context in which the leader is expected to excel."[167] Often leaders are chosen for reasons other than competencies; relationships based on ethnicity and patrimony weigh heavily in the selection of personnel for filling vacant positions. The competencies of the job holder should be related to the needs of the job. People who have demonstrated effectiveness in other roles can also develop competencies in new roles.

In the area of evangelical association leadership, Pearson proposes seven foundational competencies required for effectiveness:

i. Mission and vision
ii. Strategic plan
iii. Annual plan and measurable goals (submitted a written annual plan to the governing board with programs, products, services, budgets, calendar, etc., along with 5 to 10 "S.M.A.R.T." goals to achieve by a specific date)
iv. Membership (had segmented membership into at least three categories – and had written action plans for recruiting members and meeting the needs of members)
v. Budget and membership dues – had thoughtful discussions (based on data, not opinions) on our annual budget and understood that in most healthy associations the membership dues accounted for less than 50% of the total income
vi. Product, programs and services (menu of products, programs and services was in alignment with mission and vision and asked members for feedback and evaluation on member services at least annually)
vii. Board, staff and volunteers had written job descriptions (roles and responsibilities) for board members, staff members and volunteers and "S.M.A.R.T." goals for each person[168]

---

166. Williamson, Colvin, and McDonald, *Human Resource Management*, 36.
167. Barner, "Five Steps," 47.
168. Pearson, *Association Leadership*, 7.

Leadership of organizations requires management competencies as well. The tendency in leadership discourse is to focus on differences between leadership and management; however, good management skills and abilities are necessary for effective leadership.

In the African context, deciphering any unifying characteristics can prove difficult, perhaps without an objective way of unpacking the competencies previously outlined, since association leadership largely deals with such diverse groups of people, denominations, and other Christian organizations. Like the trait approach to leadership "no universal list of competencies exists for leaders across different organizations. However, the competencies required for organization can be classified into three broad categories of technical, human, or conceptual skills."[169]

The research seeks to identify the competencies required for leading an NEA. The research required an understanding of the essential duty or action required of the NEA leader (i.e. the task of the leader). Merriam-Webster defines task as "a piece of work that has been given to someone; a job for someone to do."[170] The task of leading the NEA is summed up into three broad categories, namely *connecting, representing,* and *equipping.* The WEA criteria for healthy evangelical associations states, "[M]ission statement shall normally (in one form or another) include the three shared missions of many national Alliances, the other WEA regions, and the WEA as a whole, connecting, equipping and being a representative voice."[171] The three tasks of connecting, representing, and equipping need further explanation to understand fully and appreciate the task of leading an NEA:

1) *Connecting* – Forming and sustainably building unity among evangelical denominations and other church organizations, positioning association to serve as platform for partnership in the gospel; a holistic vision, owned by members, clear mission and global outlook.

2) *Representing* – Representative of denominational and ethnic diversity within nation, effective public engagement adequately reflecting theological issues and guidelines within cultural context;

---

169. Moore, "Leadership," 53–54.
170. "Task," *Merriam-Webster Online.* Accessed 20 October 2014.
171. Showell-Rogers, "Regional Alliance," 2.

services to members and trusted voice of evangelicals; visible identity.

3) *Equipping* – Serving members by leading, resourcing, partnering, empowering and mobilizing constituency in living out the Good news and compassion of Jesus of Christ, resource and leadership development, office, staff and service arms.[172]

These three tasks are core to leading NEA. The project sought to discover any other tasks and the competencies required to perform these tasks of connecting, equipping, and representing in an effective manner.

Association Leadership Best Practice

Association executives serve the members of their associations. While each association has its own unique culture, member needs, and governance structure, all associations share many foundational similarities. First, the association CEO needs to be an association expert rather than a content or curriculum expert. Thus, association leadership is a specialist area of its own, even though very little is known or done to advance the development of the profession. Pearson explains that some WEA members of the national association are gifted or skilled in both association management and in national evangelical issues. This blessing also has a downside in that sometimes leaders who are evangelical experts tend not to rely on the expertise of their members and often lead with charisma and instinct instead of research and consensus.[173] Coordinating and using resources and expertise of members represents part of the tasks of the association leader.

Describing the tasks of the association expert, Pearson explains that he or she facilitates annual meetings, publishes materials, promotes best practices of the profession, distributes a membership directory, often coordinates an accreditation or certification program, and usually develops training and professional development programs for the membership. Leaders can measure the state of well-being of their associations by evaluating their associations against best practices of selected associations worldwide according to three objectives:

---

172. *Healthy Alliances: WEA International Leadership Meeting Documents*, 43–45.
173. Pearson, *Management Buckets*, 2–3.

1) To review the best practices of healthy alliances around the world and understand how to adapt the best ideas and programs so they fit the unique mission, vision and culture for country and for God's calling on alliance.
2) To understand the "Five Questions Every National Alliance Must Ask and Answer" and how to lead your alliance leaders through a "Five Questions" process to strengthen your organization, leadership and membership. Drucker postulates that there are five questions every organization should ask and answer for success.
3) To learn how to assess the true needs of your alliance members – and create cost-effective and God-honoring programs, products and services that meet those important needs.[174]

In the foreword of his book, Drucker writes the following five questions that every organization should ask and answer:
1) What is our mission?
2) Who is our customer?
3) What does our customer value?
4) What are our results?
5) What is our plan?[175]

These questions are a unique self-assessment tool applicable to almost any organization. The asking and answering of these questions are foundational to understanding the core competencies of leading an NEA.

If and when these five questions are answered according to Pearson, the national association will be well on its way to addressing the key issues upon which leadership, governors, CEOs, and staff members need to focus in order to lead the associations in an effective manner.[176] However, the five questions need to be asked and answered in the context of the NEA and ensure that the real questions the NEA leaders and their members are asking correlate with Drucker's and that the answers provide solutions to felt needs.

---

174. Ibid., 3.
175. Drucker, Five Most Important, 130–133.
176. Pearson, *Management Buckets*, 7.

Leadership Dynamics in African NEAs

AEA's governance structure consists of four key bodies as stated in its constitution and by-laws (i.e. General Assembly, Governing Council, Executive Board, and Registered Trustees). The operations of AEA are directed by a Secretariat, based at the headquarters and operations offices in Nairobi. Its operational arms are its commissions and projects. The headquarters are based in Nairobi, while the commissions are located in different countries in the continent. The decentralization of the different commissions of AEA is to enhance service to the NEAs in the different nations and regions where the commissions are based.[177] However, policies and guidelines are in place to coordinate the activities of the commissions from headquarters.

Structure and Organization

The AEA structure is the prototype of the structure of the NEA at the national level. As such, thirty-six African NEAs are associated with AEA.[178] These two bodies share common membership criteria and, to a large extent, common features and leadership challenges. Article seven of the AEA constitution states membership criteria:

> [M]embership in the AEA is extended to those who desire and meet the following conditions:
>
> i. Subscribe to the Association's Basis of Unity (Article VI).
> ii. Accept and pledge to abide by the Association's Constitution and By-Laws.
> iii. Accept any other criteria as may be prescribed by the Governing Council.[179]

The structure of the NEA includes the following: General Assembly, Governing Council, Executive Board, and the Secretariat. The General Assembly is held every year (unlike the AEA, which meets every four years) to receive reports from the chief executives and to conduct the business of the organizations. The Governing Council is responsible for the strategic and overall direction of the program of the Secretariat and

---

177. AEA Secretariat, *Strategic Review Report*, 20.
178. AEA Secretariat, *Membership Directory*, 6–15.
179. Ibid., 2.

meets every two years. The Council derives its authority from the General Assembly and elects officials that constitute the Executive Committee to oversee the work of the Secretariat directly and through the Chair of the Executive Committee.

For operational purposes, the AEA divides the continent into seven regions; each region is comprised of seven nations or NEAs on average. The region elects one of the chairpersons in the NEAs to represent the region on the AEA board. These regional presidents have some limited oversight roles for the other NEAs in the region. Their roles mostly consist of governance, especially in their particular NEA, as the board chair and employer of the leader or general secretary/CEO of the NEA. Thus, they are familiar with the recruitment and selection of the NEA CEO.

Leadership Challenges and Distortions

The NEA General Assembly meets annually or biannually to receive reports from the Secretariat through the Governing Council. The business sessions of the Assembly include receipt of reports from the general secretary, audited financial reports from the treasurer, and election/appointment of officers and the general secretary. The General Assembly, a critical time for the association, represents celebration, fellowship, inspiration, and a time that accords members to hold their leaders accountable and critically evaluate their performance. In this respect, the assembly sessions can be acrimonious and threaten the very existence and survival of unity in the movement. Good leadership is required for successful general assembly deliberations and the enhancement of the association's unity.

Election to choose or elect officers can be fraudulent or predetermined and can become a contest. Sometimes the persons at the helm of leadership can renege on holding the annual general assembly for several years, denying members the opportunity to meet and carry out the business of the association. This way, the leaders can entrench themselves in their positions indefinitely; without the general assembly, individual members hesitate to ask any question, tacitly acquiescing to the notion of sacralization of the leader. Sometimes such actions can be construed as scriptural according to biblical references such as, "touch not the Lord's anointed," (1 Chr 16:22; Ps 105:15). This major issue needs to be addressed in the church. The issues highlighted point to the leadership skills of building consensus without denying the important individual gifts of the members or dealing with conflict among members.

As in other institutions, leadership in the NEA and in the church in general has challenges or distortions nuanced by sociocultural and theological influences.[180] Concern exists regarding the absence and demonstration of even the basic managerial leadership competencies in some NEAs. Pearson highlights four basic essentials for creating a governance and leadership structure for a viable NEA, namely an environment that ensures accountability, integrity, results, and sustainability.[181] This kind of governance structure is evidenced by basic transparent and accountable organizational structure and systems, policies, and operational management guidelines in place.

Power plays exist at various levels within the structure of the NEA. The national association executives often are amazed (and frequently overwhelmed) when they attempt to use the best practices of pastoral or ministry leadership and apply them to their new roles as association executives. The pastoral skills that served them successfully in the local church may not lead to successful outcomes in their new roles as association leaders; different skills sets are required for leading the association. This difficulty is not a surprise because dramatic differences exist between local churches and denominations. Even greater differences exist between an association and a typical parachurch organization. Nonetheless, for the novice association leader, the differences are not often apparent.[182] Understanding associations and the NEA in particular will contribute to creating awareness and developing leaders for NEA role.

Another major challenge faced by association leaders is fundraising and other resource mobilization for building and sustaining the alliance. Denominational leaders depend on a certain level of denominational loyalty, history, and doctrinal distinctiveness in order to grow their movement. Associations have history, but the diversity of their members creates obstacles in working together. Denominational funding often is based on long-standing traditions and relationships. Funding the association

---

180. Okesson, "Are Pastors," 110–111.
181. Pearson, *Association Leadership*, 16.
182. Pearson, *Management Buckets*, 5.

depends on a completely different set of values. Association leaders are required to answer the annual questions from dues-paying members who ask, "What's in this for me?" For NEA members to build commitment for the association, they must be able to ask what the Bible says and what God says. Adequate responses to these questions serve to motivate evangelicals to commit to the vision of unity as their obedience to God and Scripture. The theological and biblical insights discussed in this study attempted to respond to this need.

In addition to the theological and biblical understanding of members and leaders of evangelical associations, specific leadership competencies are required for them to administer the affairs of the NEA, to achieve its objectives. The literature review highlights pertinent skills from the secular, cultural, and ecclesiastical domains and from the field of association management in general that shape the skills and competencies of NEA leaders for success.

Design of the Study

Very little research information exists regarding association leadership in the church. The objective of this research was to identify the competencies relevant to the administration or leading of African NEAs. I conducted a literature search in order to provide information on the theoretical, biblical, and theological framework underpinning the import, nature, and leadership implications for practice of running NEAs. The outcome of the literature review also provided a competency construct as a basis for exploring the competencies of current NEA leaders in Africa.

I conducted the research in two phases. First, I designed an evangelical association leadership competencies survey questionnaire. Then I administered the questionnaire to all the AEA regional presidents. I obtained consent of the regional presidents and the other group of participants (NEA CEOs) and the NEAs they serve. Then I collated and analyzed the responses of the regional presidents in the first phase of the research and generated a list of NEA leadership competencies. I organized and categorized this list, which formed the basis for developing the second instrument for rating and self-assessing the proficiency levels of the NEA general secretaries in the second phase of the project.[183] In the first phase of this entirely qualitative study, the questionnaire had open-ended questions to generate descriptive responses.

The NEA leadership competencies protocol comprised the list of competencies generated in the first phase. In the second phase, I asked the NEA general secretaries to rank the competencies in order of importance, ranging from *very important* to *least important*. I distributed the instrument by email and asked respondents to return the completed questionnaire by email within a period of one month. Next, I collated, organized, and analyzed the responses in order to identify the top competencies critical to NEA leadership as perceived by the current NEA leaders or CEOs. The third instrument was the self-assessed NEA leadership competency proficiency level in each of the competencies. The competency proficiency instrument was combined with the important competencies instrument, and participants were requested to indicate their level of competency in each area of task on the list. Accordingly, I asked the respondents to indicate how good they were in each competency, ranging from *very good* (highest level of competency) to *fair* (least level of competency). Then I collated and analyzed the responses in order to identify the levels of competency of the current NEA leaders/CEOs in Africa. The outcome of the research will inform possible future interventions for the development of future NEA leaders.

Summary

This chapter reviewed literature related to associations as unique types of organizations with unique leadership and context, effectiveness and competencies. Ecumenical associations and NEAs, in particular, with their peculiar features and challenges for achieving organizational objectives, were reviewed. The scope of literature on the latter was very limited. However, the material on association leadership developed by Pearson, consultant for the WEA Leadership Institute, was insightful. The articles and books

---

183. Plante and Boccaccini, "Psychological Assessment," 365–369; Moore, *Leadership*, 61–63.

reviewed provided useful information on the subject of leadership of organizations, including the NEA.

The review of literature established the foundation for understanding leadership as a prerequisite for any intervention for leadership developed in the NEA. The study reveals the complexity of the subject and sensitizes about the need for impact and productivity. Richard Bolden summarizes the importance of the background study:

> [W]ithout at least some understanding of the underlying principles and assumptions about leadership and leadership development, it is likely that action may be misguided – at least reducing its possible effectiveness and at worst damaging what was there in the first place.[184]

However, leadership is understood to be more of an art than a science and that leadership can be learned.

Given the African context and its beliefs and praxis, a need exists for a paradigm shift and leverage of the collectivist system of the African society to democratize leadership. Leadership is a tripartite interaction of the leader, follower, and the environment with the leader playing the catalytic role. Effective leaders have some common characteristics regardless of the particular context, but some leadership competencies are unique to the organization or context.

The review highlighted the mission of NEAs, including connecting, equipping, and representing. The mission of the NEA formed the basis for assessing leadership competencies for leading NEAs. The defining elements of each of the tasks of connecting, representing, and equipping have been outlined in various working documents of the WEA. Gordon Showell-Rogers outlines the state of a healthy NEA: "Healthy alliances are vital, viable, and visible, and to develop healthy NEAs, the tasks of connecting, representing, and equipping are required."[185] The work of NEA leader is multitasking.

Some of the characteristics of leadership competencies that stood out in the literature review included emotional intelligence, humility, servant

---

184. Bolden, "What is Leadership," 3.
185. Showell-Rogers, *Six Days*, 1–4.

and transformational leadership, strategy, management, consensus, and relation. Cultural worldview and belief systems, particularly in the African context, contributed to understanding and shaping leadership.

The heart of evangelical belief and basis of faith is Word centered, and Scripture is the standard for conduct, including leadership responsibilities. The theological and biblical overview in this study made clear the preferred style, type, and nature of leadership expected by Jesus. Exploring the leadership situation in the NEAs as significant ecumenical organizations in Africa, discovering what leadership competencies prevail and discerning how these aspects correlate with servant leadership – the model of leadership bequeathed to the church – were all of particular interest for this study.

Specifically, the research seeks to find out how best practice and factors that contributed to leadership effectiveness, highlighted in literature and Scripture, compare with what prevails in AEA. In spite of the significant growth the church is experiencing in Africa, its impact on society does not correlate to its growth. Many people believe that life and conduct of the African Christian is shaped more by cultural worldview systems than by Christian belief. Africa's sociocultural and developmental challenges are also blamed on leadership or the lack of effective leadership. The research explores the factors and influences that impact leadership and aspects that contribute to leadership effectiveness and how these can contribute to leadership development. Unity in the church is the prevailing theme of the work of NEAs. How unity is achieved in the church in the light of the different factors contributing to leadership effectiveness will be explored.

CHAPTER 3

Methodology

Problem and Purpose

Fellowship in Christ and the quest for unity within the Christian church exists not for its own sake but for the world. Furthermore, this quest for unity is missional. When believers remained united, nonbelievers would be attracted to the God of the believers. However, the church of Jesus Christ is fragmented along denominational lines and Christianity is fast losing its attraction. The world is experiencing a post-Western Christian awakening and Granberg-Michaelson underscores the challenge of disunity in the church:

> Patterns of Christian vitality and witness are shifting in breathtaking ways that are shaping the globe's religious landscape, and Christianity today seems divided in new ways and struggling to maintain a resonant and vital witness in the midst of their modern and postmodern cultures.[1]

The church cannot continue to mount walls of division and reach out with the gospel message of reconciliation. Furthermore, a need exists for building unity and strengthening cooperation among the various factions of the church. Bearing in mind that the work of the church is God's mission, Christians should seek to do mission in God's way, which constitutes a Trinitarian dimension.

---

1. Granberg-Michaelson, *From Times Square*, vii–ix.

The church in Africa needs to strengthen ways of detribalizing the church and, instead, celebrate differences as they uphold the unity they have in Christ with a deep sense of the historic Christian tradition and an ecumenical commitment to the one faith Christians confess in the one body of Christ. Beneath the veneer of Christian identity, a strong African cultural identity pervades the cultures and histories of the peoples of Africa. J. N. K. Mugambi writes, "Denominational allegiances may have eroded that identity, but they have not managed to eradicate it."[2] A visible demonstration of the spiritual unity that the church is, in Christ enhances the witness of the church. In addition, some concerns about leadership need to be critiqued to promote best practice and servant leadership as commanded by Jesus.

Effective leadership in the church is required in order to strengthen the divine heritage of a unified community. The NEA attempts to correct division in the church and provides a common platform for visible unity that Christians have in the Spirit. I undertook this research due to the leadership challenges in the African church, and sought to identify leadership competencies for effectiveness. To that end, the findings of this research will be used for possible future intervention for training and leadership development for effective NEA leadership.

The purpose of the research was to identify leadership competencies required for leading an NEA as well as needed leadership development competencies of current general secretaries or NEA leaders in Africa by interviewing current regional presidents and national leaders in the AEA.

Research Questions

With this research, I sought to capture views of AEA regional presidents regarding the leadership competencies necessary for leading an NEA. In addition, I asked NEA leaders or general secretaries to rate their competencies and assess their own proficiency levels. I achieved this task by using three appropriately researcher-designed survey instruments through which I recorded participants' responses to the following three research questions.

---

2. Mugambi, "Religions," 26.

Research Question #1

What leadership competencies did current AEA regional presidents identify as necessary for leading an NEA? I designed the questionnaire specifically to answer this question. To that end, I requested the AEA regional presidents for their views by responding to the questionnaire. I collated the competencies perceived necessary for NEA leadership from their responses to the researcher-designed questionnaire.

Research Question #2

How did current NEA leaders or general secretaries in Africa rate the competencies in order of importance for effective NEA leadership? I sought to get the opinion of the general secretaries of NEAs about the importance of the NEA leadership competencies on the list collated in the first phase of the research. I requested them to respond to a researcher-designed questionnaire, requesting the general secretaries to rank the list of competencies in order of importance. I analyzed the responses to identify the top/core leadership competencies for leading an NEA.

Research Question #3

What levels of proficiency did African NEA leaders or general secretaries attribute to themselves in each specific leadership competency for leading an NEA? The objective of this research was to identify AEA regional presidents' perceived competencies of NEA leadership. I also sought to provide information of perceived levels of proficiency, especially in the top/core competencies of the general secretaries. In achieving the stated objectives, I designed the leadership competency proficiency instrument in order to capture respondents' views. I asked the respondents to assess themselves by indicating the extent to which they were able to demonstrate each competency on the list.

Culturally, self-critique is a challenge for African leaders. For that reason, I took care in communicating and letting the respondents understand that the objective of the proficiency level self-assessment dealt with identifying training needs for the development of national association leaders and their personnel. I made the leaders appreciate the importance of their personal experiences in developing NEA leadership for the future. The participants needed assurance that my instruments were not intended to criticize their leadership, recognizing the lack of curricular and training programs for training and developing leaders for NEA leadership.

Population and Participants

Two sets of respondents were involved in the research, including a purposive population of all seven AEA regional presidents and all thirty-six general secretaries or NEA leaders from the various member countries of the AEA. The AEA regional presidents were the targeted population for the first phase of the research because they were well informed to respond to Research Question #1. The regional presidents, as chairpersons of the NEAs, have responsibility for recruiting and selecting the NEA general secretaries, and as employers, they would be familiar with the qualifications and competencies the general secretary is expected to have for effectively leading the NEA.

The administrative structure of the AEA has seven subdivisions. Each subdivision is made up of a number of countries in the region, and one of the national presidents in the region is elected by his or her peers to oversee the work of the region at an AEA general assembly held every four years. The regional presidents are also members of the governing board of the AEA.[3] The regional president doubles as chair of own national alliance and serves as a member of the board of AEA. The regional president is familiar with the job responsibilities of the general secretary as the employing authority and has additional responsibility for oversight for other NEAs within the subregion. As a member of the governance team of the AEA, he or she would be familiar with the job descriptions of a general secretary to provide the information on leadership competencies required in this research. Their views would be fairly representative of each NEA in the region and Africa as a whole.

The second phase of the research targeted current general secretaries of all the NEAs in Africa who are also members of the AEA. The general secretaries were best suited to respond to Research Questions #2 and #3, which sought to assess the importance of the competencies expected of them and the level of proficiency in each competency, respectively. The

---

3. AEA Secretariat, *Constitution*, 4.

general secretaries were in the position to provide answers to the two questions based on their experiences.

The general secretary is the chief executive officer of the national alliance and has the responsibility to build and sustain the national association. The general secretary is recruited, employed by, and held accountable to the board of the NEA through the chairperson of the board. The general secretaries could relate to their experience and give firsthand information about the quality of the competencies expected of them by their chairpersons for NEA leadership and self-assess the proficiency needs in the AEA NEAs.

The two target populations are purposive samples of the entire population of evangelicals constituting the NEA and AEA membership. Each of the two groups was a representative of the larger evangelical population. The regional presidents and general secretaries were all male adults, except for one female participant in the general secretary category in the second group of participants.

Before recruiting the participants, I sought the approval of the AEA and consent of the individuals themselves to participate in the research. I wrote to the AEA president requesting his written approval (see appendix B) and an informed consent by individual regional presidents and general secretaries, respectively (see appendixes C and D). In the request for approval and consent, I described the project and pointed out the significance and benefit to participants and the voluntary nature of their participation. I assured the participants of my respect for them and the confidentiality with which I would treat information until the end of the project when the gathered data would be destroyed.

As a requirement for doctoral research, I applied for approval from the Seminary's Institutional Review Board (IRB). The task of the IRB is to review research methodologies to assure that no harm comes to human subjects involved in research. The board carries the federal regulatory role of ensuring the well-being of human subjects participating in any research project. I completed a web-based IRB application form that included an online training seminar and examination for certification about conducting research using human subjects. Attached to the application were the relevant section of the proposal, including project description, informed consent forms, and interview questionnaires. I received IRB approval before embarking on data collection.

This project sought to identify the competencies the AEA regional presidents in Africa perceived as necessary for success and effectiveness in leading NEAs. I also sought to have the NEA leaders or general secretaries rate the competencies and self-assess their levels of competency in each competency area. I completed the literature review, including a theological reflection, in order to provide a theoretical framework and biblical foundation for the work of the NEA. Information gleaned from the literature review provided a profile from different aspects of an effective leader. The review elucidated an understanding of NEAs as organizations as well as their leadership challenges, theories, and leadership effectiveness. The literature review depicted an effective leader in various contexts of effectiveness. The literature review identified the core tasks of the NEA leader. The respondents in phase one of the project were asked to identify what they considered to be the main task of the NEA, and these tasks, identified in literature and interview, were the basis for identifying perceived competencies required for performing the tasks.

The study sought to use insights from literature to explore and depict a typical effective leader for the NEA. I conducted the research in two phases and specifically sought to identify a list of core leadership competencies in order of importance and levels of competency of current African-based NEA leaders. For the purposes of this study, I utilized an ethnographic and exploratory, mixed-method approach to gather information from the participants. I collated and analyzed the data using qualitative and quantitative methods. The first phase aimed at collating a list of competencies required for leading an NEA as perceived by AEA regional presidents. The second phase aimed at rating the competencies and self-assessing levels of proficiency by NEA leaders. I used three researcher-designed instruments. A cross-sectional survey research design collected the views of current AEA regional presidents in Africa about perceived leadership competencies for leading NEAs in the African context.[4] The researcher-designed

---

4. Creswell, *Educational Research*, 377–378.

questionnaire captured the views of the respondents in order to generate a list of competencies perceived as necessary for effective NEA leadership.

The research design had the advantage of assessing current perceptions of AEA regional presidents and NEA leaders dispersed over a vast geographic area by providing information within a short timeframe, collecting data inexpensively, and using researcher-designed instruments at a point in time. The survey was limited to small purposive populations and did not require random sampling, hypothesis testing, or inferential statistics about the entire population. Instead, only qualitative and quantitative descriptions about the populations were used.[5] The two sets of purposive populations participating in the research were familiar with the nature and context of the study and were well suited to provide the data. The AEA regional presidents were a representative group of NEA boards, the employers of the general secretaries. Thus, they were asked to state the competencies they perceived were required for selection. The general secretaries were employees capable of recognizing the importance of the competencies expected of them in their work and of self-assessing the level of proficiency in these competencies, to highlight possible gaps and training needs.

Next, a second set of participants ranked the list of competencies generated in the survey in phase one in order of importance to generate a list of top leadership competencies critical for effective NEA leadership, and I asked participants to assess their own levels of competency in each of the core competencies through the researcher-developed proficiency instrument.

Instrumentation

I conducted the research in two phases. In order to elicit the required information from respondents and in response to the research questions, I developed three instruments for use in this study:
1) AEA regional presidents' perceived competencies for NEA leadership,
2) NEA leaders' rating of competency, and
3) Self-assessed proficiency level of competency.

---

5. Ibid., 382.

The first instrument was used to collect information from the seven AEA regional presidents on the leadership competencies and attributes they believed necessary for successful or effective NEA leadership. I developed questions on the survey instrument based on the review of literature and theoretical framework (see appendix E). The questions sought information regarding background, qualification, and views on leadership competencies, skills, behaviors, and attributes of effective leadership. I utilized a semi-structured and open-ended interview protocol.

A panel of experts first reviewed the interview instrument for consistency and validity before I administered it to respondents. I obtained informed consent through a letter making respondents aware of the relevance of the study, the purpose, assurances of confidentiality, and the voluntary nature of their participation. Even though I had some perceived supervisory relationship with the respondents in the second phase of the study, I took great care not to compel participants to take part in the study. I administered the questionnaire and asked participants to return it to me via email within a time frame of one month for each phase. I maintained repeated and regular contacts with respondents from the time of distribution to the end of the period in order to ensure success in the collection of completed questionnaire.

The second instrument was the NEA leaders' rating of competency instrument. I used this instrument in order to determine the importance of specific leadership competencies for the success of current NEA leaders in each competency collated in the first phase. I asked the NEA leaders to rank the competencies in order of perceived importance in order to identify a list of top competencies deemed critical for effective NEA leadership (see appendix H).

The third instrument was the self-assessed proficiency level of competency protocol designed to assess NEA leaders' levels of competency. For ease of reference and to reduce the number of instruments for participants, I included the self-assessed leadership competency proficiency protocol in the researcher-developed important leadership competencies instrument. Both the second and third instruments are combined in this protocol (see appendix E).

Expert Review

A panel of experts reviewed the research instruments for consistency and validation. The panel of experts consisted of members of the research reflection team. These persons understood the context of the study as most of the members worked directly with NEAs. I administered the drafted research instruments to the panel of experts in order to explore unanticipated nuances in the administration of the instruments.[6] I asked the panel of experts to appraise the instruments in order to ascertain whether the instruments aligned with the purpose and research questions and to determine if any items needed to be eliminated or included. I took their suggestions into consideration in order to make the questionnaire clearer before administering them to the research participants.

The expert review panel's contribution was useful particularly in highlighting the need to craft the questions in a way the respondents in the actual research will understand and respond. The panel recommended writing out in full the attributes on the Likert scale rather than assigning numbers to the scales for rating and self-competency assessment. One of the questions on the questionnaire was identified as not related to the research questions, so I deleted it.

Reliability and Validity

The reliability ensured consistency in data collection, which resulted in outcomes that were credible or valid. To that end, I made certain the questions in the instruments were clear and unambiguous and answer options did not overlap. For consistency in design and procedures, the same questions applied to all participants. The questions on the instruments were aligned with the purpose statement and research questions to enhance validity by expert review of the protocol.

Data Collection

Following the literature review and construction of a theological and theoretical framework, I utilized an enquiry data collection approach to collect

---

6. Seidman, *Interviewing*, 29–30.

information to answer the research questions.[7] I developed research protocols in order to ensure that these instruments responded to the research questions. A panel of experts reviewed the protocols and finalized the instruments in order to ensure reliability and validity, taking into consideration any points for correction or providing clarity for consistency and user-friendly instruments. I defended the protocols together with the proposal and obtained approval by the faculty and IRB of Asbury Theological Seminary before administering the instruments to participants.

I collected the data in two phases. After obtaining approval of the project and instruments, I distributed the NEA leadership questionnaire via email, requesting the AEA regional presidents for their view about competencies they felt were required for NEA leadership. I secured the approval of the AEA and the consent of the individual regional presidents before emailing them the questionnaire. I sent letters to participants, explaining the purpose of the research, assuring confidentiality, and requesting their voluntary participation. I distributed the questionnaire on receiving the consent of the participants. I gave clear instructions regarding the manner in which participants should answer the questions and requested them to return the completed questionnaire by email within a given time frame of one month.

Within the one month, I sent reminders to any participants who had not yet returned the completed questionnaire. Furthermore, I conducted personal follow-up on each outstanding questionnaire before the close of the period. I collated the responses, organized them by themes, and analyzed and reported them in descriptive or tabular forms. In addition, I counted and clustered the themes and competencies for further analysis. The result generated a list of competencies, which AEA regional presidents perceived as required competencies for leadership success or effectiveness in NEA leadership. The number of responses and completed questionnaires received was recorded.

The list of competencies generated in the first phase was the basis for designing the second and third instruments for rating the competencies and self-assessing proficiency levels of competency of the NEA leaders. The

---

7. Creswell, *Educational Research*, 590.

two instruments were combined in a single protocol (see appendix E). The two variables of rank of competency and proficiency level were combined on one instrument to reduce the number of questionnaires participants had to complete.[8] I asked the second group of participants – the NEA leaders or general secretaries – for their voluntary consent for participating in the research in the same way I did for the participants in the first phase before distributing the questionnaire. The questionnaire was administered by email, and respondents were requested to return them to me by email within one month. Similarly, I followed up regularly with individuals who had not returned the completed questionnaire within the one-month period. I collated, analyzed the data by quantitative means, interpreted, and reported the results.

Data Analysis

The research was a mixed-method, qualitative and quantitative study, involving textual and numerical data for analysis. I took the mixed method into consideration when designing the questionnaires and when organizing and interpreting the information collected from participants' responses. I used different types of closed-ended and open-ended questions in constructing the instruments. The questionnaires ensured clarity in the way questions were framed and required only short answers from respondents. The opened-ended questions were used in the first phase of the research where respondents were required to provide answers from their own experience with no response options provided. Unlike the open-ended questions, the closed-ended questions used in the second phase of the project provided preset responses from which respondents could choose.[9] All the respondents had the same questions to make analysis and comparison of the results easy.

The first phase of the research generated textual data for content analysis and that I treated qualitatively. I tabulated aggregate responses for each item on the questionnaire and analyzed the data descriptively to identify the trend in the respondents' perceptions. I grouped together the participants'

---

8. Moore, *Leadership*, 62.
9. Creswell, *Educational Research*, 386–387.

responses to each question, especially around the perceived NEA leadership competencies for each category of NEA tasks. I analyzed each group of data, coding descriptions and themes related to competencies. Some of the themes identified from the coding, for example, were soft skills and holistic development. Respondents described the soft skills competency theme with words such as, *willing to learn, able to listen, teachable,* and described the holistic development theme with words such as, *able to initiate programs to address physical and spiritual needs of people, community development.* I presented the information in a matrix, illustrating each of four categories of NEA leadership tasks. The emerging themes and descriptions provided a list of competencies in response to Research Question #1.

In the second phase of the research competencies identified in the first phase formed the basis of the questionnaire for respondents to assign quality and indicate their proficiency levels of the competencies on a Likert scale of four and five points, respectively. For quality and level of importance, participants ranked the competencies on a scale of 1–4, from unimportant to very important. Similarly, the participants indicated their level of proficiency in each competency on a Likert scale of five points, from very poor to excellent. The responses generated data that I analyzed using qualitative descriptions and finding the mode or the frequency of the quality ascribed to each competency.

Ethical Procedures

This project was a practical action research focusing on leadership competencies for leading NEAs in Africa. The ultimate goal was to improve practice in this area of ministry. Furthermore, this research was participatory and self-reflective and required the collaboration of colleagues. Retrospective reconstruction of an interpretation as well as lessons learned formed the basis for future action. Because of the intimate and open-ended nature of the study, possible ethical issues required mitigation.[10] I had to go through ethics training to meet required minimum standards as for any other research requiring the participation of people. The history and development of international research ethics is reflective of abuses and mistakes.

---

10. Ibid., 588.

I had to have the consent of the participants, informing them about the purpose of the research, benefits, and confidentiality and letting them know their participation was voluntary.

The close relationship between researcher and participants meant data collection could not be coercive. Accordingly, I had close working relationships with participants, so the research required sensitivity and respect. In soliciting the participation of the respondents, especially for the second phase, which included NEA leaders, I clearly communicated to respondents regarding their freedom to choose not to take part in the research without consequence on their work and/or relationship (see appendixes B, C, and D). The inquiry protocols and accompanying letters made clear that the research was in the best interest of the community and reiterated core values of transparency, godly standards, and mutual commitment to democratic, nonhierarchical best practices in the community.

Mindful about ethical issues, I made every effort to convey respect for all participants as equal partners in the research process. I gave participants a comprehensive description of the project, highlighting its purpose, how results would be used, and participants' continued involvement with the project. I requested their voluntary consent to participate. I also took care to protect participants' individual identities, assuring them of confidentiality. The data participants provided was confidential and stored and secured so that other people did not have access to the information. The data was kept electronically on a personal password-protected computer, and any hard copies were kept in a locker in my office. The final report was in aggregated form, which did not identify individual participants. The information and data collected would be destroyed or deleted at the completion of the research. The Seminary IRB approval and Asbury Seminary faculty defense processes ensured the efficacy and ethics of the methodologies and approach.

CHAPTER 4

Findings

Problem and Purpose

Forging unity among the denominations and traditions of the church in the same nation is critical for effective witness of the church. However, division in the church tends to be the hallmark of the church in many nations in Africa. The different denominations and traditions of the church would be aware of the common foundation of their faith. However, perspectives in the way the factions understand and practice their faith can cause divisions among them. The people of Africa are divided by ethnicity and tribes; similarly, the church tends to be further divided into tribal factions even within the same denomination. The church will not be effective in bringing hope and proclaiming the gospel of reconciliation and peace when there is division among them. The church must be seen to be an exemplar of peace; unity in diversity as the need for oneness is also a biblical imperative.

In Africa, close affinity and unity among people exists in the community. Common ethnicity or tribal ties are particularly important in uniting people. On the contrary, the common faith Christians have does not seem to be enough incentive for a strong bond of unity as it is for ethnic and tribal considerations. Unity is limited to one's own tribe and clan with sharp divisions among tribes. This tribal unity is also one of the main sources of conflict in the region. In this case, the strength of community in Africa becomes actually a weakness, with ethnicity being the delimitation of the community. This negative ethnicity was not so much the case before colonialism but has become not only a colonial heritage but also a neocolonial political tool.

If the church should be a bridge builder and reach out to the community and the wider society with the good news of the gospel, it must do so in love, pulling down the walls of division. The body of Christ must be seen as united in purpose, as demonstrated in its conduct and ministry in spite of diversity.

The task of administrating and leading an NEA is to *connect, represent,* and *equip* members, promoting unity among the believers in spite of their ethnic backgrounds, church denominations, or tradition. WEA states, "[T]he mission of the evangelical alliance shall normally (in one form or another) include the three shared missions of many national alliances, WEA regions, and the WEA as a whole – connecting, equipping and being a representative voice."[1] Thus, the tasks of connecting, representing, and equipping, were part of the framework for exploring competencies, required for uniting church denominations and church leaders in a nation.

The purpose of the research was to identify leadership competencies required for leading an NEA as well as needed leadership development competencies of current general secretaries or NEA leaders in Africa by interviewing current regional presidents and national leaders in the AEA. In accomplishing the stated objective, I interviewed current AEA regional presidents and NEA general secretaries in Africa for their views, respectively.

I obtained the views on NEA leadership competencies of the regional presidents of AEA by administering a questionnaire through email in the first phase. The responses of the regional presidents sought to identify their perceived competencies required for leading the NEA. I also requested the general secretaries of the various NEAs in Africa in the second phase of the research, to rank and self-assess the level of proficiency of the competencies identified in the first phase by the AEA regional presidents and from the employers' viewpoint. The following report is a compilation and analysis of the responses I received from the regional presidents and the general secretaries, respectively.

---

1. Showell-Rogers, "Regional Alliance," 1–2.

Participants

Two categories of participants were involved in this research. In the first phase, all seven regional presidents of AEA were targeted for their perceived views of leadership competencies required for leading NEAs (see appendix A). The AEA regional presidents were a purposive sample of employers of the CEOs or general secretaries of the NEAs. The regional presidents were elected from a group of NEA board chairpersons from within the region, and they are the best group familiar with requirements for selecting the CEO or general secretary of an NEA and to respond to the research question in phase one of the research. The second category of participants for the second phase of the research included all the general secretaries of the NEAs that comprise the AEA. The general secretaries are better placed to respond to the research questions in the second phase of the research.

Table 4.1 shows the demographic information about the AEA regional presidents. All except one of the regional presidents responded to the questionnaire even after three reminders to the regional presidents who had not responded within the one-month timeframe given to them to respond to the questionnaire (see appendix E). I later found out that the one participant who did not respond had left his position. However, the response rate was 85.7 percent of the respondents. Although the participants were not asked to indicate their gender or age, they were all male adults; the AEA has no female regional presidents.

Table 4.1. Demographic Information of AEA Regional Presidents

Respondents N	Gender		Church Denomination			No. of Years in position		
	Male	Female	Pent.	Ind. Pent.	E. P.	1–5 yrs	6–10 yrs	10+ yrs
	n (%)	n (%)	n (%)	n (%)	n (%)	n (%)	n (%)	n (%)
6	6 (100)	0 (nil)	1 (16.7)	4 (66.7)	1 (16.7)	3 (50)	0 (nil)	3 (50)

Note: Pent. = Pentecostal, Ind. Pent. = Independent Pentecostal, E. P. = Evangelical Protestant

All except one of the regional presidents came from a Pentecostal background. The denominations included one from Assemblies of God, a classical Pentecostal denomination (simply referred to as Pentecostal denomination), and the rest of the Pentecostals were from independent Pentecostal and charismatic churches. One regional president came from an evangelical Protestant background.

Evangelicalism in Africa includes various Protestant and Pentecostal traditions. However, a host of typologies for categorizing churches in Africa exists. Classification of churches or Christianity in Africa is prejudicial and imprecise, ranging from Catholics and mainline Protestants to orthodox and heretics. Factors underlying different typologies focus around loyalty to the Western missionary-led churches and disloyalty to their African subordinates, a struggle for African identity, and association with political independence from colonialism and other cultural and religious considerations. Paul Kollman highlights some of the factors underlying the divisions:

> Differences of language and culture intensified mutual incomprehensibility, reinforcing notions of ecclesial life overtly focused on unity but rooted in colonialist prejudices that distrusted African ecclesial leadership. Nonetheless, these bases for classification, especially ecclesial dependence, cultural profile, and political engagement, have proved popular in analyzing Christianity in Africa to this day.[2]

The growth of the church and emergence of African-led churches free of Western missionary control, albeit reliant on financial support from the West, has added to the confusion on typologies in the ecclesial scene.

For the purpose of this study, classification was based on affiliation with churches planted by Western missionaries, regardless of the denomination. The Western missionary churches predating political independence and with roots from the Reformation era are referred to as evangelical Protestant.[3]

Pentecostalism lays emphasis on baptism in the Holy Spirit in addition to evangelical Protestant beliefs. Pentecostals with roots in the United States of America and Europe – classical Pentecostals – simply referred to as Pentecostals. The independent Pentecostals in Africa emphasize not only

---

2. Kollman, "Classifying," 9.
3. Okesson, *Re-Imaging Modernity*, xxi.

the baptism of the Holy Spirit but much ubiquitous spiritual power with a blending of traditional African and classical Pentecostal belief systems. The independent Pentecostals emphasize charismatic powers and add a further dimension to Pentecostalism by their emphasis on material success, particularly of interest to the followers in the African context. Okesson observes that the current growth of the church in Africa is due mainly to the segment of the church referred to as independent Pentecostal churches:

> [T]here can be no contesting the remarkable explosion of Pentecostalism on the continent as even the most cursory survey of the religious landscape reveals large churches in urban areas, amplified preachers on street corners, itinerant evangelists taking advantage of captive audiences on buses, and crowded tin buildings in rural areas effusive with congregants seemingly tapping into ubiquitous spiritual power.[4]

Charismatic leaders and individuals who claim extraordinary spiritual powers with gifts of healing and promise of material success for their followers founded most of the independent churches. This group of churches is also referred to as neo-Pentecostal.

Given the beliefs of the people about leadership and the charismatic leadership style of the Pentecostal pastors, the independent Pentecostal churches tend to have a large following. In this study, 67.7 percent of the respondents are independent Pentecostals (neo-Pentecostals and charismatic) and the evangelical Protestants and Pentecostals make up 16.7 percent each. The growth of the church in Africa is mostly within the independent Pentecostal category. However, this aspect of the growth is considered to be *sheep stealing*, where Christians are moving from the historic churches for the attraction of the more Pentecostal and charismatic churches. Another challenge with revolutionary growth of the church is the nuanced theological expressions manifested in the church. The evangelical Protestant historic churches contribute in ensuring clarity and adherence to conservative biblical beliefs. The value of the NEA is as a reference point in promoting unity and harmony among the different denominations. The NEA also serves as a guide and standards board for biblical orthodoxy.

---

4. Ibid., 145.

Half of the regional presidents (50 percent) have been in office for ten or more years, and the other half have been in office for one to five years. The length of time participants had served in the role of regional presidents ranged from four years to twenty-one years. One of the regional presidents had served on the board of his national evangelical alliance for thirty years. The regional presidents were all familiar with the work of the leader of NEA as employers. Thus, the regional presidents were suited to provide answers to the question about competencies for leading NEA.

The objective of the first part of the research was to identify the leadership competencies the AEA regional presidents perceived to be necessary for leading the NEA. First, I got the regional presidents' perceived portrait or profile of the NEA leader.

Profile of General Secretary of NEA

In attempting to identify the leadership competencies required for NEA leadership, the job profile was highlighted. Competencies and person specification constitute the job profile for any position.[5] The structure, polity, and operations of the NEA draw mostly from the global and regional alliances of the WEA and AEA, respectively. Accordingly, the job descriptions of the chief executive officers of the two associations serve as de facto templates and mirror the job description of the general secretary of the NEA (see appendices F and G). Analysis of the data shows some common elements of the profile of the NEA leader and the regional or global counterparts.

The AEA regional presidents stated their views in their responses to section B of the questionnaire regarding the perceived profile of the NEA leader. The profile included their perspective about the right kind of educational qualification, experience, and personal qualities (person specification) NEA leaders required. Table 4.2 shows the perceived educational qualification, experience, and personal qualities of the NEA leader.

In the view of the AEA regional presidents, a wide range of educational experience is expected of the NEA leader, with educational qualification ranging from diploma to doctoral level. Half (50 percent) of the respondents said a first degree was the minimum qualification required for the

---

5. Williamson, Colvin, and McDonald, *Human Resource Management*, 12.

leader of the NEA. Educational qualification at the level of a diploma had the next highest grouping (33.3 percent), and the smallest group included postgraduate or doctoral level qualifications (16.7 percent).

Table 4.2. Profile of General Secretaries of NEA

Educational Qualification			Previous Work Experience			Personal Qualities	
Levels	n	%	Vocations	n	%	Attributes	n
Diploma	2	33.3	Pastoral/Missionary	7	25.9	Teachable	1
1st degree Bachelor	3	50.0	Peacebuilding/ Conflict resolution	3	11.1	Willingness to learn	1
Postgraduate Master/PhD	1	16.7	Administration/ Management	4	14.8	Spiritual maturity	1
			Adult education	1	3.7	Relational	1
Subjects			Holistic development	2	7.4	Knowledge of ecumenism & church	1
Law			Secular work experience	2	7.4	Well respected	1
Social Sciences			Leadership/ Governance	2	7.4		
Christian ed			Advocacy	1	3.7		
Leadership & Management			Communication	1	3.7		
			Partnership/ Networking Teamwork	4	14.8		
Total number previous experience areas (N)				27	100		6

In an era when postgraduate qualifications seem to be the average educational requirement for senior leadership in many organizations, including the church, the regional leaders in Africa settled for undergraduate qualifications or less as the ideal educational qualification for NEA leaders. A large percentage of the respondents come from independent Pentecostal churches, which historically held disdain for theological education and only in recent times have realized the need for higher and graduate-level education, especially as this is deemed to confer legitimacy. Leaders in the church tend to derive legitimacy from the titles before their names (e.g. Rev, Most Rev, Dr, Bishop). At least I know of one church leader who has no university degree but refers to himself as Professor, a title of highest academic rank. Many others are looking for honorary doctoral degrees and use them as prefixes to their names.

The independent Pentecostals in Africa tend to lay more emphasis on the charisma of the leader and less on solid educational qualification, and advanced theological education is suspected of being apostasy. Ironically, this attitude towards graduate-level education could also be one of the reasons for practices in the church that would not meet the expected standards of evangelical orthodoxy, which is scandalous and a course for concern among evangelicals in Africa. The low educational standard of the top leadership and high educational achievement of those who serve under them could also be a cause for conflict in the church. The NEA plays a critical role in serving as a kind of reference point and arbiter to bring harmony and standards for the diverse theological expressions in the church.

The subject areas mentioned for the required educational experience of the NEA leader included law, social sciences, Christian education, leadership, and management. Christian education was mentioned but not theology *per se* as a subject area of endeavor. The whole question of church leaders perceiving the role of the leader of the NEA as non-ecclesial, such as the pastor of a local church congregation or overseer of the denomination, looms large. Pastoral or missionary experience constituted only 25.9 percent of the NEA leader's previous work experience before coming to the position. Expected previous work experience was quite diverse, ranging from pastoral experience to administration and strategic management, communication, advocacy, conflict management, partnership, and development (see figure 4.1).

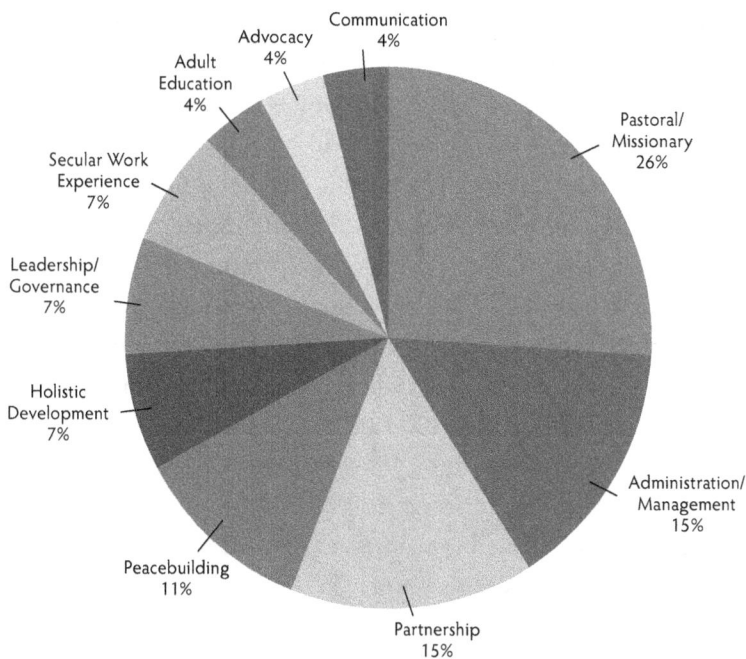

Figure 4.1. Perceived Subject Areas of Previous Work Experience of NEA General Secretaries

The bulk of the experience is mostly secular. The NEA leader is seen as more of a secular leader and not like the clergy who are called of God to provide spiritual leadership in the church. This view about pastor and NEA leader suggests the competing forces of sacred and secular dichotomy within the purview of leadership in the church. The expected work experience in diverse subject areas would not be very different from many secular vocations. However, the general secretaries are expected to be spiritually mature and relational; is no less an expectation from their pastoral counterparts.

Pastoral experience is the most frequently mentioned previous experience required of the leader, indicating that the role of the NEA leader and the NEA is missionary in nature. However, pastoral experience is only 25.9 percent among a spread of ten possible vocations. The rest of the experiences mentioned are not only limited to the church but could be acquired outside the church environment. Administration / management and partnership / team work are next in importance, each with a 14.8 percent rating, followed by peacebuilding / conflict resolution (11.1 percent) and holistic development, leadership / governance, and secular work with 7.4 percent each. Communication, advocacy, and adult education are also mentioned with the lowest rating of 3.7 percent each.

The high response rate to ostensibly secular disciplines corresponds to the prevailing socioeconomic, political, and developmental challenges in the region. Africa is the world's poorest region with a number of civil conflicts and the worst human development indices. According to the African Union Commission, "Africa and its people continue to be kept at the periphery."[6] Fifty years after independence from colonial domination, Africa still battles for emancipation and human rights.

The church is expected to play a visible and vibrant role in overcoming national challenges and enhancing the livelihood of the citizenry. In any case, a very thin line between what is sacred and what is secular in the African context. Okesson warns, "[W]e should be careful about not reading a Western, sacred-secular dichotomy into the religious landscape of Africa, by limiting this influence only to overtly spiritual forms within Christianity."[7] The African worldview creatively blends secular and sacred realities, and has hardly any such dichotomy of sacred and secular vocations.

While the church denominations may have their roots from Western missionary influence, the NEAs are mostly initiatives of the indigenous African church leaders. The dualism in the church is mostly influenced by the enlightenment philosophy, which views humans in dualistic categories – spiritual and physical. The church is expected to focus its work on what is perceived to be the spiritual aspects of humans, and the other aspects are deemed secular. However, the mostly African-initiated evangelical associations understand and approach the work of the church holistically. Therefore, the qualities and competencies expected of them to do their work are a mix of what traditionally would be considered secular and spiritual qualifications.

The expected profile of the NEA also highlights some qualities such as relational and spiritual maturity and understanding of ecumenism. These

---

6. African Union Commission. *Agenda 2063: The Africa We Want*, 41.

7. Okesson, "Sacred and Secular Currents," 40.

skills are readily associated with the church, and some may be required of a pastor or spiritual leader. Each of the attributes or qualities highlighted was mentioned only once. They are consistent with qualities highlighted in literature but may not be typical of the church leaders in Africa. The typical leader is one with charismatic powers and could hardly be described as one teachable with a willingness to learn and work on a team. The patrimonial system of leadership where the leader is placed in a class apart from the followers, would demystify the leader who demonstrates such people skills. Ecumenical knowledge has a low rating because leaders tend to view the church establishments they have founded and lead to be the only institution for which they have been called by God to reach the rest of the world with the gospel; many would argue that they would not like to have themselves being under the leadership or authority of another organization and leadership apart from their own where they preside as the boss.

A viable and visible alliance has its own governance structure, and its leadership wields a lot of authority and influence, perhaps becoming the envy of the denominational leaders. Some denominational leaders are, therefore, afraid of waning influence even in their own denominations if they stay loyal to the national alliance. The leader may be held in high regard out of fear and belief about the divine power accessible to them, and the way to maintain this power is for the leader to shy away from any situation that will demystify him or her and hold him or her accountable by some other authority in the community or nation.

NEA Leadership Competencies

In addition to the three NEA leadership task areas or specific actions required of the NEA leader – connecting, representing, and equipping – identified in literature, the AEA regional leaders were requested to self-describe the task of the NEA leader. The task of the leader is the specific role or action required to be taken and for which specific competencies are required to carry out the action. This section about self-described tasks and competencies for the NEA leader came first because this research was primarily about the perception of the regional presidents and NEA leaders. In addition to connecting, representing, and equipping, I wanted the regional presidents to designate tasks that they thought were vital to the role of leading an NEA. I wanted to know their views about the task of

the NEA leader compared to what was revealed in literature. The following were mentioned as the self-described task of the NEA leader:
- Administrating (n=2),
- Coordinating and team leading,
- Being a liaison,
- Having knowledge of NEA ethos, philosophy, and policy documents, and
- Guiding pastors.

However, only three respondents (50 percent) responded to the question of self-described tasks. These self-described tasks identified are closely related to the other three tasks – connecting, representing and equipping – previously identified in the literature review. Each self-described task is related either to the task of connecting, representing, or equipping. The list of self-described task was coded as a single theme; this theme was simply referred to as *administration*. In the list, administration was mentioned twice; the others mentioned only once. *Coordinating* is also an administrative function. In the expectations of the regional presidents for previous work experience of the NEA leader, administration and networking/partnering were ranked the next highest (14.8 percent each) after pastoral/missionary experience (25.9 percent) in table 4.2. Given the overall nature of the NEA, as a missionary endeavor and the relationship of the other self-described task to the established three task areas – *connecting, representing,* and *equipping,* the self-described task areas were assigned *administrating.*

The Merriam-Webster online dictionary defines the word administrate or administrating as "to manage the operation of (something, such as a company or government) or the use of (something, such as property)."[8] The self-perceived task of the NEA general secretary was coded as administrating the NEA. However, I could have explored the meaning of administrating further in face-to-face interviews with the respondents to shed light on what this category of task meant. Thus, I used four categories of tasks – *connecting, representing, equipping, and administrating (self-described)* – as the framework for the investigation of NEA leadership competencies. The perception of the AEA regional presidents about the competencies that

---

8. "Administration," *Merriam-Webster Online*. Accessed 20 October 2014.

Findings

were deemed to be required for leading the NEA was surveyed. The regional presidents' responses provided the answer to Research Question #1.

Research Question #1

What leadership competencies did current AEA regional presidents identify as necessary for leading an NEA? The responses of the regional presidents about the competencies they believed were required in each of the four task categories of administrating, connecting, representing, and equipping were collated and organized by themes as shown in tables 4.3 through 4.7 (pp. 118–133).

Competencies for the Task of Administrating (Self-Described)

The responses of the regional presidents to the questions posed to them about leadership competencies required for general secretaries to carry out the task of administrating were organized into themes. Thirty-three individual competencies were mentioned. Some were identical, describing the same idea or theme. Thus, the competencies were arranged by themes.[9] Eleven different themes were identified for administrating tasks (self-described) of the NEA leader. A theme comprises a cluster of competencies that are related and describe the same ability or competency. The number of competencies clustered in the same theme was identified and collated. Table 4.3 highlights the competencies outlined by the regional presidents for the task of administrating by NEA leaders by themes. The frequencies of the competencies are also shown in figure 4.2.

---

9. Sensing, *Qualitative Research*, 198–199.

Table 4.3. Competencies of the NEA Leader for Task of Administrating

#	Competencies (Grouped by themes)	Mentioned n	%
1	Resource mobilization (fundraising/other resources)	2	6.1
	Manage people and resources	5	15.1
2	Soft skills (consult, listen, teachable, reflective thinking)	5	15.1
3	Communication/inspirational speaker	3	9.1
4	Promote unity/build peace/team building and partnership/networking	5	15.1
5	Training and developing people (mentoring/making disciples)	2	6.1
6	Balanced life (spiritual maturity and professional competency in conduct)	1	3.0
7	Able to assess strength and weaknesses of the church and church leaders	1	3.0
8	Sound biblical and doctrinal knowledge	2	6.1
9	Innovative and takes risk	2	6.1
10	Motivator	1	3.0
11	Servant leadership/visionary	4	12.1
	Total number of competencies mentioned (N)	33	

The most frequently mentioned competency themes are soft skills, management of people and other resources, and promotion of unity (i.e. peace building and partnership/networking). Each of these top three themes has five clusters of competencies, and each is 15.1 percent of the total number of competencies mentioned in this area of task for the NEA leader. The frequency or percentage of theme of competency may indicate the importance of the theme of competency for leading the NEA and, in particular, in the given task of the leader. Accordingly, soft skills (i.e. consulting, listening, being teachable, thinking reflectively), managing people and resources, and promoting unity (i.e. teambuilding / partnership) are the three most important NEA leadership competencies, especially for the task of administrating. While these are important skills for the overall goal of uniting the different church denominations, the prevailing cultural perceptions of the leader would suggest skills deficit in these important competencies.

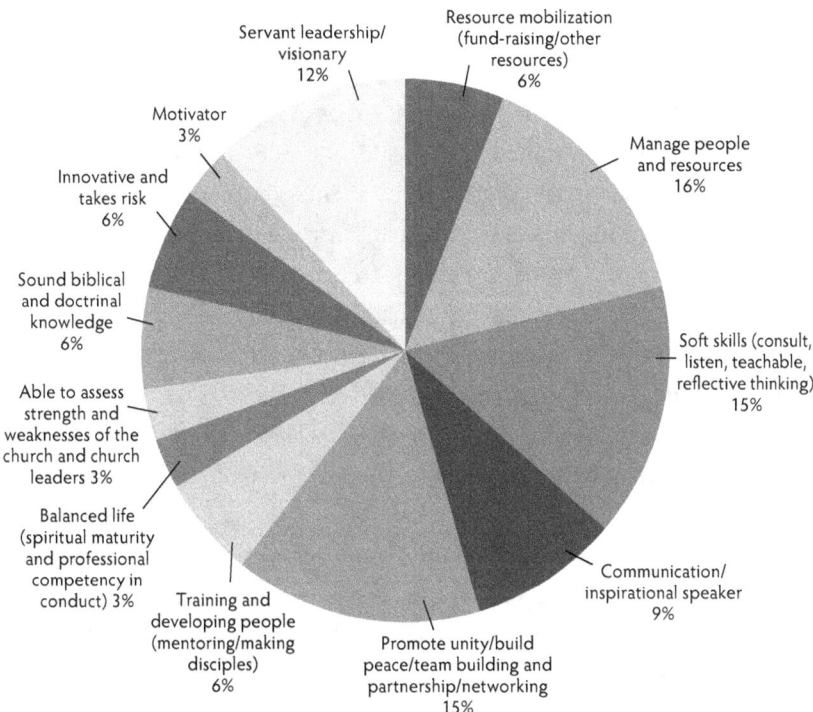

Figure 4.2. Competencies for Task of Administrating for NEA Leader

Leaders with soft skills such as listening, learning from others, and having a focus on developing others would be scarce to see in a culture where leadership is elevated to sacredness and mystery. However, these competencies were consistent with characteristics of effective leaders and biblical values espoused in chapter 2. The NEA has the challenge of cultivating leaders with these competencies. The next frequently mentioned themes of competency were servant/visionary leadership (12.1 percent), communication (9.1 percent), and resource mobilization, training/developing people, sound biblical doctrinal knowledge, and innovation (6.1 percent each). Like the top three competencies, these are also important competencies for uniting and require effort to cultivate.

The least mentioned themes, highlighted only once or 3.0 percent each, are having a balanced life (spiritual maturity and professional in conduct), having the ability to assess strengths and weaknesses of the church, and motivating others. However, these competencies are all very important for the purpose of uniting the church.

Competencies for the Task of Connecting

The competencies mentioned by the regional presidents for the task of connecting were collated and organized by themes, clustering the items that were close in meaning under one theme. Thirty-nine individual competencies were highlighted. Some of the competencies were mentioned more than once, or the same competency was described differently. Fifteen themes emerged from the organization of the data. The number of competencies clustered under each theme was identified from the list (see table 4.4).

Soft skills (i.e. listening / being willing to learn, being sensitive / flexible / cooperative, being caring and friendly) were the top competency highlighted. This theme of competency was mentioned in various forms six times or 15.4 percent of the total number of competencies. Soft skills competency is again at the top of the scale, just as it was for the task for administrating; underscoring the importance in the NEA leadership task and in the implication for leadership development in the church and in the NEAs in particular. Leadership is seen to be an interaction among the leader, followers, and the environment. The required competency highlighted has implication for the followers and the culture as well. The leadership styles and characteristics need to be accepted by the followers.

Table 4.4. Competencies of the NEA Leader for Task of Connecting

#	Competencies (Grouped by themes)	Competency n	%
1	Advocacy (voice for the voiceless/poor)	2	5.1
2	Able to convene and organize conferences	2	5.1
3	Promote holistic development in community/society	3	7.7
4	Communicate vision, mission and objectives (oral and written communication).	4	10.2
5	Deal with challenges with culturally relevant solutions	1	2.6
6	Understand ecumenism (including WEA &AEA) and engagement with other traditions without compromise	2	5.1
7	Change agent/leadership	1	2.6
8	Maintain consistent Christian values (including AEA & WEA beliefs)	3	7.7
9	Uniting (building relationships, partnering and networking)	4	10.2
10	Soft skills (Listening/willing to learn, sensitive/flexible/cooperative, caring, friendly)	6	15.4
11	Motivate	1	2.6
12	Manage/coordinate	3	7.7
13	Innovative	2	5.1
14	Mobilize resources	1	2.6
15	Able to train leaders (in theology, pastoral excellence and leadership).	4	10.2
Total number of competencies mentioned (N)		39	

Soft skills, as highlighted require a lot of humility. However, humility or meekness is associated with underlings, not the leader. These qualities are consistent with one of the characteristics of highly effective leaders – humility, highlighted in the literature review, and servant leadership commanded by Jesus Christ. These qualities are learned and cultivated, but not many training institutions or curricula exists that offer courses in the competencies highlighted. This dearth in training facilities for soft skills has implications for leadership development. Possible approaches for leadership development include spiritual formation and customized curriculum for in-service training. Leaders with soft skills may have a long cultural history in Africa due to the relational nature of leadership but also struggle to exercise these skills, due to approach to leadership.

Following the top competency were three different themes (i.e. communicating, building relationships/partnerships, and training leaders in theology, pastoral excellence, and leadership). These three themes were each mentioned four times (10.2 percent) out of the total number of competencies highlighted in this section or area of task. These competencies were also highlighted in the previous category of administrating, thus underscoring the importance for uniting the church.

These three competencies are particularly important for the task of connecting. Communication is the main means of connecting with members scattered all over the country. The most effective means of communicating, especially over long distances, is the Internet and electronic media. However, dexterity in the use of computer technology for people who are fifty and older may require some skills training. Computer hardware, electricity, and Internet facilities are a need in many of the NEAs, and these needs have implications for leadership development. However, virtual communication needs to be backed by relationship building and pastoral care.

Building relationship with pastoral skills effectively contributes to building the national unity in the alliance. These people skills require physical contact and touch with people, consistent with the principles of servant leadership as recommended by Christ.

A set of three themes – promoting holistic development, maintaining consistent Christian values (and beliefs) and managing/coordinating – were the next sets of top competencies with a frequency of three (7.7 percent) each. These competencies are service oriented; the leader is expected to demonstrate the connecting competencies practically in rendering service to people.

Figure 4.3 shows a visual representation of the connecting competencies and the percentages. The data reveals that the task of connecting requires more interpersonal or soft skills. Thus, seven competency themes are included in the top three competencies in the task of connecting:

- Soft skills (listening, being willing to learn, being sensitive/flexible/ cooperative/caring/friendly),
- Communicating, building relationships/partnerships, training leaders (in theology, pastoral excellence, and leadership), and
- Promoting holistic development, maintaining consistent Christian values and beliefs, and managing/coordinating.

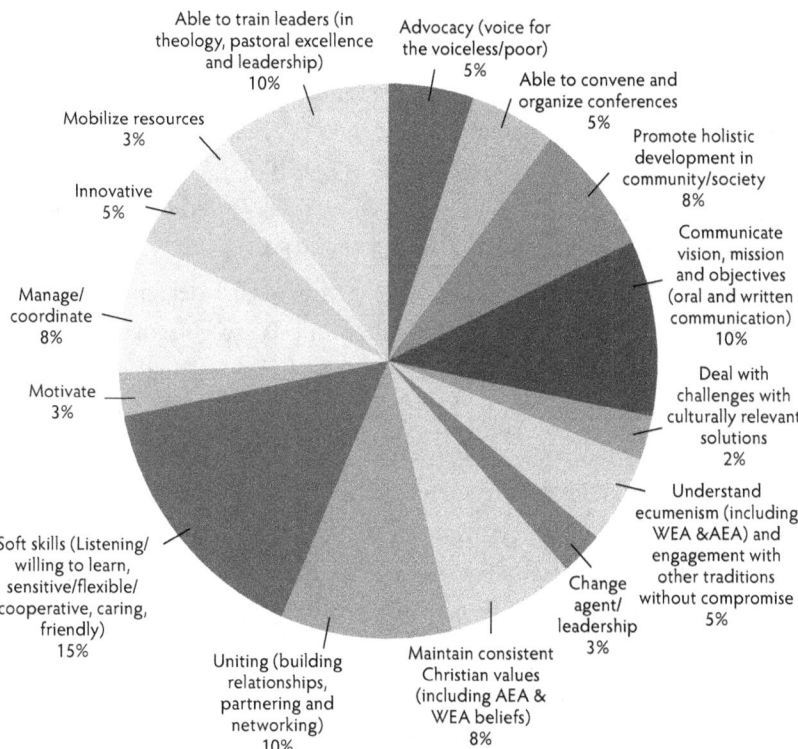

Figure 4.3. Competencies for Task of Connecting for NEA Leader

A national association with constituent members spread over a wide geographic area would need to bridge the communication gap among members to build cohesion and unity in the fellowship (association) and build relationships. These competencies contribute to uniting the body of Christ in the nation. However, effective communication requires feedback from the receiver to the initiator or sender in a timely manner. The denominational leaders at the receiving end of the communication may have similar challenges for virtual communication infrastructure as the NEA leader at the other end (sender) in the communication loop. Important as communication is, the lack in communication infrastructure could be a major challenge for the fledgling state of many NEAs.

Competencies for the Task of Representing

Table 4.5 shows the data collated and organized from the responses of the regional presidents for the task of representing. Thirty-one individual competencies were highlighted for the task of representing. The competencies were grouped into fifteen different themes. The top two competencies highlighted were a representative voice on behalf of members in the nation and knowledge about evangelicalism, especially as espoused by the regional and global organizations of evangelicals (i.e. AEA and WEA). Each one of the two competencies was mentioned five times (16.1 percent each) of the total number of competencies highlighted in this category of task.

The WEA provides the standards to which the regional and national evangelical associations look for best practices and issues for theological interpretation. Theological interpretation is one of the major causes for division in the church; therefore, NEA leaders need to be aware and knowledgeable about the positions of the global and regional associations. However, the different associations at national, regional, and global levels are independent and wary of accepting positions uncritically. The relationship is not like the papacy, with a top-down directive. Consensual positions are matters of dialogue and mutual respect and sensitivity to regional and cultural diversity. The common commitment and understanding is submission and fidelity to the authority of Scripture in the tradition of biblical or evangelical orthodoxy, which can actually help forge stronger unity.

Sound biblical knowledge and application to life was the third most mentioned competency, mentioned four times or 12.9 percent of the total number of all competencies highlighted in this section. This competency is related to the previous two competencies and they complement each other. Biblical interpretation depends, to an extent, on the view one holds of the Bible; evangelicals affirm Scripture as the Word of God, inspired by God, inerrant and infallible in all it affirms. Evangelicals subject themselves to the dictates of the Bible and seek to live in obedience as the authority for faith conduct. This affirmation is important and used as the lens for understanding and interpreting the Bible. The role of the general secretary requires knowledge on these positions and skills in contending for the faith in all matters. The member churches and denominations look up to their national alliance and the global network for guidance. The current disagreement on the issue of same-sex marriage is a typical example of where the NEAs provide a clear position and guidance for its members.

Table 4.5. Competencies of the NEA Leader for Task of Representing

#	Competencies (Grouped by Themes)	Competency Mentioned n	%
1	Sound biblical knowledge and application to life	4	12.9
2	Respect for all different traditions of the church	1	3.2
3	Able to act on decisions of members,	1	3.2
4	Peace builder	1	3.2
5	Understand ecumenism (and the global church)	1	3.2
6	Promote holistic development in churches and Bible schools	3	9.7
7	Representative voice in different platforms/connect with Government of the nation	5	16.1
8	Resource mobilization	1	3.2
9	Initiate programs that meet needs of members	2	6.4
10	Ordained minister to preach and confirm the gospel as evangelical	2	6.4
11	Knowledgeable and commitment to uphold evangelical values (AEA/WEA promote vision and mission)	5	16.1
12	Visionary leadership	1	3.2
14	Family should be role model	1	3.2
15	Advocacy (voice for the poor and marginalized on justice and social action)	3	9.7
	Total number of competencies mentioned (N)	**31**	

Holistic development and advocacy (voice for vulnerable and injustice) constituted the next two competencies with a frequency of three each (9.7 percent of the total). The NEA is not only concerned about theological positions at the conceptual level but also must demonstrate its beliefs in deed – integral mission. Faith in Christ is demonstrated by compassion and love of Christ. Holistic development and advocacy for justice are integral parts of the mission of the church in addition to evangelism and spiritual formation. An integral approach to mission is particularly important for the mission of the church in Africa. Africa is the most impoverished region of the world where people lack the basic requirements for life. The Bible encourages the church to care and be compassionate not only to its members but to strangers or unbelievers, too. Jesus warned of dire consequences for ignoring compassionate ministry:

> Then he will say to those on his left, "Depart from me, you who are cursed, into the eternal fire prepared for the devil and his angels. For I was hungry and you gave me nothing to eat, I was thirsty and you gave me nothing to drink, I was a stranger and you did not invite me in, I needed clothes and you did not clothe me, I was sick and in prison and you did not look after me." (Matt 25:41–43)

If African Christians should avoid the wrath of Jesus, they need to pay attention to the needs of the hungry, the thirsty, the refugees, the naked, the sick, and the imprisoned as in no other region in the world. The church would require shedding the legacy of dualism inherited from church plants of Western missionaries, which gives the impression that the church is only concerned with what is deemed to be the spiritual side of people.

In an effort either to correct the dualistic philosophy or respond to the needs of people according to the teachings of Christ, the phenomenon of the prosperity gospel, which itself is in error of orthodox evangelical teaching, is rampant in the church in Africa. While human flourishing (i.e. prosperity) is taught in Scripture, it also teaches about suffering and destitution. The church should teach followers of Christ about how to live in tension with the two positions in accordance with Scripture. The church should embrace holism, but it should be mindful of some dangers that it might bring to undermine the whole purpose of the church.

A representative voice requires understanding of the constituents and hearing the voice first of the people she represents. The NEA leader's role is to magnify that voice, and leaders should not just be seen to be speaking for themselves or a faction of their constituents. Building consensus informed by common values and beliefs is critical to the role of the leader. The NEA leader is an embodiment of evangelical beliefs, orthodox biblical beliefs, and therefore, the biblical knowledge theme features prominently along with the very act of representing the church to the rest of the world.

The other task areas of administrating, connecting, and equipping have to do with internal matters of the membership, working with other senior clergy and denominational leaders, and these would be looking for non-biblical materials to complement their work. In public engagement, the NEA leader is expected to portray the best of evangelicalism as a representative voice. Thus, a sound biblical knowledge, which distinguishes evangelicals, is inevitable; sound biblical knowledge is particularly important, in a world of increasing secularism when the fundamental doctrines of the Christian faith are questioned, especially in the public square. Many Christian leaders are not able to contend for the fundamental doctrines of their faith and concede to secularist views on matters such as sexuality, same-sex marriage, and abortion. Figure 4.4 shows the frequencies of the various competencies. Other themes include initiating programs to meet the needs of members, pastoral skills as in ordained ministry, and respect for different traditions of the church.

The general secretary of the NEA plays a key role in articulating the evangelical orthodox position on these matters, among others.

The NEA leader is the voice of the church, and its voice is expected to reflect what the average member of the organization would be happy to hear. The leader should be aware of a broader consensus on beliefs and evangelical orthodoxy, his or her knowledge about the AEA and WEA is an important link for the nation with the global church. The required competencies highlighted may not be the usual priority areas for which the church is probably known. Church associations such as the NEA, have their own unique nature and the competencies needed to lead effectively. The various skills are also associated with the integral approach to the mission of the church, especially from an African point of view, and the compelling humanitarian conditions of people in the church and community.

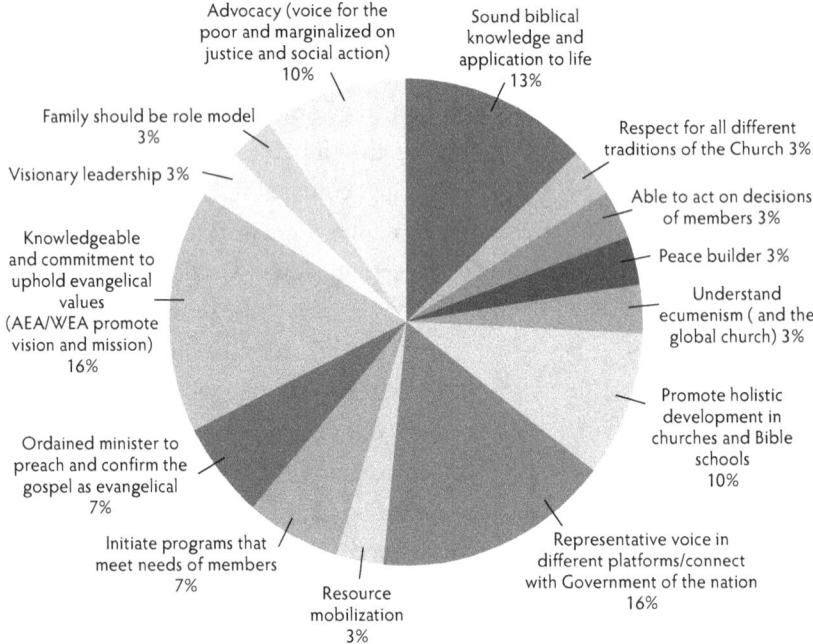

Figure 4.4. Competencies for Task of Representing for NEA Leader

Competencies for the Task of Equipping

The competencies mentioned by the regional presidents were organized and grouped into sixteen themes.

Disciple making and mentoring, creating an enabling environment for spiritual formation, and being able to organize training seminars were the top three competencies highlighted with a frequency of 5 or 10.6 percent each of the total number of competencies mentioned. These three competencies are very closely related and underscore the importance of people development. The project is about identifying competencies for the purpose of leadership development in the NEA. These first top three competencies focus on people development. The NEA is a network of denominations and other Christian organizations, and collaboration depends on relationship with people who run these organizations. Good people skills are important for uniting and encouraging collaboration among the different organizations (see table 4.6).

Table 4.6. Competencies of NEA Leader for Task of Equipping

#	Competencies (grouped by themes)	Competency mentioned n	%
1	Promote family life and prayer	1	2.1
2	Raise the standard of the church	1	2.1
3	Acquainted with needs of community	2	4.2
4	Disciple making/mentoring (and develop people)	5	10.6
5	Mobilize and empower for all classes of people in church (women, youth and children)	3	6.4
6	Facilitate NEAs to establish relief and development for poverty reduction	4	8.5
7	Resource mobilization	3	6.4
8	Plan programs in line with vision and mission	4	8.5
9	Communication skills (media and information dissemination)	2	4.2
10	Soft skills (teach and be teachable, think out of the box)	2	4.2
11	Organize training seminars/conferences	5	10.6
12	Create conducive environment for training and spiritual formation	5	10.6
13	Facilitation/training or teaching	3	6.4
14	Promote unity/strengthening ties with NEA members/ conflict resolution	4	8.5
15	Innovate and create new programs to meet needs of members	2	4.2
16	Result oriented	1	2.1
Total number of competencies mentioned (N)		47	

The general secretary's role, like any leadership role, is people oriented. Even though the role of the general secretary has a strong administrative component that requires paper work or other tasks, it needs to prioritize people. With busy people, such as general secretaries, demand for attention and time from different people could appear to be a distraction. However, people skills and meeting the felt needs of people is critical for success and effectiveness. Making disciples is not just an activity; it is long-time engagement and the leader sharing his or her life with the one being discipled, as modeled by Jesus and the band of twelve apostles. Making disciples is the core mandate of the church (Matt 28:18–20). Every true Christian call should have an element and a focus on making disciples. Often, the church limits this call for making disciple to gospel proclamation or evangelism. Therefore, the apparent secular competencies highlighted in this study and focused on people development are essential for making disciples. From a biblical point of view, no better way of developing people than making disciples of Christ.

The next set of top competencies includes facilitating NEAs for holistic development, promoting unity and conflict resolution, and planning programs in line with vision and mission. Each competency within this group was mentioned four times or 8.5 percent of the total number of competencies highlighted. Thus, the top five competencies comprised six themes because of the even ranking of the last three. Promoting unity among the churches requires healthy growth of members; the NEA leader should be able to address the needs of members holistically and have skills in conflict resolution. The leader should also mount programs in line with the vision and mission of the members. The NEA derives legitimacy from its members; it should not set objectives that do not support its members. The NEA is primarily established to serve the interest of members. Notably, the emphasis is on people development. The regional presidents' perceived competencies for leading NEA focus more on the people and less organizational structures (see figure 4.5).

The focus on people is consistent with the general perception of evangelicals shying away from conciliar and institutional development. The evangelical alliances tend to run away from organizational structures, especially from hierarchical or bureaucratic structures, as in other traditions, such as the Roman Catholic Church.

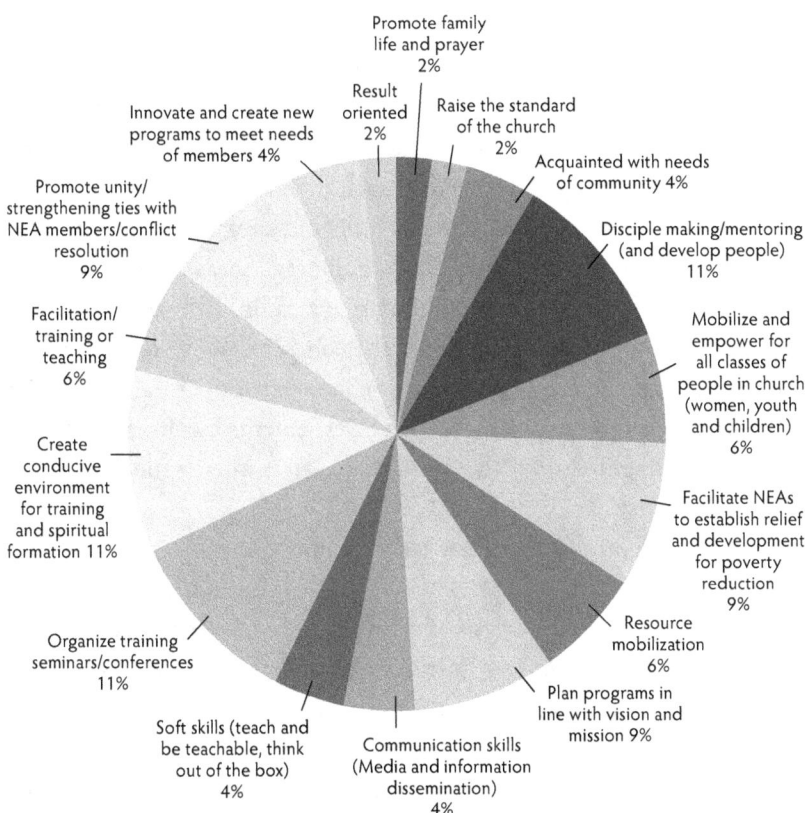

Figure 4.5. Competencies for Task of Equipping for NEA Leader

The tendency is to have flexible networks with independent parts within the whole. The independence of parts or constituents tends to undermine commitment and accountability of the alliance and is one of the possible causes for the fragility of the many national evangelical alliances. The leaders of many independent Pentecostal churches may not want to give up their independence by committing to another organization that they are not the head or leader. The tendency is to strengthen and maintain influence in their own organizations or churches because they fear losing that influence with another organization for which they are not in charge. Generally, evangelicals loathe any hierarchical authority, especially when they are not the one in charge.

Core Competencies

Further coding highlighted the core competencies for NEA leadership, which are important because they tend to be required for the different tasks of the NEA. To determine the core competencies, the number of individual competencies clustered in each theme was counted. A total of 150 competencies were mentioned in all four areas of tasks – administering, connecting, representing, and equipping. Some of the competencies highlighted recurred in more than one area or were mentioned more than once within the same category. The competencies were organized by themes, each theme comprising related competencies. A total of fifty-eight themes (i.e. cluster of similar competencies) emerged from the 150 competencies highlighted from the data collated from the responses of the regional presidents.

The regional presidents were asked to highlight the top three competencies in each section or area of task. However, only one respondent answered this question; therefore, analysis of the top three competencies was discarded. I could not figure out why only one respondent answered this question. I can only speculate about either the clarity of the question or the difficulty the respondents had in prioritizing the competencies they outlined. The objective of this question was to identify the top competencies for leading NEAs. However, the recurrent themes or cluster of competencies appearing more than once and in two or more areas of task categories give an indication of the top competencies. The top competencies are identified by the mode frequencies and percentages (see tables 4.3 through 4.6, pp. 118–129). The recurrence of a particular competency within a task area or occurrence in more than one task area was an indicator of the importance of that particular competency for leading the NEA.

The competencies with the most occurrences (mode) and occurring in more than one area of tasks were considered *core competencies* relative to the other competencies that were unique and limited to one particular task area of the NEA leader.

Table 4.7. Core NEA Leadership Competencies

#	Competency	Admin (n)	Connect (n)	Represent (n)	Equip (n)	Sum (Σn)	%
1	Sound biblical knowledge and application	2	0	4	0	6	4.8
2	Promote unity (reconciliation, peace building)	5	4	1	4	14	11.1
3	Organize training seminars	2	2	0	5	9	7.1
4	Soft skills (listen, think, teachable)	5	6	1	2	14	11.1
5	Communicate	3	4	0	2	9	7.1
6	Disciple making/mentoring	2	0	0	5	7	5.5
7	Mobilize resources (fundraising)	2	1	1	3	7	5.5
8	Manage people/resources	5	3	0	3	11	8.7
9	Promote holistic development	0	3	3	4	10	7.9
10	Advocate for justice and for the vulnerable	0	2	3	0	5	4.0
11	Be family role model	0	0	1	1	2	1.6
12	Innovate	2	2	0	2	6	4.8
13	Servant leader/visionary	4	1	1	0	6	4.8
14	Motivate	1	1	0	0	2	1.6
15	Maintain consistent Christian values and evangelical beliefs	0	3	5	0	8	6.3
16	Understand ecumenism and global Christianity	0	2	1	0	3	2.4
17	Able to teach (facilitate)/train	0	4	0	3	7	5.5
Total		33	38	21	34	126	

The competencies identified as unique only to one particular task area were categorized as *subcompetencies*. Seventeen themes of competencies that emerged in more than one category of task were identified. Table 4.7 shows the cumulative frequency for all categories. These competencies tend to be the core for the different aspects of the NEA leader's role. The cumulative totals (Σn) across the four task areas are indicators of the importance of the competency from the viewpoint of the regional presidents. The higher the sum totals of the frequency were, the greater their importance.

The frequencies generated a ranking of the competencies, indicating their importance for NEA leadership from the point of view of the regional presidents. A competency mentioned in all four task categories was an indication of its importance in the overall task of leading the NEA. However, the cumulative frequency determined the rank of the competency.

Accordingly, following is the list of core competencies for leading NEAs, in order of importance, starting with the highest ranking to the lowest as highlighted by the AEA regional presidents:

1) Promote unity – conflict resolution/partnership/network (11.1 percent),
2) Have soft skills – listen/think/be teachable/flexible (11.1 percent),
3) Manage people and resources (8.7 percent),
4) Promote holistic development (7.9 percent),
5) Communicate (7.1 percent),
6) Organize training seminars/conferences (7.1 percent),
7) Maintain consistent Christian values/evangelical beliefs (6.3 percent),
8) Work on disciple making/mentoring (5.5 percent),
9) Provide resource mobilization/fundraising (5.5 percent),
10) Be able to teach/facilitate/train (5.5 percent),
11) Have sound biblical knowledge (4.8 percent),
12) Be able to innovate (4.8 percent),
13) Demonstrate servant/visionary leadership (4.8 percent),
14) Provide advocacy for justice – voice for the poor and vulnerable (4.0 percent),
15) Understand ecumenism/global Christianity (2.4 percent),

16) Be family role model (1.6 percent), and
17) Be able to motivate (1.6 percent).

The top two competencies of promoting unity and having soft skills (listening/thinking/being flexible and teachable) have the highest total frequency, fourteen each (11.1 percent). These top competencies are especially needed for task of connecting and representing and were highlighted in all four categories of NEA leaders' tasks. Soft skills require a lot of humility on the part of the leader and in consonance with servant leadership – the style of leadership modeled and recommended for Christians. The leadership characteristics exhibited, and as highlighted in this research, by the regional presidents are at variance with what they expect of the NEA general secretaries. Although the roles are different, the NEAs would be stronger if its presidents also modeled the qualities expected of the general secretaries.

Next in rank of competencies is the management of people and resources with a total occurrence of eleven (8.7 percent) of the total number of competencies mentioned, followed by holistic development with ten occurrences (7.9 percent) of the total competencies. People management and holistic development provide a set of competencies for holism. People management requires more than technical skills and has implication for making disciples, requiring spiritual nurture and care for the well-being of the person.

The next two competencies were communication and the ability to organize training seminars, each occurring nine times (7.1 percent) each of the total number of competencies. These were all important skills for the purpose of uniting and building a vibrant NEA. The NEA leader must be able to communicate as a mouthpiece for the church in the country. As a representative voice, the NEA leader must be heard literally. The role involves public engagement, speaking on behalf of the association. Communication competency would include written communication, presentations and technology, and general comportment or behavior of the leader.

Figure 4.6 illustrates the frequency distribution of the core competencies. Thus, the top six competencies may not be what traditionally would be the expected core competencies for leadership in the church. However, the findings point to the increasing concern among evangelicals of biblical illiteracy and the rise of modern cultural values rather than biblical values. One of the key activities of the NEA leader is organizing conferences and being able to facilitate training or teach, passing on knowledge and skills to members. African view of spirituality is integrative – all of life has a spiritual dimension. Holistic development, resource mobilization and management, peace building, and other activities are as important as the traditional activities in the church for disciple making.

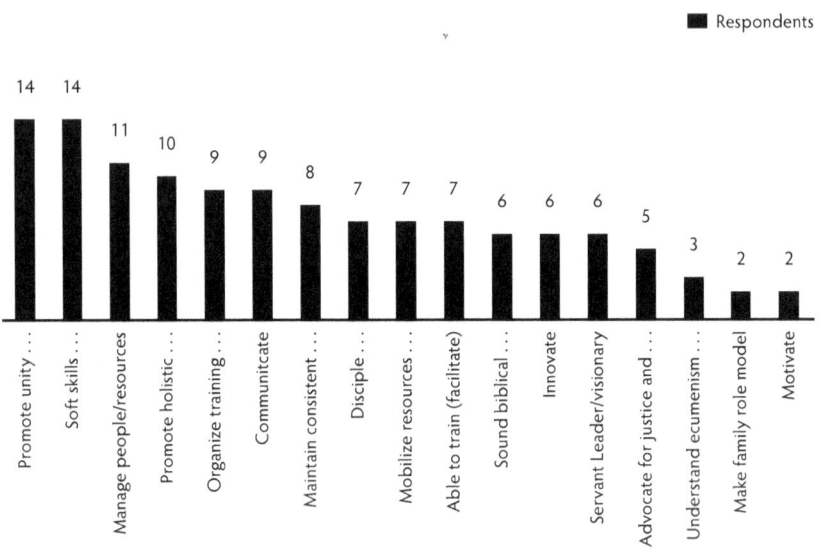

Figure 4.6. NEA Leadership Core Competencies

Africans look for spiritual reasons for every aspect of life: when the harvest is plentiful or lean, in birth or in death, for better or for worse; hardly a dichotomy between what is spiritual and what is physical. Every aspect of life has spiritual implications, and the Bible should be able to speak to every situation in life. Thus, the six top competencies mentioned palpable areas of need for an organization of national stature and influence, except that the competencies may not readily appear to be ecclesial in the traditional mindset of the church.

The more traditional areas of leadership competency in the church start appearing in seventh place on the list. Maintaining Christian values (evangelical beliefs) was the seventh core competency with a frequency of eight (6.3 percent). Disciple making/mentoring was in eighth position, along with resource mobilization and the ability to teach/facilitate with a frequency of seven (5.5 percent) of the total number of competencies. Making disciples and maintaining Christian beliefs are foundational evangelical convictions that serve to strengthen identity and unify the alliance for collaboration. However, disciple making and maintaining values are not just programs and activities. These are the very essence of being a Christian, and much more so, a Christian leader. Whether in holistic development or, managing people or other resources, as mentioned at the top end of the scale, elements of manifesting evangelical values and making disciples should be evident to be truly holistic and missional.

Sound biblical knowledge was in eleventh place on the list, along with servant/visionary leadership and the ability to innovate, each occurring six times (4.8 percent) of the total number of competencies. Evangelicalism is rooted in sound biblical worldview; it is the lens through which evangelical Christians view all of life. The leader of the NEA is not only expected to have a sound biblical knowledge but to live out and promote it. Sound biblical knowledge is basic to the work and witness of the church.

The last three core competencies at the bottom end of the list are advocacy for justice (voice for the poor and vulnerable), understanding ecumenism/global Christianity, being family role model, and the ability to motivate. Surprising that holistic development is ranked in the top four competencies and advocacy for justice is in the bottom. Holistic development has to do with issues of justice, and promoters must have a strong voice for advocacy. The disparity may be evidence of a gap in understanding two concepts, needing further exploration especially in training interventions for NEA leaders.

Subcompetencies

The other competencies that emerged from the study and were unique for only one task category and not another were considered to be *subcompetencies*. The subcompetencies are summarized in table 4.8. The total number of competencies unique only to one particular task area was eleven. Most of these subcompetencies were mentioned only once and for a particular task area, except for the task of equipping.

Table 4.8. Subcompetencies for NEA Leadership

Tasks	Subcompetencies
Administering (self-described)	1. Balanced life (spiritual maturity and professional competency in conduct)
	2. Able to assess strength and weakness of church
Connecting	1. Deal with challenges with culturally relevant solutions
Representing	1. Reverence (respect) for all churches,
	2. Act on decisions of members
	3. Ordained minister to preach gospel
Equipping	1. Raise the standard of the church
	2. Plan programs in line with vision and mission (n=4)
	3. Result oriented
	4. Create conducive environment for training and formation (n=5)
	5. Acquainted with needs of community (n=2)

In the task of equipping, most of the competencies highlighted occurred multiple times, except for *result oriented* and *raising the standard* of the church, which were mentioned once each. Planning programs in line with vision and mission and creating conducive environments were mentioned four and five times, respectively. Acquaintance with needs of the community was mentioned twice.

The competencies have been organized into clusters of themes to eliminate multiple occurrences in the final list of competencies for the next phase of the study. Most of the competencies mentioned occurred in more than one category of tasks. The total number of themes or clusters of competencies (core competencies) was seventeen, and the total number of subcompetencies occurring in only one area of tasks was eleven. Thus, these responses constituted a total of twenty-eight individual competency themes highlighted by the regional presidents.

The twenty-eight competencies, without overlap or recurring counts, formed the data for crafting the research instrument in appendix H for the second phase of the research. The data was the basis for surveying the views of participants, the general secretaries or NEA leaders of the National Evangelical Associations that were constituent members of AEA.

Research Question #2

How did current NEA leaders or general secretaries in Africa rate competencies in order of importance for effective NEA leadership? The responses of the general secretaries of NEAs in Africa, in the second phase of the research, provided answers for Research Question #2. The second phase of the research required the general secretaries or NEA leaders in Africa, to rank the competencies identified in tables 4.7 and 4.8 (pp. 133, 138) in order of importance. The competencies listed constituted the core competencies and subcompetencies, respectively and each appeared only once on the competencies instrument in appendix H.

Demographic Information of NEA General Secretaries in Africa

The NEA general secretaries in Africa participated in the second phase of the project. The competencies highlighted by the AEA regional presidents were representative views of employers of the general secretaries who were the employees of the NEA. The general secretaries were, therefore, most suited to provide answers to Research Questions #2 and #3 in this project. Tables 4.9 and 4.10 highlight the demographic information about the participants. I received responses from twenty participants out of thirty-one (64.5 percent) of the targeted participants. The responses I received were recorded, organized, and presented. All but one respondent or NEA general secretaries were male. Leadership tends to be male dominated in the NEAs and very much like the rest of society in Africa. The question of women in leadership continues to be a subject of interest for human rights and development workers.

Table 4.9. Demographic Information of NEA General Secretaries (N=20)

Gender		Church Denomination			No. of Years in Position			
Male n (%)	Female n (%)	Pent. n (%)	Ind. Pent. n (%)	E. P. n (%)	0–4yrs n (%)	5–9yrs n (%)	10–14yrs n (%)	15–19yrs n (%)
19(95)	1(5)	2(10)	5(25)	13(65)	10(50)	7(35)	2(10)	1(5)

Note: Pent. = Pentecostal; Ind. Pent. = Independent Pentecostal; E. P. = Evangelical Protestant.

Table 4.10. Age Range of NEA General Secretaries in Africa (N=20)

40–44yrs n (%)	45–49yrs n (%)	50–54yrs n (%)	55–59yrs n (%)	60–64yrs n (%)
3 (15)	5 (25)	6 (30)	4 (20)	2 (10)

The church has traditionally contributed to discrimination against women. However, this position does not reflect mainstream thinking in the church; therefore, the NEA should be clear and seen to be presenting an unambiguous position on this matter. The biblical and church's position on gender issues should be clear. People in Africa can sometimes take extreme positions on gender issues, questioning whether women are equally human as men. Men can divorce their wives for childlessness, which means that their wives have not given birth to male children even if that those women have given birth to girls. In many communities in Africa, women have no inheritance rights, and many other rights are denied them. The church should be championing the cause for redemption in these matters and should not give tacit support to these cultural positions on women.

The denominational affiliation of the NEA general secretaries is mostly the evangelical Protestant tradition: thirteen out of twenty (65 percent) said their denominational background was mainline evangelical. Five of the NEA general secretaries (25 percent) said they were independent Pentecostals (and charismatics). Pentecostals were two of the total number of respondents (10 percent).

The denominational backgrounds of the two sets of respondents in this research are quite different. The first set of respondents, the AEA regional presidents, were mostly independent Pentecostals with interest in power and control. They have established themselves in leadership roles, often as founders and presidents of an existing independent Pentecostal denomination of prominence and influence in the country. The qualification for selection or election to the position of regional president is being president of an NEA. Thus, the regional presidents are influential people and are well respected among their peers and followers. To illustrate the influence of these leaders, one of them was named among the one hundred most influential people in the world in even within the period of this research.[10] In contrast, the general secretaries came mostly from the evangelical Protestant denomination, known for ecclesial loyalty and amenable to submission to authority. Whereas the general secretaries wield significant influence of their own, they are disposed to service and hold themselves accountable to the executive committee and councils of heads of denominations. The general secretaries come to the position with endorsement from their local church pastors or/and denominational heads but often with not much influence of their own. Denominational heads who have been appointed as general secretaries have not fared well in the position. As former denominational heads and coming into the position with certain perceptions and dispositions, they tend to be less motivated to serve former colleagues.

The general secretaries have been in their current positions for a varying length of time, ranging from two months to nineteen years. Half of the general secretaries (50 percent) have been in the position for four years or less, and 85 percent of the general secretaries have been in post for seven years or less.

The short stay in the post for the NEA general secretaries suggests a high turnover rate in the NEAs, which is one possible reason, among others, for the fledgling state of many NEAs in Africa. The working conditions of employment could also be unfavorable, especially in terms of remuneration, which may be a cause for the high turnover. General secretaries are expected to demonstrate a lot of humility in their service to senior church leaders. In addition, they are expected to raise funding to run the alliance, both the overhead and the programs. Unlike their counterparts in pastoral ministry,

---

10. Wallace, "Imam Omar Kobine Layama."

they do not have full-time congregations; rather, they run the alliance part-time and do pastoral ministry or some other work for their livelihood.

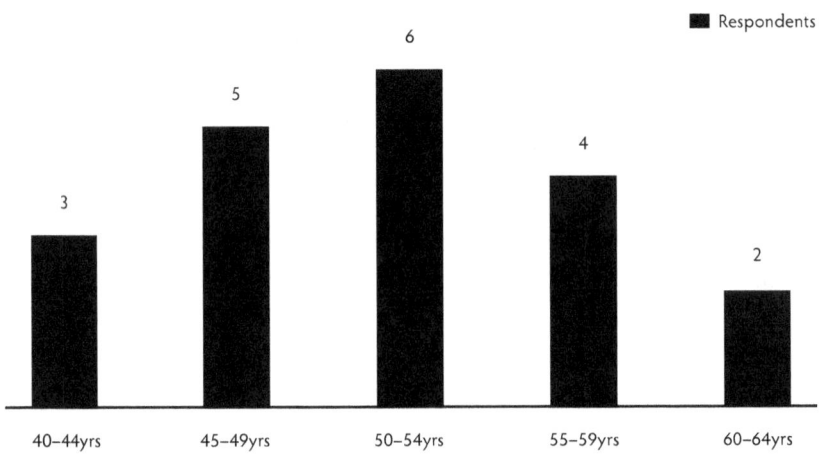

Figure 4.7. Age Range of NEA General Secretaries

The ages of the general secretaries were between 40 and 61 years. More participants were within the age bracket of 50–54 years (30 percent). The participants aged between 45–59 years constituted 75 percent of the total number of participants (see figure 4.7). The average age of the NEA general secretary tends to be fifty years and older, and given the youthful population of Africa, the average general secretary would tend be a male adult who is older than the average person in the church. According to Abdoulie Janneh, Under-Secretary of State for the Economic Commission for Africa, "[t]he median age, which is the age that divides the population into two equal groups, is 19.7 in 2012 and will increase to 25.4 in 2050."[11] The population of Africa is very young, but leadership tends to favor the older male adult. One leadership challenge is to bridge the generational gap between the leader and the followers for effectiveness, more so when the task of the leader is service oriented. However, the general secretaries' main

---

11. Janneh, *Statement*, 1.

customers are denominational leaders who may be older or in the same age bracket as the general secretaries.

Educational Qualifications of NEA General Secretaries

The educational qualifications and subject areas of training and post-qualification or in-service training are shown in table 4.11. The academic qualifications of the general secretaries were divided into three categories: diploma/certificates rated less than a first degree, undergraduate training or first degree, and postgraduate degrees (i.e. master and doctoral qualifications). Fifteen of the general secretaries (75 percent) had postgraduate degrees. Three of the postgraduate degrees were doctorates, and twelve were at the master's level. Three people had first degrees, only two with diplomas / certificates who, unsurprisingly, came from independent Pentecostal backgrounds. The attitude of the adherents of this church denomination towards higher education is generally negative. They perceive preparation for ministry coming not from human effort but as a spiritual endowment from God. This perception is at variance with evangelical, orthodox teaching on the nature, work, and doctrine of the Holy Spirit, which acknowledges both the work of the Holy Spirit and the need for training. The call of God not only includes the impartation of the Holy Spirit but also a period of preparation and training. Jesus modeled the place of the Holy Spirit and preparation and training in ministry; in his own life on earth and in the life of the apostles he trained and mentored.

The educational experience of the general secretaries is broad in terms of range of subjects. The general secretaries with postgraduate qualifications had the most diversified subject areas. Their undergraduate training was not necessarily in the same subject area as the postgraduate level. Theology was the most popular subject offered by the general secretaries with postgraduate degrees as a major in at least one of the two or three academic qualifications mentioned. Seven of the fifteen postgraduate-qualified general secretaries studied theology.

Table 4.11. Educational Qualification (Profile) of NEA General Secretaries

Academic Qualification	Subject Area	n	%	Other Training	n
Diploma/ Certificate	Theology/Bible	1		Project management	1
	Ministerial training	1		Leadership	1
	Total	2	10	Evangelism	1
1st Degree/ Bachelor	Administration	1		Development/ peace building	1 1
	French	1		Preaching	1
	Theology	1		Bible translation	1
	Total	3	15	Holistic development	1
Postgraduate	Theology	7		Management	1
Master's (n=12)	Admin/ Management	2		Accounting	2
PhD (n=3)	Pure & applied science	3		Computing	3
	Engineering	1		Leadership	4
	Commerce	1		Project management	5
	Leadership	3		Development	3
	Law	1		Administration/Management	4
	Development	1		Organizational development	1
	Mathematics			Communication	2
	Total	15	75	Evangelism	2
				International relations	1
				Training of trainers	1
				Advocacy	2

Other subject areas included pure and applied science, engineering, commerce, law, development, mathematics, and leadership. The diploma-qualified general secretaries had their training in ministry or Bible. Those with first degrees had only one with Bible or theology training. The diversity in skills sets of the general secretaries is consistent with the nature of the tasks required for their role.

The post-qualification or in-service training to enhance the leadership capacity of the general secretaries further were in the areas of project management, leadership and management, computing and development, accounting and communication (with evangelism and advocacy), international relations, and training of trainers. The subject areas are diverse, and many of these subjects will ordinarily not be included in Bible school or seminary curriculum, which is used to train people for various leadership positions in the church. The limited or nonexistence of training curricula and institutions suggests a growing trend of church leaders coming from non-theological backgrounds, hence the concern for biblical illiteracy in the church and the need for biblical engagement in all aspects of human endeavor. The challenge is a balance between sound biblical knowledge and practical skills for performing tasks that contribute to achieving the goals of the association.

Ranking of NEA Leadership Competencies in Order of Importance

In the second phase of the research, the NEA general secretaries were required to assign a value to indicate the importance of each competency on the list presented to them (see appendix H). The questionnaire was distributed by email to thirty-one general secretaries that were said to be active on the AEA Directory 2013.

The NEA general secretaries' ranking of the competencies was done using a Likert scale of fixed choices to measure the importance of each competency identified by regional presidents (see tables 4.7 and 4.8, pp. 133, 138) and shown on the questionnaire (see appendix H).

Table 4.12. Ranking of Core NEA Leadership Competencies

#	Competency	Level of Importance and Frequency			
		Unimportant n (%)	Of Little Importance n (%)	Important n (%)	Very Important n (%)
1	Sound biblical knowledge and application	0	0	5(25)	15(75)
2	Promote unity (reconciliation, peace building)	0	0	5(25)	15(75)
3	Organize training seminars	0	0	9(45)	11(55)
4	Soft skills (listen, think, be teachable)	0	1(5)	6(30)	13(65)
5	Communicate	0	0	2(10)	18(90)
6	Disciple making/mentoring	0	0	3(15)	17(85)
7	Mobilize resources (fundraising)	0	0	5(25)	15(75)
8	Manage people/resources	0	0	2(10)	18(90)
9	Promote holistic development	0	1(5)	3(15)	16(80)
10	Advocate for justice and for the vulnerable	0	2(10)	8(40)	10(50)
11	Be family role model	0	0	3(15)	17(85)
12	Innovate	0	0	7(35)	13(65)
13	Servant leader/visionary	0	0	4(20)	16(80)
14	Motivate	0	0	0	20(100)
15	Maintain consistent Christian values and evangelical beliefs	0	0	4(20)	16(80)
16	Understand ecumenism and global Christianity	0	0	7(35)	13(65)
17	Able to train (facilitate)	1(5)	0	8(40)	11(55)

The general secretaries were requested to indicate the importance of a competency by choosing on the Likert scale one description, ranging from unimportant, of little importance, important, to very important.

Each competency was rated *important* or *very important*. The ratings affirm the seventeen competencies highlighted by the regional presidents as important. However, all the competencies were ranked and listed in order of importance, starting with most important to the least important. For each of the seventeen competencies, the modal frequency falls in the *very important* category. The frequency and percentage scores for the attribute: *very important* ranged from ten (50 percent) to twenty (100 percent), advocating for justice for the vulnerable competency was mentioned ten times (50 percent) and motivating was mentioned twenty times (100 percent). Generally, the ratings of the general secretaries show the importance of the competencies and indicate which ones are core competencies for leading the NEA (see table 4.12 and figure 4.8).

The importance of the competencies in order of rank was indicated by the percentages scored in the columns for *important* and *very important*. The higher the scores were in the column for *very important* with no scores in the *unimportant* and *of little importance* columns, the higher the competency was ranked in order of importance. Thus, the top five most ranked competencies fall in the top three highest percentage points in the *very important* column. This list included the following five competencies in descending order of importance:

1) Ability to motivate (100 percent),
2) Communication (90 percent),
3) Resource management (90 percent),
4) Disciple making/mentoring (85 percent), and
5) Being a family role model (85 percent).

The five top competencies the general secretaries deemed most important integrate traditional biblical competency subjects (e.g. making disciples and family life) and secular subjects (e.g. motivation, communication, and resource management).

Comparison of the responses of the regional presidents and the general secretaries in ratings of the top five competencies shows some disparity. The difference in perceptions has to do with the fact that the regional presidents perceive the general secretaries' role as more administrative rather than being focused on the core mission of the church, which is to make disciples.

The general secretaries perceive their role as missional, and their approach may be more holistic than that of the regional presidents.

Given the nature of the task, this assessment is not unexpected. Motivating is a people skill, although not clustered with the soft skills and all the respondents rated motivation as *very important*. Resource management includes human resources. The general secretaries emphasized people skills as the most important ones for leading an NEA. This finding is consistent with the highlights of major characteristics of effective leaders in the literature review, including Goleman's description of emotional intelligence[12] and Collins' Level 5 leaders.[13] All but four of the competencies were ranked either *important* or *very important*, exclusively.

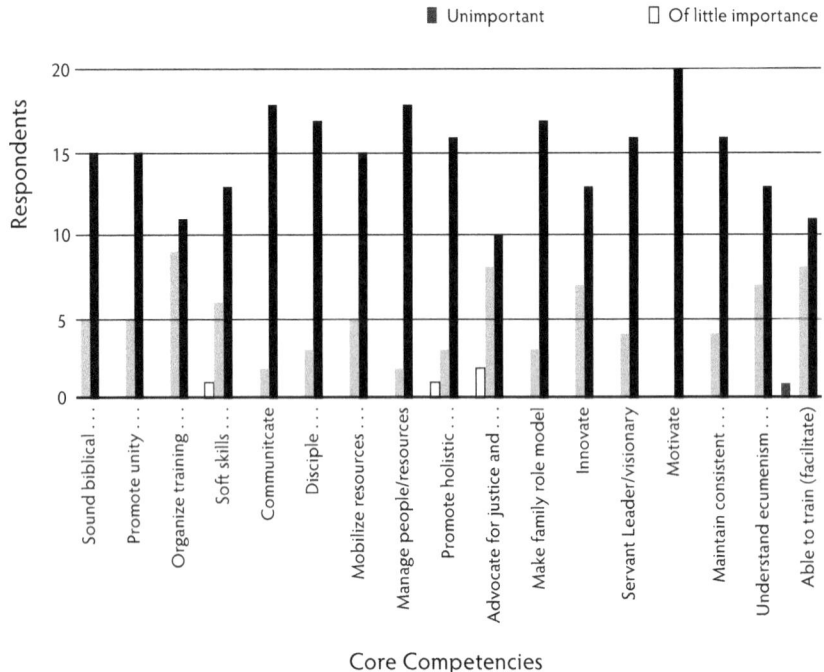

Figure 4.8. Ranking of Core Competencies by NEA General Secretaries in Order of Importance

---

12. Goleman, "What Makes a Leader," 2.
13. Collins, "Level 5 Leadership," 116.

To assess the order of importance of the rest of the competencies, I took into consideration the spread of attribution or ranking across the scale. A combined ranking of *important* and *very important* for each competency, with no other responses given, was ranked higher than competencies with scores of 80 percent in those same combined scores. Thus, following the five top competencies, the rest of the competencies ranked in descending order of importance included:

1) Servant leadership (80 percent),
2) Consistency in maintaining Christian values (80 percent),
3) Holistic development (80 percent),
4) Sound biblical knowledge (75 percent),
5) Promoting unity (75 percent),
6) Resource mobilization (75 percent),
7) Understanding ecumenism (65 percent),
8) Innovation (65 percent),
9) Soft skills (65 percent),
10) Organizing training seminars (55 percent),
11) Ability to train (55 percent), and
12) Advocacy for justice for the vulnerable (50 percent).

Competency in advocacy for justice for the poor is ranked least important, which is surprising given the significantly high rating holistic development has in the ranking. Holistic development is motivated by concern for justice and expected to rank close to holistic development. However, the two categories of *important* and *very important* account for 90 percent of the total ranking. Overall, the NEA general secretaries consider the identified core competencies important. The competencies are a mix of skills sets that enhances holistic engagement and missional effectiveness in the church.

Four competencies were not ranked exclusively as *important* or *very important*; their rating included a range of rankings from *unimportant* to *very important*. The four competencies that were ranked either as *unimportant* or *of little importance* were soft skills, promoting holistic development, advocating for those who are vulnerable, and the ability to train. The rating of the last four competencies as *unimportant* or of *little importance* is surprising, given the high rating the competencies received elsewhere in this study. This perception could be in tandem with views of church leaders who perceive nontraditional skills for the mission of the church, such as evangelism and making disciples, as unimportant or of little importance. Advocacy was mentioned twice (10 percent) as *of little importance.* The ability to train was the only competency ranked *unimportant,* although was only 5 percent of the total while 95 percent ranked it as *important* or very *important.*

The other category of competencies unique to only one area of task was considered as subcompetency. The subcompetencies were also on the questionnaire, and the general secretaries were requested to rank these, too, as in the previous section (see appendix H). The highest ranked competency in the subcompetency category was an acquaintance with the needs of the community (85 percent); mentioned for the task of equipping. Having a balanced life (spiritual and professional) and being resulted oriented were the next two top subcompetencies, each ranked by 80 percent of the respondents to be *very important* and mentioned under the tasks of administering and equipping. Six of the eleven competencies mentioned were either important or very important. The remaining five were spread between *of little importance, important,* and *very important* and in all four task areas. None of the competencies mentioned as subcompetency was ranked *unimportant* (see table 4.13). The least ranked competency was ordination. Ordained minister was ranked by 50 percent of the respondents as important, and 25 percent thought ordination was *of little importance.* A similar number of respondents (25 percent) thought ordination was *very important.* Although ordination is a status issue rather than a competency, the ordained person is expected to carry out certain functions as a leader without which he or she cannot perform the role. Ordination for some denominations also means that the ordained minister would have gone through certain training to build competencies that befit a minister of the gospel in order to play some leadership role in the church.

Conducting marriage ceremonies and the premarital counseling services that go with weddings in Africa is an instance when the NEA leader is expected to perform the role as spiritual leader and mentor for young couples and which skills are preserved for the ordained minister.

Table 4.13. Ranking of Subcompetencies by NEA General Secretaries in Order of Importance

Task	Competency	Level of Importance and Frequency			
		Unimportant n (%)	Of Little Importance n (%)	Important n (%)	Unimportant n (%)
Administrating	Balanced life (spiritual and professional)	0	0	4(20)	16(80)
	Able to assess strength and weakness of church	0	1(5)	14(70)	5(25)
Connecting	Deal with challenges with culturally relevant solutions	0	2(10)	7(35)	11(55)
Representing	Reference (respect) for all churches	0	0	12(60)	8(40)
	Act on decisions of members	0	2(10)	6(30)	12(60)
	Ordained minister to preach gospel	0	5(25)	10(50)	5(25)
Equipping	Raise the standard of the church	0	0	6(30)	14(70)
	Plan programs in line with vision and mission	0	3(15)	6(30)	11(55)
	Result oriented	0	0	4(20)	16(80)
	Create conducive environment for training and formation	0	0	6(30)	14(70)
	Acquainted with needs of community	0	0	3(15)	17(85)

The opinion of the general secretaries about the importance of ordination as a required competency for leading an NEA is split. Similar discordance occurs in the opinion about planning programs in line with vision and mission, dealing with challenges with culturally relevant solutions, acting on decisions of members, and having the ability to assess strengths and weaknesses of the church. However, the competencies were all ranked as important, on average. Like the core competencies, the subcompetencies were also people focused. Leadership generally has to do more with working with people than doing paper work or the impersonal side of administrative and organizational management.

Comparison of the Ratings of Competencies by the Two Sets of Respondents

Juxtaposing the two lists of competencies in order of importance by both the regional presidents and general secretaries reveals some similarity and disparity in perception of the two groups of respondents in this research. Although the criteria for establishing the order of ratings of the two lists of competencies are different, some disparity in the ratings for the core competencies coded from the responses of the regional presidents and the general secretaries is evident.

The most divergent view is on the ability to motivate. The general secretaries highlighted the ability to motivate as the most important competency for leading an NEA, but the regional presidents highlighted this competency as the least important. The difference in perceptions may mean more clarity about the role of the NEA leader. However, motivating is consistent with the overall ratings, which have an emphasis on people skills. The objective is for the leader to accomplish his or her task through people, and the leader needs the ability to motivate people to accomplish the work. The contrary view of the regional presidents may be due to the perception of the nature of the NEA leader's role – administration. The job of administration is generally perceived as task-oriented jobs and paper work, rather than people oriented.

Some other striking differences in perception included ranking *holistic development* in fourth place on the regional presidents' list and *making disciples* as the competency in fourth place on the general secretaries' list. The reverse is the case in eighth place with *making disciples* on the regional presidents' list and *holistic development* on the general secretaries' list. Similarly, *resource mobilization* was in ninth place on the regional presidents' list while *sound biblical knowledge* was ninth on the general secretaries' list. These two competencies are reversed in the eleventh position on the lists of ranking. This parallelism is an apt illustration of the extent of the dualistic mindset of evangelical Christians. Even the brain is dualistic, profoundly split into two. One side of the brain is sacred and the other secular. In addition, the differing views of the two sets of leaders in the NEA reveal the need for addressing this split for harmony and guidance in the church.

Table 4.14. Comparison between Regional Presidents' and General Secretaries' Ratings of Core NEA Leadership Competencies in Order of Importance

#	Regional Presidents' Rating (%)	#	General Secretaries' Ranking (%)
1	Promote unity (11.1)	1	Ability to motivate (100)
2	Soft skills (11.1)	2	Communication (90)
3	Manage people and resources (8.7)	3	Resource management (90)
4	Promote holistic development (7.9)	4	Disciple making/mentoring (85)
5	Communicate (7.1)	5	Be family role model (85)
6	Organize training seminars (7.1)	6	Servant leadership (80)
7	Maintain consistent Christian values/evangelical beliefs (6.3)	7	Consistency in maintaining Christian values (80)
8	Disciple making/mentoring (5.5)	8	Holistic development (80)
9	Resource mobilization (5.5)	9	Sound biblical knowledge (75)
10	Able to teach/facilitate/ train (5.5)	10	Promoting unity (75)
11	Sound biblical knowledge (4.8)	11	Resource mobilization (75)
12	Able to innovate (4.8)	12	Understanding ecumenism (65)
13	Servant/visionary leadership (4.8)	13	Innovation (65)
14	Advocacy for justice (4.0)	14	Soft skills (65)
15	Understand ecumenism (2.4)	15	Organizing training seminars (55)
16	Be family role model (1.6)	16	Able to train (55)
17	Able motivate (1.6)	17	Advocate for justice for the vulnerable (50)

Some similarities were also evident in the two lists of ratings. Resource mobilization was rated as the third most significant competency on both lists. The rating for *maintaining consistent Christian values* was the same for both groups of respondents in seventh place.

Overall, the general secretaries tended to rate the traditional competencies for mission of the church (e.g. making disciples, family values, sound biblical knowledge) higher than the regional presidents. The recurring theme of the difference in perception of the regional presidents on the role of the general secretary as less of a missional vocation could be the underlying factor in the difference in perceptions (see table 4.14).

Two competencies (i.e. management of resources and communication) appear in the top five competencies on each list. Selecting the top two competencies on each list in addition to the two competencies that were common to both includes the following:

- Management of resources,
- Communication,
- Promoting unity,
- Ability to motivate, and
- Soft skills.

The general secretaries rated communication and resource mobilization, which were mentioned on both lists, as the second most important competencies; therefore, only the top competency, motivating, was selected from the general secretaries' list of important competencies. Promoting unity and soft skills were the two top competencies selected on the regional presidents' list. These five competencies would be important competencies, assessing from the perspectives of both the regional presidents and the general secretaries. The more traditional qualifications of the church leader, making disciples, sound biblical knowledge, Christian values, being family role model, and understanding ecumenism, all of which appear on the list of core competencies, are conspicuously absent on the reconciled list of top five competencies. These top five competencies were mostly secular although they are needed in the church as well. Emerging from this study is the emphasis on nontraditional biblical or theological competencies for NEA general secretaries.

Findings

This project did not only seek to view the perception of the general secretaries about the importance of the leadership competencies identified by regional presidents but also to have the general secretaries' self-assessed levels of proficiency in each of the competencies highlighted in the questionnaire for ranking.

Research Question #3

What levels of proficiency did African NEA leaders or general secretaries attribute to themselves in each specific leadership competency for leading an NEA? The NEA general secretaries were asked to self-assess levels of proficiency in the competencies identified for ranking.

The level of proficiency was indicated on a five-point Likert scale, using poor, fair, average, good, and excellent (see appendix H). Table 4.15 shows the self-assessed levels of proficiency of the general secretaries in the core competencies highlighted in the first phase of the project. In analyzing the ranking of the self-assessed proficiency levels, I gave more weight to the combined scores of *good* and *excellent*, especially when ratings of the competency were spread into the different categories of attribution. Analysis of the data revealed that overall 50 percent and more of the general secretaries rated their proficiency levels as *good* or *excellent* in all competencies. When the competencies were rated only *good* or *excellent*, weighting of the competency tended towards the top end of the scale, indicating higher proficiency in that competency. The proficiency rating of competencies ranked only as *good* or *excellent* were the competencies the general secretaries believed were most proficient. The top three competencies were rated 100 percent when the ratings of *good* and *excellent* are combined. The rating for *excellent* was 25 percent, 20 percent, and 15 percent, respectively.

Table 4.15. Self-Assessed Proficiency Levels of NEA Leadership Core Competencies

#	Competency	Level of Proficiency and Frequency (and %)				
		Poor n (%)	Fair n (%)	Average n (%)	Good n (%)	Excellent n (%)
1	Sound biblical knowledge and application	0	0	7(35)	11(55)	2(10)
2	Promote unity (reconciliation, peace building)	0	0	6(30)	13(65)	1(5)
3	Organize training seminars	0	0	3(15)	14(70)	3(15)
4	Soft skills (listen, think, teachable)	0	0	4(20)	12(60)	4(20)
5	Communicate	0	0	0	15(75)	5(25)
6	Disciple making/mentoring	0	0	3(15)	16(80)	1(5)
7	Mobilize resources (fundraising)	0	2(10)	6(30)	10(50)	2(20)
8	Manage people/resources	0	0	2(10)	15(75)	3(15)
9	Promote holistic development	0	1(5)	4(20)	10(50)	5(25)
10	Advocate for justice and for the vulnerable	0	1(5)	4(20)	10(50)	5(25)
11	Be family role model	0	0	0	16(80)	4(20)
12	Innovate	0	0	4(20)	15(75)	1(5)
13	Servant leader/visionary	0	0	2(10)	16(80)	2(10)
14	Motivate	0	0	1(5)	15(75)	4(20)
15	Maintain consistent Christian values and evangelical beliefs	0	0	0	17(85)	3(15)
16	Understand ecumenism and global Christianity	0	0	5(25)	13(65)	2(10)
17	Able to train (facilitate)	0	2(10)	3(15)	10(50)	5(25)

The following is the list of competencies ordered by level of proficiency by the general secretaries, starting with most proficient to the least proficient:
1) Communication
2) Being family role model
3) Maintaining consistent Christian values/evangelical beliefs
4) Motivating
5) Managing resources
6) Servant leadership
7) Organizing training seminars
8) Disciple making/mentorship
9) Soft skills
10) Innovating
11) Holistic development
12) Advocating
13) Understanding ecumenism
14) Ability to train
15) Promoting unity
16) Sound biblical knowledge
17) Resource mobilization

They had no score in the other three categories of *poor, fair,* and *average* for these three competencies. Communication, the top competency in which the general secretaries were most proficient, is a key competency for running a national association that cuts across the nation. Communication also bridges the link with other international and global partners, especially in an era of information technology. However, I was surprised that information and computer technology did not appear in the list of competencies highlighted by the employers' representative group: the regional presidents. The omission to mention communication technology could be an oversight or an indication of an ability to get work done in more traditional and conservative ways without the technological hype. Effective communication requiring contact with recipients scattered all over the country would hardly be effective without the use of computer technology and the various means communication technology avails. Perhaps a face-to-face interview could have explored further the non-mention of computer and technology.

The next two competencies of the top three are equally important to the role of leading the NEA. Family values and Christian beliefs are defining elements to the whole task of promoting evangelicalism and unity in the church, which is the main subject of the research. The behavior and characteristic elements of people are determined mostly by their worldview. If the worldview is informed by Christian and biblical beliefs, the behavior and leadership qualities would be informed by Christian values and, thus, manifest the qualities of the servant leader. The mark of a good leader is shown in the conduct of the leader's family. The leader whose family is dysfunctional and has a bad reputation in the community could hardly be a good and effective leader.

Three of the reconciled top five competencies highlighted were among the top five competencies that the general secretaries thought were most proficient; these include management of resources, communication, and the ability to motivate. The other two competencies in the top five most proficient competencies were maintaining biblical values and being family role model. In terms of the perception of the general secretaries, they assessed themselves to be fairly evenly balanced in terms of proficiency in traditional biblical competency and secular competencies. This assessment is similar to the ranking of competencies by the general secretaries, although the perception weighs more towards the nontraditional biblical competencies.

The general secretaries' proficiency ratings were generally more *average* and *fair* than they were *excellent* in the rest of the competencies. The general secretaries need improvement in the proficiency level of each competency. The last seven competencies in the bottom end of the proficiency rating are particularly important when compared to the top end of the list of competencies ranked in order of importance. Resource mobilization was self-rated as the competency in which the general secretaries were least proficient. The general secretaries have the key responsibility for mobilizing resources to run the NEA; therefore, the inability to mobilize resources is an important and significant gap in the operations of the NEA. In all the ratings emerging from analysis of the two sets of data collected from the two phases of the research, resource management, which is closely linked with resource mobilization, was always ranked in the top five of the lists and competencies. The low rating of the proficiency level points to a significant need for the training and development of NEA general secretaries. The need has implications for training curriculum and the methodology for training, including the place or training institutions required.

Closely following the gap in skills sets for resource mobilization are the following competencies:

- Sound biblical knowledge,
- Promoting unity,
- Holistic development,
- Advocacy for justice,
- Understanding ecumenism, and
- Ability to train.

All these competencies are core and vital skills for effective leadership in the NEA. The gap in biblical knowledge is particularly important for a leader who embodies the evangelical movement in the nation. The very act of uniting the body of Christ reveals a deficiency in skills. This gap is an important contributing factor for the fledgling state of many of the NEAs in the region. Given the high rating of holistic development in this study, its low proficiency level rating is also an important gap. These gaps also have the same implications for training as highlighted for resource mobilization. No *poor* proficiency rating was recorded in any of the competency.

The educational profile of the general secretaries shows they were fairly well educated, 75 percent of them with postgraduate qualifications. In spite of the fact that these were a well-educated group of people, the need exists for skills development for their role in leading the NEA. Schooling and educational credentials alone may not be adequate for charging people with leadership responsibilities in the church. Apparently, current formal educational credentials do not necessarily confer competencies in every situation, thus the need for other methods of training and continuing education. The findings have implications for personnel development and curriculum for training of NEA leaders.

Table 4.16 shows the proficiency ratings of the subcompetencies unique for the different tasks of the NEA leader. Using the same criteria as for the core competencies in table 4.15, the self-assessed proficiency levels of the general secretaries in the different competencies unique for each task of the

NEA leader were rated. The data shows that the general secretaries' proficiency ranged from *average* to *excellent*, except in one case (i.e. ordination), where proficiency ranged from *poor* to *excellent*. One could argue that ordination is a status and not competency and proficiency issue, thus making it a curious entity among the others. However, given the expectations of any senior personnel in the church in Africa, ability to perform a role is often contingent on status. In the case of ordination, many denominations offer particular training to qualify for ordination; therefore, ordination could be considered a competency.

As highlighted in chapter 1, many would argue that the NEA leader, such as senior pastors or denominational heads, should be ordained ministers of the gospel. Ordination not only confers status but assumes some competencies for performing an important ecclesial role as general secretary of an NEA, representing and leading other senior clergy in the role. The general secretaries had a wide divergent view about their ability in the area of ordained ministry. This subject could be of interest for further exploration.

Considering the combined proficiency rates of *good* and *excellent* (90 percent good; 10 percent excellent), balanced life (spiritual and professional) stands out the most. The other two competencies that were rated high were acting on decision of members and creating conducive environments for training/formation with a combined score of 85 percent proficiency rating each. Acquaintance with needs of the community was the competency with the least combined proficiency rating (55 percent). Close to this competency at the bottom of the combined ranking are the ability to assess strengths and weaknesses of the church, planning programs in line with vision and mission, maintaining stand of church, and being result oriented, each with a combined rating of 65 percent. Overall, the average proficiency rating was good. However, an average of 25 percent of the respondents rated themselves as average with more room to improve proficiency in all the competencies. Evangelical associations are a unique type of organization and different from other organizations by nature. They require certain competencies unique to them. However, very few institutions, if any, in Africa have training or leadership development programs that focus on such organizations.

Table 4.16. Self-Assessed Proficiency Levels of NEA Leadership Subcompetencies

Task	Subcompetency	Level of Proficiency and Frequency				
		Poor n (%)	Fair n (%)	Average n (%)	Good n (%)	Excellent n (%)
Administrating	Balanced life (spiritual and professional)	0	0	0	18(90)	2(10)
	Able to assess strength and weakness of church	0	0	7(35)	10(50)	3(15)
Connecting	Deal with challenges with culturally relevant solutions	0	0	5(25)	12(60)	3(15)
Representing	Reference (respect) for all churches	0	0	5(25)	12(60)	2(10)
	Act on decisions of members	0	0	3(15)	10(50)	7(35)
	Ordained minister to preach gospel	2(10)	1(25)	2(10)	8(40)	7(35)
Equipping	Maintain the standard of the church	0	0	7(35)	9(45)	4(20)
	Plan programs in line with vision and mission	0	0	7(35)	10(50)	3(15)
	Result oriented	0	0	7(35)	6(30)	7(35)
	Conducive environment for training/formation	0	0	3(15)	16(80)	1(5)
	Acquainted with needs of community	0	0	9(45)	5(25)	6(30)

The general secretaries were requested to highlight any comments about leadership competencies, especially any important competency not mentioned by the regional presidents. This question was optional, and only four of the twenty respondents (20 percent) responded to this question. The following is what each of the four said:

> For core competencies where our proficiency is either weak or average, we need an institutional support especially for capacity building. This support also applies where there is room for improvement to reach an excellent proficiency/expertise on all the above listed competencies. Let's add that this tool is very useful and we would appreciate receiving a similar feedback from another point of view on how we can better improve the leadership of our NEAs.
>
> Hi Aiah: two areas I miss: first, the managerial competency of actually managing a flourishing and sustainable organization. This is a mix of organizational theory as well as strategic and operational management. Secondly, I miss the critical qualities of discernment. National alliances in Africa are vulnerable to succumbing to the dictates of the West, both due to donor dictatorships or simply to be overrun by the glamour of programs imported from the west. Eg March for Jesus. Good luck, and every blessing for your studies.
>
> One of the areas of competencies that might be needed in working with the evangelical alliance would be the ability to exhibit maturity and calm under extreme pressure and challenges.
>
> Knowledge and ability to maintain a balance between the global south view of the church and the global north view of the church and ensure that these remain authentic to the work of the gospel and experience in holistic ministry and church development.

These comments underscore the diversity and complexity of the need and challenge for understanding and leading the NEA. Even though the comments are a small sampling, they lend qualitative voices to the quantitative data collated from the general secretaries. They also underscore the importance of this project and the contribution the findings may contribute to this area of ministry of the church in Africa.

The few comments highlight management skills and the need to improve competencies and personnel development. Attention is also drawn to a need for maturity and independence of the church from other influences. Two of the respondents suggest North-South divide and an unsavory Western influence in the affairs of the church in Africa, and struggles with self-actualization in various aspects of life. Political colonization had some correlation with missionary influence in the church in Africa. The general perception is that even after political independence, African leaders have not been totally free to make their own choices to lead their nations without interference by Western partners, especially former colonial masters, and thus Africa continues to be in a state of neocolonialism. As with colonialism, neocolonialism correlates with continuing Western influence in the church in Africa in spite of the phenomenal growth of so-called African instituted or independent churches. In tandem with the views expressed by the two respondents with regard to external influence in the church in Africa, I made this observation: "As it was with the geographical space, the ecclesial space is Balkanized into pieces. It is difficult to pinpoint the one African church I will be talking about in this presentation."[14] The historical divisions of the Western church are reflected in the church in Africa. The walls of division caused by ethnicity or tribalism compounded divisions in the church in Africa. Lydia Mwaniki observes, "[C]olonial ideology is about power and control."[15] The neocolonial era finds new ways of maintaining power and control.

Influence of the West in the church in Africa continues in the form of sponsorship or funding and peddling all quick-fix answers to African missional challenges with solutions made in the West and expected to be applied uncritically in Africa, thus stifling indigenous innovation for homegrown solutions to local challenges. Thus, African voices need to be heard in theologizing and missiological approaches in the global church. Leading NEA is a call for mutual respect and reverence and consensus building. This assessment does not mean the days of Western missionary endeavors in the church in Africa are over. However, a change in approach and recognition that leadership has changed from being Western led to being indigenous African leadership. The role of the NEA in providing leadership

---

14. Foday-Khabenje, *Church of Africa*, 1.
15. Mwaniki, "Ethnicity," 191.

in the current era of globalization in which the church thinks globally and acts locally is very important.

Summary of Major Findings

This chapter sought to organize, present, analyze, and interpret data collected from research participants with regard to their perception on competencies required for leading NEAs, especially in the African context. The findings highlighted the different sections from the two phases of the study, designed to respond to the research questions. The following list is a summary of the major findings:

1) The profile of the general secretary was well suited for holistic ministry in the church and was not the typical profile of the traditional church leader with pastoral competency. However, gender parity and favoring younger people with leadership positions are needed.
2) The regional presidents mentioned administering more times than any other, as task of the NEA leader.
3) The AEA regional presidents mentioned 17 core competencies for leading NEAs, the five topmost being: management of resources, communication, promoting unity, ability to motivate, and soft skills.
4) The general secretaries ordered the NEA leadership competencies slightly differently from the regional presidents, focusing first on the ability to motivate. There is difference in perspective between the regional presidents and general secretaries about the NEA general secretary's role and qualification.
5) The general secretaries believed, on average, that they make good use of the competencies identified for leading NEAs. However, they found need for improvement in each competency. There are identifiable gaps in skills set for training and development.

CHAPTER 5

Discussion

Major Findings

The local church congregation or church denomination needs to look outside its own structures for standard practice in ministry and biblical and doctrinal guidance. The church councils have provided for this need in the history of the church. The practice and importance of a guiding and standards institution of the church was illustrated in the New Testament (Acts 15) when the council met to resolve disagreement about the need for circumcision in the church. The ancient councils in the early church – Nicaea 1 in AD 325, Constantinople 1 and 11 in AD 381 and AD 553, Ephesus in AD 431, and Chalcedon in AD 451[1] were forums for establishing the fundamental doctrines of the Christian faith that have been formulated into creedal confessions of the church and handed down to the church over ages. These councils served as the standards board for defining Christian doctrines and creeds that the church affirms as the basis of the Christian faith, even in the contemporary church. Thus, the need for ecumenism has both biblical and historical precedence.

In the contemporary church, the need for such church councils is met by ecumenical organizations such as the NEAs that also come together in regional and global associations such as the AEA and WEA, respectively. The contemporary church has three main traditions at the global level, shaping ecumenism, including the Vatican, the World Council of Churches, and the World Evangelical Alliance. These global organizations

---

1. Tanner, "African Church," 202–208.

have national expressions such as the NEAs within the WEA family. Africa has thirty-six NEAs, but a number of them are either inactive or not very effective in connecting, representing, and serving their members or constituents. The NEAs provide an important platform and a crucial service for the unity and witness of the church in the nation.

The unity of the church is a biblical or divine imperative rather than being optional. Jesus wanted his followers to be one so that he and God the Father would be glorified and the world will believe. Jesus Christ likens the unity of the church to the Trinity; as the three persons of the Godhead are one, so should the church be one.

However, the church continues to be divided along denominational lines with all manner of disagreements even on the very issues that provide a common identity and witness as the one body of Christ. The NEAs seek to promote unity among the different church denominations within the country, but their effort at this task depends to a large extent on the leadership in the NEA. The NEA needs effective leadership for equipping the local church and developing leaders.

Leadership is a complex concept and involves an interaction of the leader, the followers, and the context or environment. The goal of NEA leadership is to promote unity in diversity. Unity does not necessarily mean unanimity, but the leadership challenge is to maintain a creative tension between divergent views and making progress for the attainment of organizational goals. Leading organizations, especially associations such as the NEA need a team. Teamwork is required at all levels of the organization. To work in a team demands much humility on the part of the leader and members of the team and is in sharp contrast to the patrimony practiced in Africa, even if the system has some strengths within cultural context.

Associations are a type of organization, different from other organizations. This study sought to investigate the leadership of the NEA from the perspective of associations that comprise different and independent organizations. The purpose of the research was to identify leadership competencies required for leading an NEA as well as needed leadership development competencies of current general secretaries or NEA leaders in Africa by interviewing current regional presidents and national leaders in the AEA.

Profile of the NEA Leader

Two sets of respondents were involved in the study; these were the key leaders in the NEA at both governance and management levels (i.e. the regional presidents and the general secretaries). The study explored perceptions of these two sets of leaders about NEA leadership competencies. The person specification for a role and their competencies constitute the job profile. John P. Kotter asserts that the leader's task includes "looking for the right fit between people and the vision and motivating them to overcome barriers to change toward the desired future."[2] The profile and skills of the person constitute the qualification for the job. In exploring perceived competencies, the profile of the leader in the context of the NEA was necessary.

The regional presidents were all adult males, and 66.7 percent of these came from independent Pentecostal denominational backgrounds. The expectation of the general secretary, in terms of educational background, was varied with qualifications ranging from diplomas to doctorates. Half of the respondents (50 percent) said a first degree was the minimum qualification required for the leader of the NEA. Educational qualifications at the level of a diploma had the next highest response (33.3 percent), and the qualification with the fewest number was postgraduate or doctoral qualifications (16.7 percent).

However, actual data analysis of the general secretaries' profiles reveals higher educational qualifications than expected by the regional presidents, their employers. More general secretaries (75 percent) had postgraduate qualifications, and 15 percent had only a first degree. The educational experience of the general secretaries was broad in terms of range of subjects and level of academic achievement. The general secretaries with postgraduate qualifications had the most diversified subject areas; their undergraduate and postgraduate level trainings were not necessarily in the same subject areas. Theology was the most popular subject studied by the general secretaries with postgraduate degrees, being offered as a major in at least one of the two or three academic qualifications mentioned. Seven of the fifteen general secretaries with postgraduate qualification studied theology. Other subject areas included pure and applied science, engineering, commerce,

---

2. Kotter, "What Leaders Really Do," 40.

law, development, mathematics, and leadership. The general secretaries with diplomas had their training in Bible or theology. This group constituted only 10 percent of the general secretaries.

The disparity in the expectations of the regional presidents and the actual educational qualifications of the general secretaries is due to the growing trend of emphasis on higher education. Many of the evangelical Bible schools offer degree courses rather than certificate and diploma programs. Furthermore, the Bible schools are becoming full-fledged universities with wide subject options rather than theological courses. However, many would-be pastors are training with an eye on non-governmental organizations for possible employment. When these leaders enter the church, they are found wanting for adequate theological training. Currently, the tendency is for more personnel with higher academic qualifications than their counterparts in the past, but ironically, these individuals have less theological training to meet the need of the church.

Additional training, including in-service and formal academic training, also had a wide range of subject matter, such as human resources management, accounting, computing, leadership, project management, development, administration/management, organizational development, communication, evangelism, international relations, advocacy, and training of trainers. Notwithstanding the popular offering of theology for the NEA, the general secretaries had a lot of interest in acquiring skills from secular subjects rather than from theological or seminary offerings. Bible schools, turned Christian universities, should consider the need of the church in planning curricula and ensure that the people serving the church are well equipped.

The educational profile of the general secretary is generally not very different from any typical leadership role in the wider society. Many vocations require specialist areas of qualification that are unique to that particular area of vocation. The role of the general secretary is fairly generalist and may not be well understood and defined. A growing need for different skills sets in different subject areas is apparent, and the lack of adequate training facility or curricula is being addressed by participation in several informal training programs.

Not only is academic qualification necessary for training and building competencies for the diverse and demanding task of leading a national association, but it is also a status symbol. People may be given leadership positions in the church because of academic qualifications. Given the nature of the curriculum and the educational philosophies of the institutions available for training, graduates of these institutions may lack understanding and competencies in dealing with local realities in the church. People with high educational qualifications may be alienated from those they lead, resulting in ineffective leadership.

Education is also used as a means of gaining credibility; apparently many pastors in senior positions in the church want to be addressed as Reverend Doctor, and many are seeking the title by every means, even if through an honorary degree and from establishments that are not necessarily credible as a way of addressing the educational challenge associated with leadership positions. Conversely, credible educational attainment at the highest level of the academy is good for the church. The church in Africa needs leaders who can resource the church at the conceptual and intellectual level and be trained to review values, assumptions, and beliefs about the Christian faith and conduct. The contemporary church in Africa needs its own thinkers to match and sustain the growth of the church.

The indigenization mission theory of self-supporting, self-propagating, and self-governing churches should explicitly be inclusive of indigenous theologizing and biblical engagement consistent with evangelical orthodoxy. Neo-orthodoxy, mostly among liberal African theologians, in the name of inculturation theology, and erring on the side of syncretism and extolling African traditional religious values is increasing. At the other end of the intellectual spectrum are the prosperity preachers and faith healers or miracle workers whose claim for spiritual powers and exegesis of Scripture on these matters defies critical thinking. The leadership of the NEAs needs to address these theological conceptions or doctrines in the African context from an evangelical orthodox point of view. These liberal teachings require sound biblical scholarship and spiritual formation shaped by Christian theology. The work of guiding the church in this way cannot be left to individual denominations and independent churches and requires a platform such as the NEA for consensus building on theological positions.

Educational qualification needs to be integrated with other human qualities, such as underlying values, assumptions, beliefs, and expectations highlighted by Clawson,[3] humility highlighted by Collins,[4] and emotional intelligence by Goleman.[5] While these are qualities that can be learned, formal educational institutions that confer status credentials are not necessarily the only places or means where these qualities are acquired. Leadership development involves spiritual formation, and the foundation of spiritual formation in the church is premised on making disciples and nurturing people in the church. The most effective way the church could accomplish building these values in people is to prioritize ministry to children, inculcating these values in the formative stages of human life is easier (Ps 22:6). Character formation is better achieved when people are younger. The desire for a better world and change for the better, means raising up a new generation of leaders as change agents.

The contemporary world is that in which those who preceded the current generation invested. The present generation desires a change for the better, requiring investment of resources on the development of children more than what has been done in the past to see the change society wants. The church, in particular, should take the teachings of Jesus seriously and prioritize the holistic development of children. The biblical values and doctrines of unity espoused in this study guarantee missional effectiveness and transformation of society.

The demographic data of the current general secretaries of the NEAs also show nineteen (95 percent) were male and one (5 percent) female. The literature review described the dominance of the male gender in the area of leadership. Only one female general secretary participated in this study. Further investigation showed there have previously been two other general secretaries in the history of the AEA. Given the nature of the NEA as a bridge builder and promoter of unity in diversity, it must be seen to be intentionally providing answers to the gender question and women in leadership. The church in Africa should not uncritically adopt the general perception about the image of the leader in the society who is typically a

---

3. Clawson, *Level Three*, 9.
4. Collins, "Level 5 Leadership," 118.
5. Goleman, "What Makes a Leader," 2–5.

male. The oneness and unity of the body of Christ is based on a solid biblical foundation that does not discriminate the call of God for service based on gender.

The age of the general secretaries ranged from 40 to 61 years with 30 percent of the respondents in the 50–54 year age bracket, which was the modal age range. The general secretaries were, on average, aged 50 and over. People in this age bracket were expected to be well experienced, influential, and well established. The general secretaries come to their current positions with significant previous experience, which may be in similar field or completely different vocation. In contemporary African churches, educational attainment tends to be prioritized over age for leadership positions. Victor Cole observes, "In African context, the leaders of the people are traditionally old, experienced and married. However, in the church a role reversal often occurs because of this schooling approach."[6] The preference for elderly leadership is consistent with the general perception of the leader.

The literature review describes how the leader is viewed – a mediator between the community and ancestors and venerated as super human and one closer to the gods. A relatively younger generation of leaders with postgraduate educations tends to be in contention with the more conservative and traditional leaders. The society also expects the younger to defer to the older and, thus, expect older people in leadership to whom the followers are expected to submit. Even well-educated, older males may not be depositional for acquiring soft skills, which require lots of humility and contribute to leadership effectiveness. Emerging young leaders would have to contend with these cultural tensions in the church in Africa.

The biblical and theological framework of this study highlights a profile of the leader in the church. In particular, Paul's letters to Timothy and Titus outline the characteristics of the leader – elders and deacons (1 Tim 3:2–10; Titus 1:6–9). Maturity and experience are highlighted in Paul's admonition for qualifying for leadership. Maturity may be seen to mean chronological age only. However, Paul was writing to young Timothy and expressly encouraged him not to let others look down on him as a leader

---

6. Cole, "Concepts, 1.

because of his youthfulness (1 Tim 4:12). The leadership image created by Jesus Christ in the Bible is slave and servant. As evangelicals, biblical imperatives take precedence over tradition and human culture, especially when these are contradictory. Biblical Christianity redeems culture, affirming culture as God's creation and healing aspects of creation that have been ruined by sin.

Ministry leaders' expectation of maturity should take into consideration appropriate ministry experience more than the chronological age of the leader. The average age of the NEA leader was above that of the average person in Africa, but age was not necessarily a measure of maturity from a biblical viewpoint. A disposition for servant leadership is particularly necessary for the NEA role, which is mostly service oriented. Indeed, leadership is about service to followers, and leaders should not be enamored with the adulations of followers and the community around them, regardless of age, education, or qualification. However, people's identity and power are intertwined with status, which people guard carefully. Leaders need to be assured of their new identify in Christ and learn the way to greatness by being the least and servant of all (Luke 22:25–29).

The profile of the general secretary may not be inconsistent with the image described of conservative patriarchal leaders and charismatic Pentecostal leaders in the church. The evangelical leaders need to demonstrate a paradigm shift and exercise leadership that is different from the world. The God-man, Jesus Christ, provides the example for his followers and admonishes them not to follow the way of the world. Jesus recommended servant leadership, and some of the skills sets, such as soft skills and humility, highlighted in this study are helpful competencies for the NEA leader's role. The complex task of leading the NEA requires that leaders be trained in multiple disciplines and be versatile in several fields of human endeavor.

The Task of the NEA General Secretary

The literature review identified three categories of NEA leader's tasks. According to the WEA, the tasks of the NEA leader include connecting, representing, and equipping its members. In addition to these three task categories, administrating was evident in coding the responses of the regional presidents' description of the NEA general secretary's task. The task of the NEA leader is to manage the operation of the national evangelical association. Among other tasks mentioned by the regional presidents, administrating was mentioned more times than the others. In describing the problem of the study, management or administration was highlighted as a general perception about the role of the NEA leader. Managing and leading tend to be synonymous; however, discourse on leadership focuses more on the difference between the two. Olan Hendrix opines that managers need leadership skills as much as they need management skills:

> When we define management as the work one does to get work done through others, it is difficult not to include leading in our thinking. How can we expect to cause people to accomplish tasks apart from influence? Leading is influence.[7]

Management is integral to the task of the leader, and the distinction made of the two concepts may not be very helpful; both good management and good leadership skills are required for institutional/organizational and program effectiveness. Good leaders should be able to incorporate both leadership and management skills and vice versa, even if leaders have a bias toward one or the other.

Perceived Competencies for Leading the NEA

The regional presidents' responses provided answers for Research Question #1 for perceived competencies for leading the NEA. Coding and analysis of the responses generated a list of competencies for each task area for leading the NEA. However, some of the competencies highlighted appeared in more than one task area. The competencies were coded from an original list of 150 individual competencies highlighted to a more condensed list of twenty-eight competencies, which were further classified into two categories of competencies.

The recurrent competencies appearing in more than one category of task for the role of the NEA leader were deemed essential to the overall task of leading the NEA and were classified as core competencies. The other group, which was highlighted in only one task area and not the others, was classified as subcompetencies.

---

7. Hendrix, *Management That Leads*, 2.

Seventeen core competencies were identified in the study. The core competencies are listed in order of importance as indicated by the frequency with which they were mentioned:

1) Promote unity – conflict resolution/partnership/network (11.1 percent),
2) Have soft skills – listen/ think/teachable/flexible (11.1 percent),
3) Manage people and resources (8.7 percent),
4) Promote holistic development (7.9 percent),
5) Communicate (7.1 percent),
6) Organize training seminars/conferences (7.1 percent),
7) Maintain consistent Christian values/evangelical beliefs (6.3 percent),
8) Make disciples/mentor (5.5 percent),
9) Provide resource mobilization/fundraising (5.5 percent),
10) Be able to teach/facilitate/train (5.5 percent),
11) Have sound biblical knowledge (4.8 percent),
12) Be able to innovate (4.8 percent),
13) Demonstrate servant/visionary leadership (4.8 percent),
14) Advocate for justice – be voice for the poor and vulnerable (4.0 percent),
15) Understand ecumenism/global Christianity (2.4 percent),
16) Be family role model (1.6 percent), and
17) Be able to motivate (1.6 percent).

I endeavored to explore and elucidate the importance of the competencies highlighted in this study. I compared the list as ordered with the ranking of the general secretaries. The top core competencies of promoting unity and people or soft skills are not surprising. The vision and mission of the NEA is centered on promoting unity. Unity of the church is at the heart of this study and identified as the topmost core competency on the list of competencies highlighted. Promoting unity include a range of skills, including peace building, conflict resolution, empathy, reverence, and social skills. These require emotional intelligence, among other qualities, as described by Goleman.[8] The theological basis for unity is indeed the main subject for this study.

Although the church was divided in history, it has a common purpose and is urged to be one. More compelling biblical rationale exists, for the oneness of the church than what divides it. The world recognizes the power of unity and endeavors to promote unity for social cohesion, peaceful coexistence, and advancement of humanity and society as a whole. The quest for unity is manifested in the establishment of institutions such as the United Nations, regional and economic blocs, and social, professional, and community associations. The diversity within Africa is actually one of the greatest resources for fostering a richer, thicker kind of unity, and organizations such as the NEA contribute a primary influence in this regard.

Unity is an imperative for the church from God as part of Christian worship to glorify Jesus Christ and missional strategy to make Christ known to the world. Exercise of leadership is a test of commitment to the teachings of Christ and quality of the leader's faithful Christian witness. Therefore, promoting unity is an essential leadership competency in the church. The doctrine of the Trinity shapes the mind of the body of Christ – the church. Independent churches will achieve more if they work together. Generally, humans know they can achieve more together than individually.

Soft skills are more consistent with the servant image of leadership than the popular image and notion society has of the leader as having more power or higher status than others. Leadership literature supports people skills as important competencies for highly effective leaders. The core business of the church is to connect people to God. Leadership in the church should enhance making disciples and mentoring people to realize their God-given potential, which requires people skills.

The next four core competencies on the list (i.e. managing people and resources, promoting holistic development, communicating, and organizing training seminars/conferences) are all essential skills oriented to developing people. One characteristic about the booming churches in Africa compared to historic and Western missionary church plants is the embrace of holistic mission. In addition to preaching and teaching the Word

---

8. Goleman, "What Makes a Leader," 4–6.

of God, the local church is also involved with programs that address the economic and social needs of its members and the community. The early church was concerned for both the preaching and teaching of the Word and serving the material needs of its members (Acts 6:1–7). Even then, this approach led to phenomenal growth and even greater obedience to the faith by the priests themselves (Acts 6:7). A similar growth in the church is taking place in Africa.

Africa's socioeconomic challenges are due in part to poor management of resources. The reason for the poor management could be due to incompetency and also vices such as corruption and nepotism (encouraged by a patrimonial system of leadership). The church could make a difference to impact society when it adds to faith competency and sound management skills. On the contrary, the preaching and impact of the gospel in the nation is undermined if the church cannot manage its own resources. Similarly, the church should demonstrate aptitude in holistic development as a means to demonstrate Christ's compassion for societal transformation. Communication skills is another effective tool for building unity within the church but also making the work and message of the church heard, enhancing the work of the church.

The list comprises competencies that were mainly people, technical, and conceptual skills in connecting, equipping, and administering. These competencies are not unique to the NEA or ministry in the church; they are in demand in the secular work environment, too. However, the competencies are higher up the scale than the more biblically oriented competencies that start appearing in seventh place on the list and continuing to the end. The seventh competency was maintaining consistent Christian values followed by making disciples/mentoring (with mobilizing resources and having the ability to teach/facilitate), having sound biblical knowledge, and being a servant leader. These competencies highlighted in the middle of the list and lower are undisputedly critical competencies for ministry in the church. Traditionally, these competencies would be the ones the church leaders would require in a prospective candidate for any leadership role in the church. The tendency is to regard these competencies as domain of the pastor or evangelist or those who are ordained to preach the Word of God and lead people to Christ. Any function in the church that is not directly connected with preaching and evangelism is not seen as core to the mission of the church.

There needs to be a balance between the traditional view and what the current reality is. The implication is to ensure adequate biblical and theological material informs praxis in demonstrating the top competencies highlighted. The whole of the Christian's live is a life of witness and seemingly biblical competencies like disciple making and maintaining evangelical beliefs should not be in isolation from other activities.

In this research, the biblical support for the missional importance of the NEA has been established in chapter 2. An overview of the nature and competencies required for association leadership was also discussed in the literature review. Both secular and Christian leadership literature highlight people skills for effective leadership and unity.

Servant leadership is the type modeled and recommended by Christ for his followers to adopt. This view of leadership is at variance with that of the world and its relatively low ranking on the list of core competencies could be an indication of worldly influence by secular or business models of organization rather than by biblical models. In addition, the nature of ministry in the NEA may not be well understood, and perception about the vocation tends to be more generalist. Inquiry into this area of ministry in the church needs further exploration and development.

However, secular research on effective leadership also supports the principle of servant leadership. Greenleaf's servant leadership theory was developed at AT&T and later taught at Harvard Business.[9] Collins' Level 5 leadership theory identifies humility as the most outstanding characteristics of effective leaders.[10] The descriptions of Collins' Level 5 leaders and Greenleaf's servant leaders have some affinity to the biblical servant leader. However, the world's thrust on leadership and the church's vision may be different, and servant leadership and humility may have a distinct biblical expression, modeled by Jesus, from the secular vision of servanthood and humility.

---

9. Greenleaf, "Servant Leadership," 454.
10. Collins, "Level 5 Leadership," 122–123.

Many church leaders talk about servant leadership in Africa, but very little is observed as characteristic servant leadership behavior of the leaders. However, African church leaders may be servant leaders at heart, but their followers do not want to see their leaders as underlings.

Leaders tend to be superhuman, strong and mystical. Karlström observes that seemingly unhelpful leadership practices are encourage by followers. Followers alienate leaders by their expectations of the leader. Even if the expected behavior is to their detriment, followers complain about this behavior in private and continue to support it in the open.

For instance, pastors are criticized and condemned if they do not carry their own Bible, and carried by someone else, usually a mentee. I learned about this issue and sympathized with pastors criticized for this behavior from a personal experience with a junior colleague in my office. I resisted his attempts many times to carry my bag from the car for a short walk to my office. One day, he said that I was preventing him from being blessed, suggesting that I was selfish and did not mean well for him. I was shocked by this revelation, and from that time on, I could not refuse his attempt to carry my bag. However, I found a way to make up for my opulence when I also insisted that we change places at the gate, which he manned as a security guard, while he takes his tea with other staff in the commons. Allowing people to honor each other is an important cultural and even biblical value, but this way of honoring the leader should not undermine the Christological essence of servant leadership.

If the follower believes carrying the leader's bag is means of grace, carrying the pastor's Bible would even be better, and wonder how and why any leader could deny the follower to do so in these circumstances. This episode is similar to Peter denying Jesus from washing his feet, but when Jesus pointed out what the foot washing meant, Peter was ready not only to have his feet washed but also his whole body (John 13:1–9). Leadership, indeed, is complex, and Clawson points out that leadership behavior occur at three levels – (1) visible, (2) cognitive, and (3) subconscious.[11] Others can only observe what happens at level 1 and may not know what is below the surface.

---

11. Clawson, *Level Three*, 33.

Sound biblical knowledge and maintaining consistent Christian values have been highlighted in the biblical framework section of this study God's principles and demands are the same for all of humanity and may be foreign to all cultures, but as Christ followers, the church is expected to domesticate biblical imperatives without compromising the integrity of biblical values. Clinton insists that the Christian leaders' knowledge of the Word of God enhances effectiveness.[12] The knowledge and right application of the Word of God guarantees equipping (Isa 40:8). Training in biblical courses is vital to the development of people for the NEA leadership role.

What makes evangelicals different from other traditions is the high view of Scripture and commitment not only to hear and say it but also to do what it says in loving obedience to Jesus Christ: "All Scripture is God-breathed and is useful for teaching, rebuking, correcting and training in righteousness, so that the man of God may be thoroughly equipped for every good work" (2 Tim 3:16–17). Every Christian leader should be conversant with Scripture and able to teach or preach it. Paul further admonishes: "Do your best to present yourself to God as one approved, a workman who does not need to be ashamed and correctly handles the word of truth" (2 Tim 2:15). Sound biblical knowledge is not only for the pastor but for every Christian, especially the Christian leader.

Disciple making is at the middle of the scale. Competencies higher up the list were deemed to be more important than those competencies at the bottom of the list. Not to have the core business of the church placed at the top of the scale was surprising. The disparity may be due to differences in perception of denominational leaders and pastors concerning the general secretary's role as mainly administrative. Nevertheless, the use of the people skills highlighted at the top of the list could enhance disciple making. In addition, the Africans' worldview and integral approach to mission of the church could be the reason for the apparent low rating of the disciple-making competency.

The low rating of competencies such as advocacy for justice (i.e. being a voice for the poor and vulnerable), understanding ecumenism, and being family role model was surprising. These competencies would be expected

---

12. Clinton, *Ministry That Lasts*, 17.

to be at the top of the list. Understanding ecumenism is critical to promoting unity and is expected to be rated at the top end of the scale, close to promoting unity. Unity of the different denominations in the church requires understanding of the different streams, their differences and commonalities, and how they could work together in harmony, in spite of the differences. Understanding the global church also promotes collaboration and unity in the body of Christ.

Similarly, advocacy for justice is closely related to holistic development that is at the top of the scale. The discrepancy may also be an indication that the concepts of ecumenism and holistic development and advocacy are less understood, with implication for curriculum and leadership development. The lowly rated competency of *being family as model* is another indication of increasing worldly influence creeping into the church. The NEA is essentially a representative entity of the church; its engagement with the wider society should not diminish its primary mission of sharing the gospel of Jesus Christ. In fact, the NEA exists to enhance the mission of the church and be effective in its impact on society. However, the competencies were all expected to contribute in accomplishing the task of the NEA leader, as these were all core competencies highlighted from analysis of the regional presidents' responses. The competencies are in essence, God's equipping of the church as whole, individuals may have multiple endowments. Individuals within the team would be equipped uniquely, demonstrating certain competencies and abilities more effectively than others (Eph 4:11–13), so that all may work effectively towards maturity in Christ.

A total of eleven subcompetencies highlighted in all four task areas were identified. In this category of competencies, planning in line with mission, creating a conducive environment for training and acquaintance with needs of community were the only competencies mentioned multiple times, and all dealt with the task of equipping. The importance of the competencies has been established mainly using frequencies; therefore, the single occurrences were discarded for any meaningful analysis. However, all twenty-eight competencies were highlighted in the instrument for the second phase of the research for the general secretaries to rate and self-assess proficiency levels.

NEA Leadership Competencies in Descending Order of Importance

The final list of competencies identified by the regional presidents comprised twenty-eight competencies, which were classified into two categories: the core competencies – competencies highlighted in two or more task areas of the NEA leaders' role, and subcompetencies – competencies highlighted in only one task area.

NEA leadership core competencies. The following was the aggregated ranking of the core competencies by NEA general secretaries, listed in order of importance, starting with most important:

1) Ability to motivate,
2) Ability to communicate,
3) Ability to manage resources,
4) Ability to make disciples/mentor,
5) Be family role model,
6) Servant leadership,
7) Consistency in maintaining Christian values,
8) Holistic development,
9) Sound biblical knowledge,
10) Promotion of unity,
11) Resource mobilization,
12) Ability to understand ecumenism,
13) Innovation,
14) Soft skills,
15) Organization of training seminars,
16) Ability to train, and
17) Advocate for justice for the vulnerable.

Although the definition for leadership is contentious, leadership as influence seems to be more popular than other definitions. Thus, motivation is an important skill for influencing and commanding a loyal following. However, further exploration could establish whether the approach to motivation on the part of the general secretaries is transactional or transformational.

The first ten competencies ranked by the general secretaries are a blend of what traditionally would be considered biblical competencies and important for accomplishing the mission of the church and competencies for secular work. The traditional biblical competencies include disciple making, family values, servant leadership, Christian beliefs, and sound biblical knowledge, to name a few. The nontraditional competencies include management of resources and holistic development. The blend of competencies makes for a more holistic approach to the mission of the church than the traditional approach, which tends to dichotomize ministry into two parts: the spiritual – the responsibility of the church, and the physical – outside of the church's responsibility. Approaching ministry holistically is particularly important for the church in Africa where people look for spiritual solutions for every aspect of life and do not differentiate about what aspects of life are spiritual and what aspects are not. Thus, the church's witness is enhanced when it involves an integral mission to reach out to the whole person.

The approach to integral mission is not only relevant to the church in Africa; the global evangelical church has now embraced the holistic concept as the biblical understanding of mission. The Lausanne Movement has endorsed the integral approach to mission:

> We embrace the witness of the whole Bible, as its shows us God's desire both for systemic economic justice and for personal compassion, respect for and generosity towards the poor and needy. We rejoice that this extensive biblical teaching has become more integrated into our mission strategy and practice, as it was for the early church and the Apostle Paul.[13]

The approach to integral mission, however, should not just be a confessional statement but should be seen in the way the church ministers to the members and the community in which the church is located. Therefore, leadership development should include development of the competencies required for effective holistic ministry. This approach was demonstrated in the New Testament church (Acts 4:32–37; 2 Cor 8–9; Gal 2:9–10; Rom 15:23–29) and required skills beyond the preaching and teaching of God's Word.

---

13. The Lausanne Movement, *The Cape Town Commitment*, 33.

The next seven competencies at the bottom of the list are also important for enhancing integral mission and promoting unity in the church. The competencies highlighted for effectiveness are mostly service oriented. However, the approach and understanding of leadership in many African societies dictates followers serving and adoring their leaders and not the other way; leaders serving followers. Building the competencies require a paradigm shift and training. Training may also require the integration of important skills with biblical knowledge.

A review of the job descriptions of the general secretaries of the WEA and the AEA, which serve as de facto job description templates for the general secretaries of NEAs, reveals some similarity in the job profile of the NEA leader (see appendixes F and G). The job description templates outline most of the competencies identified in the study and are notably strong on competencies that traditionally are not the kinds for which the church looks in the leader. These are more generalist or secularist. The WEA needs to take seriously the implications for doing theology and training and development of people for the church, especially in the NEAs.

Notwithstanding the different parameters used to establish the order of the lists of competencies, differences exist in the ordering of the competencies by the two sets of respondents: the regional presidents and the general secretaries. Management of resources is the only core competency that was mentioned in the top three competencies on both lists – perceived competencies, listed in order of frequency, and competencies ranked in order of importance. In fourth place on the general secretaries' ranking is making disciples, which correlates with holistic development on the list of the regional presidents. The general notion about the general secretaries' role being less missional is reflected again in the two sets of rankings. The two groups of leaders agree in their rating of *management of resources*.

Perhaps while the regional presidents may consider their role as senior clergy to make disciples, they expect the general secretaries to complement that role with the other aspect of what would constitute an integral ministry – holistic development. Often the holistic ministry implies more focus on social action, thus continuing to perpetuate the dualism dichotomy – the sacred and mundane, the spiritual and the physical. The imbalance in emphasis about the spiritual and physical aspects of the mission of the church is a misconception of integral or holistic ministry, prevalent among evangelicals and Pentecostals. Like servant leadership, holistic ministry is a popular notion, but how it is expressed and demonstrated is confusing and contentious.

Generally, the disparity in ordering of the competencies by the regional presidents and the general secretaries could be due to the difference in perceptions of the role of the NEA leader or general secretary as stated in the description of the project. The disparity in the perception of the two sets of leaders is important. While the general secretaries thought motivation was the most important competency, the regional presidents thought it was the least. The cultural perception about leadership could well be at play in this case, where the key leaders, regional presidents, do not perceive their subordinates, the general secretaries, in the commanding role of influencers of the followership in competition with regional presidents.

The disparity in perception may further underscore the importance of the problem of little understanding of the nature of the NEA and the task of leading. The difference in the responsibilities of the two sets of leaders could also have resulted in the differences in perception. This study was an attempt to bring more clarity and understanding into this aspect of ministry of the church in Africa.

Subcompetencies. The competencies mentioned in only one of four categories of the NEA leader's task were
- Acquaintance with needs of members and community equipping,
- Result-oriented equipping,
- Balanced life administering, and
- Ordination, planning.

The most important subcompetency was acquaintance with community needs, followed by balanced life and result-oriented equipping. The least rated competency was ordination, also about which the general secretaries' views were most divergent.

Level of Proficiency in Core Competencies of Current NEA General Secretaries

The general secretaries' proficiency levels in the core competencies ranged from communication, the most proficient, to resource mobilization, the

least proficient. Following is the list of core competencies ordered from most proficient to least proficient:
1) Communicating,
2) Be family role model,
3) Maintaining consistent Christian values and evangelical beliefs,
4) Motivating,
5) Managing resources,
6) Providing servant leadership,
7) Organizing training seminars,
8) Disciple making/mentoring,
9) Using soft skills (e.g. listen, teachable, flexible),
10) Innovating,
11) Working for holistic development,
12) Advocating,
13) Understanding ecumenism,
14) Having the ability to train,
15) Promoting unity,
16) Having a sound biblical knowledge, and
17) Mobilizing resources.

The self-assessed proficiency levels provide further insights about the competencies and gaps in skills in the Africa-based NEA general secretaries.

While the general secretaries' ranking of the top ten important competencies reflected a balanced list of competencies in favor of integral mission, the top ten competencies in which the general secretaries were self-assessed to be most proficient were skewed. Making disciples and some other traditional biblical skills are highlighted in the top ten most proficient skills along with some people skills. However, holistic development and sound biblical knowledge are highlighted in among the seven least proficient skills. Promoting unity, understanding ecumenism, and mobilizing resources competencies were also highlighted in the seven least proficient skills.

Communicating was the competency in which the general secretaries were self-assessed to have the highest level of proficiency. Communicating is an important competency for connecting and building relationships with members from the different parts in a nation. However, in spite of what Internet technology provides in the current era to enhance communication, no mention was made of communication technology on the list of competencies. Communication was also not highlighted for the task of representing, although it appeared in the other three tasks areas of NEA leadership. Thus, further exploration of what the general secretaries ascribe to communication as the most proficient competency could have been done in face-to-face interviews.

The assessment reveals a sufficient gap in the proficiency of the general secretaries in the core competencies for leading NEAs. Overall, the self-assessment proficiency levels reveal room for improvement in proficiency levels in each core competency. Every core competency could at least be improved from good to excellent. The gap includes skills in both traditional biblical competencies and the seemingly secular competencies. The self-proficiency assessment of the general secretaries showed that resource mobilization, very closely related to resource management, was the competency in which the general secretaries were least proficient. The fledgling state of the NEAs, highlighted in literature review section, could partly be due to lack of resources accentuated by the inability of the leaders to mobilize resources.

The churches tend to be dependent more on outside resources especially from the West or the United States of America, in particular. This dependency has some implication for authentic leadership and relevance of African church leaders. The leader's ability to initiate programs to address felt needs of their communities is undermined and instead they focus on programs determined by donors. Often, the community does not have ownership of the foreign-initiated programs, and these programs are unlikely the solution to the local needs. The ability to mobilize the people around a vision they share and own is the key to resource mobilization and effectiveness of the leader. However, the reality is that the resources of the church, as a whole is concentrated in the West, in spite of the dwindling population of Christians in that part of the world and the growing population of Christians in Africa and the global South. Partnership and collaboration of the church in Africa will continue, but African leaders should ensure true partnership and mutuality, rather than just be recipients of donor funds and subject themselves in servitude to the dictates of donors.

In spite of the high level of educational credentials, the self-assessed proficiency levels reveal gaps in theological knowledge. Theology as a subject may not be a strong area of previous training of the general secretaries. General secretaries also ranked theology in the middle of important competencies list. The NEA is expected to give direction for biblical engagement for all the evangelical denominations in the nation, and sound biblical knowledge of the leaders is critical to the role. The low level of proficiency is a manifestation of the challenge in the church with biblical literacy and rising secularism and worldly influence. The church should take theological education seriously in the development of leaders. Sound theological education is required to engage with seemingly secular domains, such as resource management, advocacy, and holistic development for the church to create any significant impact in the society.

Most of the competencies in which the general secretaries thought they were least proficient were rated highly in the ordered lists of important competencies. This low proficiency rating of important competencies has implication for equipping the church, for curriculum development and training of leaders in the church. The profile of current general secretaries shows an appreciable level of training or academic qualification; however, the proficiency levels in the competencies perceived to be required for their role in leading NEAs show a need for training. The nature of the training needed was multidisciplinary.

The self-assessment of the subcompetencies showed that the general secretaries' proficiency ranged from average to excellent, except in one case, ordination, where proficiency ranged from poor to excellent. The rating for proficiency for subcompetencies was

- Having a balanced life,
- Acting on decision of members and creating conducive environments for training/formation,
- Having the ability to assess strengths and weaknesses of the church, planning programs in line with vision and mission, ability to raise and maintain standards in the church and be result oriented, and
- Being acquainted with the needs of the community.

Overall, the proficiency rating was good. However, 25 percent of the respondents rated themselves as average with more room to improve proficiency in all the competencies.

Skills and competencies are important requirements for leadership effectiveness and could be developed through training. Character formation of people in their childhood is important and contributes to the preparation of effective leaders.

Implications of the Findings

Globalization and trends in organizational theory tend to favor structured networks rather than hierarchical and pyramidal organizational structures. Associations such as the NEA are structured networks, unlike the denominational hierarchical or bureaucratic structures in the church. Thus, the future of global Christianity tends towards structured networks such as the NEA. Therefore, a healthy NEA requires good and competent leadership. The goal of this research is to contribute to the understanding and strengthening of the NEA and the ministry of the church. Therefore, the findings of the research have implications for ministry at various levels of the church – global, regional, and national. In particular, the findings provide insights about the current state of ministry in the NEAs in Africa and material for possible interventions for personnel development for more effectiveness.

The profile of a typical NEA leader, at governance and management levels, revealed a preponderance of males. Only one female general secretary was among thirty-one respondents that were targeted, and no female was among the regional presidents. The profile of the NEA is inconsistent with its reconciliatory nature, in view of the long-standing disagreement about exclusion of women in leadership, in the church. The dominance of males in the NEA leadership reflects the cultural practice but as an evangelical and biblical institution the NEA should demonstrate redemptive message of Christ and provide equal opportunities for all people.

The NEA is a network of networks and has flexible relationships with the different members in the association for effectiveness. However, patrimony, especially in terms of exclusion of females from leadership, is an aspect of the culture that may require a paradigm shift. Jesus warned his followers about the kind of leadership he expected of them and also made clear the purpose of leadership. Leadership is about serving others, but African cultural perspectives focus on authority and power, which tend to have a corrupting influence especially in the context of the church. NEAs should endeavor to change the outlook of leaders and be sensitive to the gender question for cohesiveness in the NEAs.

While the average or modal age bracket of 50–54 years would be considered as an ideal matured age group, it is higher than the average age group of the population of the different countries in Africa, and indeed the overall average age group for the whole region of Africa. Africa has a very youthful population and will remain so for the next several decades. The greater the age difference between the leader and the followers, the greater the possibilities of disconnect and ineffectiveness of the leader. The church should consider trusting the younger generation with leadership and must be seen to be preparing the young generation adequately for leadership roles in the church.

With the fast-changing communication and technological era, people in the age bracket of fifty years and over, tend to be less technologically savvy than their younger counterparts. These emerging technological competencies required for effectiveness in organizations could render older people ineffective. The older and aged leaders would require a large investment in terms of training to acquire current and needed skills than the younger generation.

However, the general secretary works directly with the different denominational heads and pastors of local churches who may have identical profiles in terms of age and gender. From empirical observation, the tendency is to have denominational heads – bishops, national superintendents, and overseers – who are older than the general secretary of the NEA. Therefore, a generational gap and disconnect between the leadership of the church and the followership in general exists. The tendency to have all male leaders who are much older than the average person in the church may lead to ineffectiveness. Notably, the effect of this disconnect is dwindling church attendance; this phenomenon is currently observed in the historic Protestant churches. Young people have an attraction to newer charismatic church plants that have an appeal to contemporary culture and the youths.

The purpose and task of the general secretary of the NEA is not well understood. However, a threefold task – connecting, representing, and equipping – has been identified. The African regional presidents' perception about the task of the general secretary was to administrate. The NEA, like other church organizations, is both an organism and an organization. The aspect of organism has to do with the whole life of people, including the spiritual life. The organizational aspect deals with management structures and systems that define relationships between different activities of the members and their roles and responsibilities within the organization. NEA leaders need to have management or administrative competencies to run the organizations effectively.

The competencies that have been identified by the regional presidents for leading NEAs are diverse and multidisciplinary. NEA leadership competencies include the traditional skills or competencies for ministry in any church organization: making disciples (but also mentoring), teaching (ability to train others), and communicating. In addition, the NEA leader requires competencies in areas such as peace building and conflict resolution (for promoting unity), management, advocacy, development, and visionary leadership. In addition, the NEA leader's lifestyle and that of his or her family was an important qualification for the respondents. This blend of competencies equipped the NEAs for holistic or integral mission in the church.

Generally, most of the core competencies highlighted in the study were secular and different from the traditional biblical competencies for leadership in the church. The emergence of the nontraditional biblical competencies requires an approach to theological education that seeks to prepare leaders to reach out to the people, especially in the public square. The holistic approach to ministry is likely to make the church more missional and impact the society more than the traditional dualistic approach, which is concerned more with what is supposedly the spiritual side of humans.

The findings are expected to inform the assessment criteria in the recruitment and selection of candidates for leadership role in the NEA and similar organizations. The competencies can be part of the content of the job description for assessing candidates for selection for the NEA leadership role. Human resource management skills are required for job analysis, assessment of candidates, and finding the best fit – the human resource management doctrine of having the best person for the job.

Some church denominations that consist of independent local congregations that have a general overseer or superintendent may need similar competencies to perform their roles effectively. Like the NEA, they would need to build unity and harmony among the various local congregations and reflect their common distinctive as a denomination. Other regions of the world within the WEA family may also find these competencies useful for leading the NEA in their regions. The NEAs in Africa have much in common with NEAs around the globe and in other regions. They are all members of the WEA, which informs many aspects of their operations. In addition, the findings may be useful to those responsible for curriculum development in the WEALI, seminaries, and Bible colleges and those responsible for leadership development in the church.

The findings show that the ability to motivate others was the most important competency the NEA general secretaries believed was needed for leading the NEA. Other priority skills were the ability to communicate and manage resources. Thus, the three competencies of motivating, communicating, and managing resources were prioritized before disciple making, the key call and purpose of the church. The competency for making disciples was even lower in frequency of occurrence on the list of competencies identified by the regional presidents.

Making disciples is not only the core task of the church but is also its biggest challenge in Africa. If the church should effectively impact the nation with the gospel, it has to prioritize and be effective in making disciples. The growth of the church in Africa does not correlate with the church's transformational impact. The following statements are popular for describing the ineffectiveness of the church: "a mile long but only an inch deep; blood of ethnicity is thicker than waters of baptism; Christians go to church on Sunday but look for the witch doctor Monday to Saturday." These scathing commentaries about the church can only be countered with effective discipleship in the church to bring about meaningful transformation in society, as individual lives are shaped by the teachings of Christ and the gospel.

The combined priority list of the two sets of NEA leaders shows the five most important top competencies as resource mobilization, communication, promotion of unity, ability to motivate, and soft skills. These top five competencies should be prioritized in equipping leaders. The competencies could be learned and acquired, but they may not be found in the curriculum of schools where the churches traditionally train leaders. To address this need, schools may have to review their curricula and integrate traditional Christian educational curricula and/or devise a customized approach for personnel development to ensure that needed skills that contribute to effectiveness could be acquired. The skills should be integrated with biblical and theological competency.

Whereas the role of the NEA leader may be complementary for traditional pastoral leadership in the church, the two roles seem to be different. The difference can be seen in the fact that the immediate recipients or beneficiaries of the services of the NEA leaders were the denominational leaders and the local pastors, first, and second, the larger community. However, as Paul spells out in the Pastoral Epistles, the spiritual qualifications of the church leaders (i.e. pastors) and deacons (i.e. those called to complement the work of the leaders/pastors) were the same. The priority on competencies that seem to be secular may well be a gift for the effective functioning of the church as in the early church when the church grew as a result of the work of the deacons (Acts 6:1–7).

The findings also show that the NEA leaders needed to improve their proficiencies in all the competencies identified. The general secretaries' proficiency ranged from average to excellent except in one case (i.e. ordination) where proficiency ranged from poor to excellent. Although resources management was rated high as one of the most important competencies, general secretaries were least proficient in resource mobilization. Thus, skills in resource mobilization, was one of the areas of need, in terms of training and development of leaders for the NEA and similar organizations of the church. The inability of the leader to mobilize resources for the work of the church makes the leader and the church vulnerable to be dependent. Dependency would also lead to less ownership of the programs of the church and programs that may not meet the felt needs of members.

Similarly, promoting unity (e.g. peace building and conflict resolution) was one of the competencies among the least three proficient skills after resource mobilization and sound biblical knowledge. The goal of the NEA was promoting unity. The low proficiency level in promoting unity is highly important, since much of the focus of this study has to do with unity. The findings underscore the fragility of the NEAs and the need to strengthen NEAs. Building the capacity of the NEA leaders in this area of competency is, therefore, a priority.

The church generally depends on both secular colleges/universities and seminaries or Bible colleges for leadership training. Neither of the two types of educational institutions provides a curriculum or training that adequately addresses the subject matter of the competencies highlighted in this research. Therefore, general secretaries tend to be perpetual students with a quest to acquire one skill or the other to build their capabilities. The need to build proficiency in the various competencies may be ameliorated by recruiting qualified staff. The role and responsibilities of each member of the staff team should be clearly defined. The need for a team of qualified staff would require sustainable resources to maintain and retain them. However, with the perceived inability to mobilize resources it may be a challenge for the NEA leaders to attract staff or for the NEA, to even employ a general secretary to lead the NEA. The inability or poor ability for resource mobilization may be a key factor for the fledgling state of several NEAs in the region, revealing a great area of need for capacity building and partnerships. This need should be of particular importance for many global Christian and international partners whose mission was to assist to the church in Africa.

The findings of this research would be useful to the NEAs in Africa and especially for leaders involved in recruitment and staff training and development in the NEA. Similar NEAs in other parts of the world could also benefit from this work, as they would have similar organizational objectives and challenges. The findings would also be of interest to WEA, especially the WEA Leadership Institute, set up to provide training for leaders in the NEAs around the world. Other ecumenical associations of other church traditions, such as the Council of Churches and the Pentecostal fellowships could also benefit from the findings of this research.

The findings have a wider application for curriculum planners for leadership development and Christian education in other institutions, universities, seminaries, or Bible colleges. The findings would be of interest to denominational heads with responsibility for overseeing independent local congregations.

Limitations of the Study

The findings and their applicability could be enhanced by improvement in the design, instrumentation, and a more robust implementation of the project. The purposeful sample of participants, especially in the first phase, was relatively small, and the findings may not be applicable in every NEA in Africa. The study could be conducted with a larger population, including other members on governance and management, such as those of the NEAs. The denominational heads and pastors of the local congregations, direct beneficiaries of the services of the NEA leaders, could also participate in the research.

The study was mostly quantitative in nature, especially in the data collated in response to Research Questions #2 and #3. Face-to-face interviews could have been more exploratory and aid further understanding the meanings of some of the responses received, especially from the regional presidents in the first phase of the research. The regional presidents' responses to the questions were stated in writing, which were brief notations. Some of the responses could have been probed further by secondary or follow-up questions for clarification in interviews.

Unexpected Observations

I had some assumptions about the perceptions of leadership and competencies for leading NEAs, especially in the African context. I assumed that the personnel specification described by the participants would be similar to a typical pastor. However, the findings show fundamental differences, especially in the goal and focus of ministry and the priority areas of competency required.

The NEA leader's focus and ministry objectives were the equipping of pastors, and the pastor tended to focus on shepherding the flock: teaching, preaching, evangelism, and discipleship. These traditional competencies were perhaps the core tasks of pastoral training and ministry. However, the church needs to be missional, impacting society holistically. Often, the evangelical pastors lay more focus on the soul and spiritual issues while neglecting the burning issues of justice and human flourishing. This issue of dualism is particularly important in Africa where little or no dichotomy exists between spirituality and the physical and material aspects of life. Therefore, the NEA leaders have a tendency to have focus more on the gap in skill sets of the church leaders. The least ranked competency was ordination, ranked by 50 percent of the respondents as important and by 25 percent as of little importance. A similar number of respondents (25 percent) thought ordination very important. A marked split in the views of the general secretaries is observed about the importance of ordination as a required competency for leading NEA, reflecting the difference between the role of the pastor and the general secretary.

No computer technology competency was mentioned among the competencies highlighted, especially taking into consideration the fact that the contemporary world is part of a communication and technology era. Even more intriguing that communication was highlighted as the competency in which the general secretaries were self-assessed to have the most proficient level of competency ability.

Given the general perception about the leader, especially in the African context, soft skills, including the ability to listen and being teachable, was rated as a priority for leaders. Soft skills require much humility, and in the perception of the society a leader with these characteristics is considered to be a weakling. Christian leaders are faced with the challenge of reconciling societal and cultural expectations with sound biblical principles and best practice leadership characteristics for effectiveness. The low rating of advocacy for justice for the poor and vulnerable as *least important* was surprising while holistic development, which is a justice issue, was rated closer to the top of the list of important competencies. The disparity in the ratings of the competencies is a manifestation of the need for further exploration of these subject matters in order to gain clarity and understanding of the competencies.

Recommendations

In relation to the findings of the research, the following recommendations were made with a view to enhance understanding and improving this area of ministry of the church. In addition, recommendations for further research that could be done to provide more information are highlighted.

The NEA as a reconciliatory establishment, promoting unity among the diverse and conflicting factions of the church, should reflect best practice of equal opportunities in the work place. The NEAs should be intentional about attracting females for the position of general secretary for a more reconciliatory posture in view of the women-in-leadership controversy in the church and wider society. Staff recruitment and development in the NEAs must take into consideration the age factor, as well, and target people in the younger age bracket for leadership roles. Regardless of social status or gender, Christians were one in Christ (Eph 2:14), and the NEA should be seen as an organization that pulls down walls of division, mounted by cultural considerations rather biblical, in the church while promoting unity in diversity.

The core competencies identified in this study, especially the top ten, should inform the content of the job description of the NEA general secretary in the recruitment and selection process. The core competencies should also be integrated into the operation, training, and development process in the organization, including staff appraisal and promotion. The staff training and development program should focus on building proficiency in these competencies and pay attention particularly to developing capacity in competencies that the general secretaries rated as very important but in which they were also least proficient.

The competencies should be of interest to curriculum planners to develop teaching curriculum or content for training people for ministry in the NEA or similar organizations, such as other ecumenical organizations, denominational conferences, confederations, or dioceses. Seminaries or Bible colleges should also be interested in the findings and training curriculum, ensuring training needs of the church in this area of ministry. The seemingly secular competencies but deemed necessary requirements for holistic or integral mission do have a theological basis and should be systematized and inform the curriculum content for training and people development.

WEALI, recently established to train people for association leaderships, should field test the findings of competencies for NEA leadership in other regions of the world with a view to integrating these into their training curriculum. The application and use of findings in this research has professional human resource management implications. The WEALI institute should do job analysis and develop assessment centers for recruitment and selection. WEALI should take into consideration the findings in the whole process of staff training and development.

Missional and transformational leadership development begins with discipleship and mentorship in the church. Like an integral approach to mission of the church, the discipleship program of the church in Africa needs a paradigm shift. The churches' discipleship program for new believers, especially children, should aim at self-discipline and nurture in emotional intelligence. Further research is recommended to bring more clarity and consensus to the role of the NEA leader and indeed on the function of the NEA for ministry of the church. Future research could include a bigger population of participants, including other staff and denominational heads that benefit directly from the work of the NEA general secretary. In the current era, the use of technology seems to be inevitable and could be particularly important for NEA leaders given the dispersion of their constituents within the nation. Research on the use of technology and how it will impact the NEA could be an important undertaking.

Postscript

This project was conceived out of twenty years of experience in ministry with evangelical associations, both at national and regional levels. In this role, I have also interacted with leaders of other regional alliances or associations around the globe and within the WEA. The fragile state of many evangelical associations in the region and how they could be strengthened is a growing concern. The thesis of this project was the need to understand the NEA as an organization and identify the leadership competencies required to effectively run the NEA. Very little in information exists in literature from which to glean on this subject. However, getting the views of key regional evangelical leaders and current general secretaries of the National

Evangelical Associations provided useful insights about the person specification for NEA leadership.

My experience in carrying out the research was a growing understanding of the fundamental issues relating to the fledgling state of the NEAs. Identifying these issues was a step in the direction of finding solutions to the challenges, thus strengthening the NEAs for effectiveness. I thought NEA general secretaries had a call similar to that of pastors in the church. The experience and findings of the research helped me review my position on this thought. While both pastoral and NEA leadership were important calls to ministry, I realize a difference between the two. The pastor's role required contact with people from all backgrounds, necessarily including nonbelievers, with a view of reaching them with the gospel and bringing them to the church for discipleship. The NEA leader works mostly with Christian leaders, presenting a representative image and voice of the church to the rest of society.

However, while the role of the NEA leader may seem to be secular, it is critical to the witness of the church as a whole. The role demands both the character of a pastor and best practices of leadership and management principles as in business, governance, and public service. A blend of the pastoral, best leadership, management, and public service principles, in practice, provide a model for a missional church and its impact on society. The purpose of the NEA is focused on the church and building the capacity of the church to be missional. The demand for engaging with the pastors assumed significant previous pastoral training and required skills from other human endeavors for a more holistic approach to the work of the church for an impact in society.

I have a better appreciation of the giftedness of the church: the purpose of individual gifts at individual, denominational, and organizational levels and how these could be earnest as one body of Christ for the mission of the church. Approach in ministry was not all about getting people to do work and achieve program objectives but how to bring out the God-given passion and gifting in individuals for the good of all. The skills needed are in people and waiting to be recognized and developed as communities of individuals complement one another. A way to develop and improve abilities is to learn from one another; no amount of formal schooling will ensure acquisition of all the skills required for ministry. In-service training and receiving coaching from other people would be one approach to integrate with staff development.

Finally, while the conception and description of this project was conducted in the catacombs of the academic environment, the closing reflections were crafted in the wild, watching animals for the third time in the last two years of engaging with the project, from Amboseli Game Park to Masai Mara and Salt Lick Game Parks in Titativeta, all in Kenya. I was enriched from insights of the social life of the different species of animals and their associations in the wild. This project is about leadership, associations, and unity. I could not help being fascinated with the social life of the different species of animals in the wild. Similarities and contrasts of human civilization and other mammals in the jungle were apt from the narratives of the tour guides about the exercise of leadership, associations, and unity of the animals in the jungle. I could discern the paucity of real effective and impactful leaders in the park. Of the hundreds of animal species, the *big five* – the African elephant, lion, leopard, buffalo, and rhinoceros – stand out in the jungle. The *big five* are renowned for their survival instinct, claim on territorial habitat, and show of strength rather than size. Effective and impactful leaders, such as the big five, are critically endangered species even among *homo sapiens,* hence the quest for real leaders – Level 5 leaders – to stand up or be made.

APPENDIX A

AEA Regions: Article IX of AEA Constitution

A. Purpose

1. To advance the Association's vision, mission and objectives.
2. To promote regional cooperation.
3. To facilitate cross-border ministries.
4. To promote formation of National Fellowships or networks in nations without any in the Region.
5. To strengthen the weak Member Fellowships in the Region.
6. To tackle Regional issues.
7. To elect regional presidents from their rank who sit on the Board and the Council.

B. Distribution

1. **North West**: Algeria, Cape Verde, Gambia, Guinea Bissau, Guinea Conakry, Mali, Mauritania, Morocco, Senegal and Western Sahara [10].
2. **North East**: Libya, Tunisia, Egypt, Sudan, Eritrea, Djibouti, Ethiopia [7].
3. **West Africa**: Nigeria, Togo, Benin, Ghana, Côte d'Ivoire, Liberia, Sierra Leone, Burkina Faso and Niger [9].

4. **Central Region**: Cameroon, Central Africa Republic, Democratic Republicof Congo, Congo Brazzaville, Chad, Equatorial Guinea, Gabon, SãoTomé-Principe and St. Helena [9].
5. **Eastern Africa Region:** Kenya, Uganda, Tanzania, Somalia, Burundi,Rwanda, [6].
6. **Southern Region:** Malawi, Mozambique, Angola, Namibia, Botswana,Zimbabwe, Zambia, Swaziland, Lesotho, Republic of South Africa [10].
7. **Indian Ocean:** Seychelles, Comoros, Mayotte, Madagascar, Mauritius, Re-Union [6].

All together 57 nations and territories, when Western Sahara has been recognized.

APPENDIX B

Request for Approval from AEA to Conduct Research

Association of Evangelicals in Africa
7, Valley Road, P.O. Box 49332, 00100
Nairobi, Kenya

Dear _____

RE: Request for Approval to Conduct an Investigation into Leadership Competencies for Leading National Evangelical Associations in Africa.

I am a Doctor of Ministry candidate at Asbury Theological Seminary in the USA, and conducting research on leadership development. Particularly, I am investigating the competencies needed for successfully building and sustaining National Evangelical Associations particularly in the African context.

I would like to interview the Chairpersons and General Secretaries of the various national associations you have in Africa and may require information related to my research from your headquarters in Nairobi. The study will seek to get the opinion of the Chairpersons and general secretaries about the required competencies that lead to success.

I am writing to kindly request your approval for the conduct of the research and for the leaders of the national associations to participate in the research. The leaders would be required to respond to a questionnaire designed for easy completion and would approximately take one hour to complete.

The objective of the study is to assist in identifying the leadership competencies unique to building and sustaining National Evangelical Associations and required for developing and supporting leaders for the national associations in Africa, in particular.

The data participants provide and any information gathered from the office will be confidential and the final report will be in aggregated form, which does not identify individual participants. The data will be kept electronically on a personal password-protected laptop computer and any hard copies will be kept in a locker in my office. The information and data collected will be destroyed or deleted when the research is completed.

The participation of the leaders is voluntary and their consent will be sought in addition to your approval.

I would be grateful if you would convey your response in writing. Feel free to contact me for any further information or clarification you may require.

Yours sincerely,

Aiah Foday-Khabenje

APPENDIX C

Consent Form for AEA Regional Presidents' Participation

Dear _____

RE: Introduction and Request for Consent to Participate in Project: Investigation into Leadership Competencies – Case Study for African-Based National Evangelical Associations.

I am a Doctor of Ministry candidate at Asbury Theological Seminary in the USA, and conducting research on leadership development. Particularly, I am investigating the competencies needed for successfully building and sustaining National Evangelical Associations particularly in the African context.

I would like to interview the seven regional presidents of the Association of Evangelicals in Africa (AEA) who are familiar with recruitment, job descriptions and work of the general secretaries or the chief executive officers of National Evangelical Fellowships or Associations. The study will seek to get the opinion of the regional presidents about the required competencies or capabilities that lead to success.

I am writing to kindly request you to participate in the research by responding to a questionnaire, designed for easy completion and would approximately take one hour to complete the questionnaire. The objective of the study is to help us identity the leadership competencies unique to building and sustaining national evangelical association and used to developing and supporting leaders for the national fellowships in Africa. Your honest and objective opinion based on your real life experience will help in finding ways to strengthen the national evangelical fellowships in Africa and other regions within the World Evangelical Alliance.

The data participants provide will be confidential and the final report will be in aggregated form, which does not identify individual participants. The data will be kept electronically on a personal password – protected laptop computer and any hard copies will be kept in a locker in my office. The information and data collected will be destroyed or deleted when the research is completed.

I realize that your participation is voluntary and I greatly appreciate your willingness to being a part of this study. You are also free to not answer any questions you do not want to answer.

To indicate your voluntary participation, please indicate below your consent or otherwise, at the end of this letter. Feel free to contact me for any further information or clarification you may require.

Thank you for your kind assistance.

Yours sincerely,

Aiah Foday-Khabenje

I, _____, volunteer/decline to participate in the study described above.

Date: _____

APPENDIX D

Consent Form for General Secretaries' Participation

7 Valley Road,
P. O. Box 49332, 00100
Nairobi

Date

Dear_____

RE: Introduction and Request for Consent to Participate in Project: Investigation into Leadership Competencies Case Study for African-Based National Evangelical Associations.

I am a Doctor of Ministry candidate at Asbury Theological Seminary in the USA, and conducting research on leadership development. Particularly, I am investigating the competencies needed for successfully leading National Evangelical Associations particularly in the African context.

    I would like to interview current general secretaries or CEOs of the various National Evangelical Associations in Africa. The study will seek to get the opinion of the general secretaries with regard to the value they place on perceived competencies for leading National Evangelical Associations by AEA regional presidents and assess the level of proficiency of current general secretaries of each of the competencies.

    I am writing to kindly request you to participate in the research by responding to a questionnaire, designed for easy completion and would approximately take about 30–40 minutes to complete the questionnaire.

The objective of the study is to help us identity the top leadership competencies unique to building and sustaining national evangelical association. The outcome of this research would be used in developing and supporting leaders for the national fellowships in Africa. Your objective and honest opinion, based on your real life experience will help in finding ways to strengthen the national evangelical fellowships in Africa and other regions within the World Evangelical Alliance.

The data participants provide will be confidential and the final report will be in aggregated form, which does not identify individual participants. The data will be kept electronically on a personal password – protected laptop computer and any hard copies will be kept in a locker in my office. The information and data collected will be destroyed or deleted when the research is completed.

I realize that your participation is voluntary and I greatly appreciate your willingness to being a part of this study. You are also free to not answer any questions you do not want to answer. To indicate your voluntary participation, please indicate below your consent or otherwise, at the end of this letter. Feel free to contact me for any further information or clarification you may require.

Thank you for your help.

Yours sincerely,

Aiah Foday-Khabenje

I, _____ volunteer/decline to participate in the study described above.

Date _____

APPENDIX E

Questionnaire to Be Completed by AEA Regional Presidents

Thank you again for agreeing to participate in this study of leadership competencies needed by general secretaries of National Evangelical Associations in Africa. For the purposes of this study, we are defining competencies as the various factors including personal attributes, knowledge, experience, skills, behavior, and other relational and contextual factors which in your opinion contribute to success in leading the national evangelical association.

As Chair and President of your national association and the subregion respectively, you would be familiar with the task of selecting the general secretary of the national evangelical association. I am particularly interested in your thoughts and ideas about what specific leadership competencies or capabilities individuals need in order to be successful as general secretary of the national evangelical association.

I would be very grateful if you would kindly respond to the following questions. It will take about 30 minutes to complete the questionnaire:

A. Demographic Information: (your personal details)

Name: _____

How long have you served as president?

Gender: _____ Region: _____

Denomination: _____

B. Profile of Leader of Nation Evangelical Association (the following questions solicit your input regarding the necessary qualifications of a leader of a national evangelical p or association).

1. **Education:** What level and type of formal education/qualification do think is required for leading an NEA? (E.g. Certificate, Diploma, Higher Diploma, BA, etc).
2. **Experience:** (Please state the kind of experience you think is essential for the task of leading a national evangelical fellowship):

C. Leadership Competency Questions: (This section explores the task of the leader or general secretary of a national evangelical association and the leadership capabilities required of the leader to carry out the task, especially in the African context).

1. **Perceived Task:** What do you consider to be the main task of the general secretary or leader of the national evangelical fellowship in Africa?

    1.1 What five leadership abilities do you think a general secretary of a national evangelical association need to carry out the task stated in C1 above?

    (Please list as capability statement; i.e. Able to ....
    [*State action word*])

    1.1.1 Able to

    1.1.2 Able to

    1.1.3 Able to

    1.1.4 Able to

    1.1.5 Able to

Questionnaire to Be Completed by AEA Regional Presidents   211

2. It is generally believed in the global context that the key tasks of the general secretary of an NEA are threefold; **connecting, representing and equipping** their members.

    What five leadership abilities do you believe a general secretary of a National Evangelical Association need to successfully carry out each of the three main tasks of **connecting, representing** and **equipping** members?

    2.1 **Connecting:** (Forming and sustainably building unity among evangelical denominations and other church organizations, positioning association to serve as platform for partnership in the gospel): Please list five abilities to *connect as defined*:

    (Please list as capability statement; i.e. Able to ………
    [*State action word*])

    2.1.1. Able to

    2.1.2. Able to

    2.1.3. Able to

    2.1.4. Able to

    2.1.5. Able to

2.2 **Representing** (Effective public engagement and serving as trusted voice of evangelicals; influencing public policy and advocating for religious liberties, poverty alleviation and vulnerable and disadvantaged groups): Please list five abilities to *represent as defined*:

(Please list as capability statement; i.e. Able to .... [*State action word*])

2.2.1. Able to

2.2.2. Able to

2.2.3. Able to

2.2.4. Able to

2.2.5. Able to

2.3 **Equipping** (Serving members by leading, resourcing and partnering; empowering and mobilizing constituency in living out the Good news of Jesus of Christ and transforming their nation): Please list five abilities to *equip as defined*:

(Please list as capability statement; i.e. Able to .... [*State action word*])

2.3.1. Able to

2.3.2. Able to

2.3.3. Able to

2.3.4. Able to

2.3.5. Able to

Please underline what you think are the top three of the perceived abilities, in each of the four tasks of perceived (as in C1), connecting, representing and equipping and as listed above.

Thank you for taking the time to respond to these questions.

APPENDIX F

Job Description: Secretary General and Chief Excutive Officer of WEA

The World Evangelical Alliance is a global association of national alliances, regional alliances, global partners and associated ministries who gather to advance the good news of Jesus Christ, strengthen the evangelical church around the world and seek holiness, justice and renewal at every level of society – individual, family, community and culture – so that God is glorified and the nations of the earth are transformed.

Purpose

To support the objectives of the WEA by:
1) Serving the members of the WEA with vision, cultural and spiritual sensitivity, God-honoring leadership, integrity and humility.
2) Creating, recommending and executing the rolling three-year strategic plan (and detailed annual plans) based on the mission, vision, values and policies approved by the International Council.
3) Recruiting and empowering senior staff to serve WEA members and partners in the fulfillment of the WEA objectives.
4) Representing the WEA as its primary spokesperson to the global evangelical and Christian community, the global interfaith community, the media, the public, governmental bodies, and non-governmental organizations.
5) Cultivating, educating, inspiring and serving the members and donors of WEA so the funding of WEA is sustainable.

Relationships

Reports to: WEA International Council and (in financial matters) the North American Council

Supervises: The Executive Team

Responsibilities

Strategy, Vision and Leadership

- Collaborate with the International Council (IC) and (in relation to financial matters) North American Council (NAC) to refine and implement the strategic plan while ensuring that the budget, staff and priorities are aligned with WEA's core mission and vision
- Cultivate a strong and transparent working relationship with the IC and NAC and ensure open communication about the measurement of financial, programmatic, and impact performance against stated milestones and goals
- Provide inspirational leadership and direction to all executive staff, and ensure the continued development and management of a professional and efficient organization; establish effective decision-making processes that will enable WEA to achieve its long- and short-term goals and objectives

Representation

- Represent WEA and serve as WEA's primary spokesperson to the global evangelical and Christian community, the global interfaith community, the media, the public, governmental bodies, and non-governmental organizations
- In collaboration with the Associate Secretaries General, represent and connect the WEA to its members of regional and national alliances, commissions and initiatives, associate members and church networks, etc.

Development
- Ensure that the flow of funds permits WEA to make continuous progress towards the achievement of its mission and that those funds are allocated properly to reflect present needs and future potential
- In collaboration with the Director of Development and Director of Communications, formulate and execute comprehensive marketing, branding and development strategies that will ensure consistency throughout the organization and enhance revenue from major donors, foundations, government agencies, and corporations

Strengthening Infrastructure and Operations
- Ensure the delivery of high quality services while managing for current and future growth
- Support and motivate the organization's staff
- In collaboration with the Chief Operations Officer (COO), facilitate cross-departmental collaboration and strengthen internal communications with staff throughout the organization; create and promote a positive, multicultural work environment that supports consistency throughout the organization's strategy, operational methods, and data collection needs
- In collaboration with COO and Director of Finance, oversee the financial status of the organization including developing long and short range financial plans, monitoring the budget and ensuring sound financial controls are in place; set financial priorities accurately to ensure the organization is operating in a manner that supports the needs of the program and staff

Program Development
- Rationalize the delivery of programs through new and existing departments and partnerships
- In collaboration with the Director of Strategic Programs, increase efficiencies and consistency throughout the organization by developing and implementing standardized programs, services and program office marketing

Position Requirements

The International Council has established the following requirements for this position. This person will have demonstrated in his or her previous positions the characteristics and abilities necessary to the successful performance of the duties of the Secretary General. These include:

- Exemplary Walk with God: The SG/CEO of WEA must be a committed follower of Jesus Christ who affirms WEA's Statement of Faith and who demonstrates continuing growth in his or her Christian faith. This person will seek to be a fully devoted follower of Christ and a mentor and spiritual guide for others
- Long-term Commitment: The SG/CEO should be willing to make a commitment of at least five (5) years to WEA.
- Location: While it would be helpful for this person to reside in New York, NY, it is possible that the SG/CEO could operate from his or her home country or another location of his or her choice, subject to International Council approval.
- Education: A college or university masters or doctoral degree would be an advantage. Bachelor's degree is required.
- Experience: The preferred candidate will have relevant experience as a CEO in either ministry leadership, the not-for-profit world or in the marketplace.
- Core Competencies: The SG/CEO should be able to demonstrate prior effectiveness in the following leadership areas:
    i. Vision Casting and Championing of the Vision, Mission and Core Values
    ii. Team Building and Inspirational Leadership of the Executive Team; Able to Work in a Team
    iii. Management; Program/Operations/Financial Oversight
    iv. Strategic Thinker and Ability to See the Big Picture
    v. Fundraising and Resource Development
- Builder of People and Relationships: The SG/CEO must have documented experience in building teams of inspired staff members, board members, and volunteers for both current and future global opportunities. The SG/CEO must be an excellent

delegator, with clear goals and objectives for both paid and unpaid team members.
- Inspirational Team Leader: This person must be highly gifted as the leader of a team – specifically in the cultivation, recruitment, orientation and engagement of direct reports. There must be prior evidence that staff, volunteers and board members have experienced joy and fulfillment working alongside him or her.
- Association Leadership Core Competencies: Since WEA is a member-based alliance/association, the SG/CEO must have prior experience serving on an association board or as staff, or demonstrated experience in his or her ability to quickly learn new skills sets in unique arenas and niches (such as the unique arena of the association world). The successful SG/CEO will become a mentor and recognized association expert and trainer to the association community in WEA (the general secretaries, staff, volunteers and board members of WEA's regional and national associations and alliances).
- Knowledgeable Influencer/Leader in Global Evangelical Circles: The SG/CEO will have enough background and theological and cultural understanding to become a widely recognized and trusted spokesperson and influencer for the global evangelical movement.
- Models a God-honoring, Balanced and Healthy Lifestyle: The SG/CEO will have demonstrated a balanced life and the ability to maintain a consistent God-honoring life in every arena: physical, spiritual, emotional, and psychological. The SG/CEO will ensure that he or she has accountability partners that will help monitor family and marriage issues, travel days, health and wellness, hobbies and leisure time, professional development, time management, work and personal priorities, local church, and other relationships.

APPENDIX G

Job Description: General Secretary of AEA

AEA General Secretary Profile: An Executive Summary

Preamble
The Association of Evangelicals in Africa (AEA) as a Movement uniting evangelical churches, mission agencies and parachurch organizations was born in February 1966. It is committed to making disciples and advancing the Kingdom of God throughout Africa. As of AD 2001, it commands a membership of over 70 million believers in 47 African nations.

Its vision is to unite evangelicals in Africa for holistic ministries that will make a difference.

Position Description
The general secretary is the Chief Executive Officer and the Team Leader of the Movement. The primary function of the general secretary is two-fold:
- To lead the Movement to greater heights.
- To provide management oversight for its ministry Commissions, their projects, the branch offices, and the Nairobi-based Headquarters.

Personality Traits
As a team leader of a Christian movement, the general secretary of AEA must be characterized by the following traits:

- Christlikeness: a life controlled, led, guided, and empowered by the Holy Spirit. A life of obedience and humble submission to God.
- Conviction: adherence to the inspiration and trustworthiness of the Bible as God's Word, and an acceptance of AEA's Statement of Faith.
- Character: bearing the composite fruit of the Spirit, namely: love, joy, peace, patience, kindness, goodness, faithfulness, gentleness and self-control (Gal 5:22–23). A person of integrity.
- Capability: able to display high energy and a large capacity to perform. Blessed with good health.
- Courage: Capacity to face challenges, accept responsibility, and forge ahead.
- Compassion: possessing passion for souls and for believers' unity; able to bridge denominational divides.
- Commitment: a person of vision and focus; a committed Christian called of God to the AEA mission.

Personal Qualifications

- Spiritual: one with a personal relationship with Jesus Christ as Savior and Lord; maintains a consistent spiritual growth through regular Bible study, prayer, and witness; and a healthy local church membership and involvement.
- Social: one who is above reproach, temperate, self-controlled, respectable, hospitable, able to teach, not given to drunkenness, not violent but gentle, not quarrelsome, not a lover of money, a team leader, manages own family well (where married), and not a recent convert.

- Scholarship: a student of the Word with an understanding of contemporary cultural, socio-political, moral and theological issues of the world in general and Africa in particular. One who is a clear thinker and a good communicator. A formal theological education up to a master's level minimum will be an advantage.

Leadership-Management Tasks

As a team leader, the general secretary is expected to:
- provide vision
- plan for growth: setting goals and using resources wisely
- pioneer new ministries e.g. new fellowships
- promote teamwork: investing in people, inspiring, empowering, and delegating responsibility cum authority
- perform funds development
- pave the way for a successor

As a manager, the general secretary is expected to:
- ensure that records and documents are kept
- ensure that accurate financial records are kept and the books are audited by external auditors
- coordinate the Movement's continental operations and offices
- maintain strong staff morale
- strengthen the spiritual vitality and financial health of the Movement
- at least be bi-lingual (English and French)

Specific Constitutional Duties

These are taken from AEA By-Laws, Article V H of the new constitution

1. To execute through the Headquarters' machinery the policies and resolutions of the Board and to report to the Board.
2. To preserve the Association's seal, official records and historical documents.
3. To handle official correspondence to and from Headquarters.
4. To coordinate the activities of the various Ministries of the Association.

5. To receive reports of the Commissions and Program Executives, and chair the meetings of the Leaderships Team.
6. To attend or be represented at meetings of the Commissions, the Projects and National Fellowships' Annual General Meetings whenever possible.
7. To send out periodically to all members, newsletters and prayer bulletins and other publications.
8. To employ within the limitation of the budget and in consultation with Board, whenever necessary, any necessary assistance to carry out the purpose of the Association.
9. To uphold the constitution and By-Laws at all times and perform any other duties assigned to this office by the same documents and as may be assigned by the Board from time to time.
10. To serve as a godly example to the public in general and the Christian community in particular.

Reporting

The general secretary reports to the Executive Board of AEA through its chairman.

APPENDIX H

General Secretaries' Ranking and Self-Assessed Proficiency Levels of Competencies Instruments

Code #_____

Thank you very much for agreeing to participate in this study. The purpose of the study is to determine from your point of view, the importance of competencies or abilities AEA regional presidents perceived as essential to successfully lead a National Evangelical Association or Fellowship.

Also, I want you to self-assess your level of proficiency in these competencies. The self-assessment of proficiency level is to help us determine how well your previous experience; training and development had equipped you in each competency. This is to determine what level of training is required for any intervention for staff development for national evangelical fellowships in our region and share our experience with the rest of the world.

Your responses will be kept completely confidential. The code number on the front of this instrument will be used only for follow-up by email to those individuals who do not respond. However, your participation in this study is completely voluntary, but it is my hope that you will take just a few moments to complete the instrument and share information that will better help us prepare future National Evangelical Association leaders. Thank you again for your participation.

Directions:

The instrument consists of two main sections. The first section solicits demographic information about you, as the respondent. The second section solicits your opinion on the importance of the competencies and level of proficiency in each of the main areas of the general secretary's tasks.

Section 1: Demographic Information

Please complete the following demographic questions:

1. What is your gender? (Please check) __ Female __ Male

2. What is your age (in years)? _____

3. Please indicate how long you have been in your current position within National Evangelical Association: _____

4. How long (in years) have you been employed within the national evangelical association? _____

5. Denomination _____

6. Please state your academic qualification(s)

_____

_____

7. What trainings have you attended that have helped build skills for your work?

_____

_____

_____

_____

_____

Section 2: Rating and Proficiency Levels

In each of the following subsections and tables below, please rate the level of importance of the competencies listed in the first column to your left, using the scale in the center column and your current proficiency level in column to your right, by placing a mark (X) in the square that corresponds to your level of rating of each competency and your level of proficiency for each competency.

Level of Importance:

Please rate the level of importance of each competency listed using the scale below and the center column in the table below:

1 = Unimportant
2 = Of little importance
3 = Important
4 = Very important

Level of Proficiency:

Please assess your current level of proficiency for each competency (in the first column) in the third column and to your right, using the scale 1 to 5; 1 being very poor and 5 being the best possible ability/skill (i.e. Excellent).

1 = Poor
2 = Fair
3 = Average
4 = Good
5 = Excellent

Section 2.1: Competencies Unique to Self-described Task of the NEA Leader: The role of the NEA Leader or general secretary as perceived by AEA regional presidents (administering, catalyst and team leading, Liaison, knowledgeable about NEA ethos/philosophy and guiding pastors).

Competencies	Rating Level of Importance				Level of Your Proficiency/Expertise				
	Unimportant	Of little importance	Important	Very important	Poor	Fair	Average	Good	Excellent
1. Balanced Life (spiritual maturity and professional competency)									
2. Assess strength and weakness of church and talents of leaders									

Section 2.2: Competencies Unique to Role of Connecting of the NEA Leader: Forming and sustainably building unity among evangelical denominations and other church organizations, positioning association to serve as platform for partnership in the gospel.

Competencies	Rating Level of Importance				Level of Your Proficiency/Expertise				
	Unimportant	Of little importance	Important	Very important	Poor	Fair	Average	Good	Excellent
1. Deal with challenges with culturally relevant solutions									

General Secretaries' Ranking and Self-Assessed Proficiency Levels   229

Section 2.3: Competencies Unique to Role of Representing of the NEA Leader: Effective public engagement and serving as trusted voice of evangelicals; influencing public policy and advocating for religious liberties, poverty alleviation and vulnerable and disadvantaged groups.

Competencies	Rating Level of Importance				Level of Your Proficiency/Expertise				
	Unimportant	Of little importance	Important	Very important	Poor	Fair	Average	Good	Excellent
1. Reference for all churches									
2. Acts on decisions of members									
3. Ordained minister of gospel									

Section 2.3: Competencies Unique to the Role of Equipping the NEA Leader: Serving members by leading, resourcing and partnering; empowering and mobilizing constituency in living out the Good news of Jesus of Christ and transforming their nation.

Competencies	Rating Level of Importance				Level of Your Proficiency/Expertise				
	Unimportant	Of little importance	Important	Very important	Poor	Fair	Average	Good	Excellent
1. Raise the standard of the church									
2. Plan programs in line with vision and mission									
3. Result/goal oriented									
4. Create partnership and network (enable)									
5. Acquainted with needs of community									

Section 2.4: Core Competencies of the NEA Leader: Competencies that cut-across the various categories of task mentioned above.

Competencies	Rating Level of Importance				Level of Your Proficiency/Expertise				
	Unimportant	Of little importance	Important	Very important	Poor	Fair	Average	Good	Excellent
1. Sound biblical knowledge and application									
2. Promote unity (reconciliation, peace building)									
3. Organize training seminars									
4. Soft skills (listen, think, teachable)									
5. Communicate									
6. Disciple making/mentoring									
7. Mobilize resources (fundraising)									
8. Manage people/resources									
9. Promote holistic development									
10. Advocate for justice and for the vulnerable									
11. Be family role model									
12. Innovate									
13. Servant leadership/visionary									
14. Motivate/interpersonal skills									
15. Maintain consistent Christian values and evangelical beliefs									
16. Understand ecumenism and global Christianity									
17. Able to train (facilitate/teach)									

Thank you for your participation! If you believe there are things we have not addressed that are important to leadership competency, please use the following space to record your comments:

Bibliography

Adeyemo, Tokunboh. *Africa's Enigma and Leadership Solutions*. Nairobi: WorldAlive, 2009.

———. *Is Africa Cursed? A Vision for the Transformation of an Ailing Continent*. Revised edition. Nairobi: WorldAlive, 2009.

"Administration." *Merriam-Webster Online*. Merriam-Webster, n.d. Accessed 20 October 2014. Web.

AEA Secretariat. *Constitution: Amended*. Nairobi: AEA, 2010.

———. *Membership Directory*. Nairobi: AEA, 2013.

———. *Strategic Review Report*. Nairobi: AEA, 2008.

African Union Commission. *Agenda 2063: The Africa We Want: A Shared Strategic Framework for Inclusive Growth and Sustainable Development & a Global Strategy to Optimize the Use of Africa's Resources for the Benefit of All Africans*. Addis Ababa: African Union Commission, 2014.

"Afroscope." *AEA Newsletter* 1, no. 4 (Apr–June 2010): 1–5.

"Association FAQ." *Asaecenter.org*. ASAE Center for Association Leadership, n.d. Accessed 10 February 2014. Web.

Barna, George. "Nothing Is More Important than Leadership" in *Leaders on Leadership*. Edited by George Barna. Ventura, CA: Regal, 1997.

Barner, R. "Five Steps to Leadership Competencies." *Training & Development* 54, no. 3 (2000): 47–51.

Bloomberg, Charles, and Saul Dubow. "Christian-Nationalism and Rise of the Afrikaner Broederbond in South Africa." *Book Notes for Africa: A Review Journal* 24 (2009): 5–6.

Bolden, Richard. "What Is Leadership?" *Leadership South West Research Report 1*. 3–36. Exeter: Leadership South West, 2004.

Bongmba, Elias K. "Rethinking Power in Africa: Theological Perspectives." *Religion and Theology* 11, no. 2 (2004): 103–138.

Breman, Christina. "The Association of Evangelicals in Africa: Its History, Organization, Members. Projects, Localization and Message." Dissertation Utrecht University, 1995.

Caperig, Joel A. "Enhancing the Leadership Competency of CAMACOP (Christian and Missionary Alliance Churches of the Philippines) Pastors through the Course on Leadership in Urban Ministry in Ebenezer Bible College and Seminar." Dissertation Asbury Theological Seminary. 2008.

Carpenter, Joel A. "The Christian Scholar in an Age of Global Christianity." Christianity and the Soul of the Church Conference, Baylor University, Waco, TX. 25–27 March 2004.

Cassidy, Michael. "Problems and Possibilities of Fellowship." Cassidy and Verlinden 72–79.

Cassidy, Michael, and Luc Verlinden, eds. *Facing the New Challenges: The Message of PACLA*. Kisumu: Evangel, 1978.

Chalk, Jack. *Making Disciples in Africa: Engaging Syncretism in the African Church through Philosophical Analysis of Worldviews*. Carlisle, UK: Langham, 2013.

Choi, Sanghan. "Democratic Leadership: The Lessons of Exemplary Models for Democratic Governance." *International Journal of Leadership Studies* 2/3 (2007): 243–262.

Clawson, James G. *Level Three Leadership: Getting Below the Surface*. 5th ed. Boston, MA: Prentice, 2012.

Clinton, J. Robert. *Having a Ministry That Lasts: Becoming a Bible Centered Leader*. Altadena, CA: Barnabas, 1997.

Cole, Victor. "Concepts of Pastoral Leadership in Africa: A Case Study." *AJET* 9, no. 2 (1990): 1–12.

———. "Sharing the Opportunity of Ministerial Spiritual Formation." In *Confronting Kingdom Challenges*. Edited by Samuel T. Logan, Jr., 169–196. Wheaton, IL: Crossway, 2007.

Collins, Jim. "Level 5 Leadership: The Triumph of Humility and Fierce Resolve." *HRB's 10 Must Reads*. 115–136.

Creswell, John W. *Educational Research: Planning, Conducting, and Evaluating Quantitative and Qualitative Research*. 4th ed. Boston, MA: Pearson, 2001.

"Denominationalism." *Merriam-Webster Online*. Merriam-Webster, n.d. Accessed 14 February 2014. Web.

Dickson, Roger E. *Biblical Research Library*. Hutchinson: Africa International Missions, 2012.

Dockery, David S., ed. *Christian Leadership Essentials: A Handbook for Managing Christian Organizations*. Nashville, TN: Broadman, 2011.

Dodd, Brian J. *Empowered Church Leadership: Ministry in the Spirit according to Paul*. Downers Grove, IL: InterVarsity, 2003.

Drucker, Peter F. *The Five Most Important Questions You Will Ever Ask about Your Organization*. San Francisco, CA: Jossey-Bass, 2011. Kindle file.

———. "What Makes an Effective Executive?" *HRB's 10 Must Reads*, 23–36.

Foday-Khabenje, Aiah. *The Church of Africa Today: Challenges and Opportunities*. Africa Advocacy Leadership Summit 2014, Compassion International, Addis Ababa. 23–27 February 2015.

Foster, Richard J. *Streams of Living Water*. New York: Harper, 1998.

Foulkes, Francis. *Ephesians: An Introduction and Commentary*. Tyndale New Testament Commentaries. Rev. ed., edited by Leon Morris. Downers Grove, IL: InterVarsity, 2001.

Fuller, W. Harold. *People of the Mandate: The Story of the World Evangelical Fellowship*. Grand Rapids, MI: Baker, 1996.

Gifford, Paul. "Africa's Inculturation Theology: Observations of an Outsider." *Hekima Review* 38 (May 2008): 18–34.

Giltinane, Charlotte Louise. "Leadership Styles and Theories." *Nursing Standard* 27, no. 41 (2013): 35–39. Accessed 11 April 2013. Web.

Githiga, Gideon. *The Church as the Bulwark against Authoritarianism: Development of Church-State Relations in Kenya, with Particular Reference to the Years after Political Independence 1963–1992*. Oxford, UK: Regnum, 2001.

Goleman, Daniel. "What Makes a Leader?" *HRB's 10 Must Reads*, 1–21.

Granberg-Michaelson, Wesley. "Foreword." In *Revisioning Christian Unity: Journeying with Jesus Christ, the Reconciler*. The Global Christian Forum. Edited by Huibert van Beek. Oxford, UK: Regnum, 2009. vii–ix.

———. *From Times Square to Timbuktu: The Post-Christian West Meets the Non-Western Church*. Grand Rapids, MI: Eerdmans, 2013.

Greenleaf, Robert. "Servant Leadership." In *The Leader's Companion: Insight on Leadership through the Ages*. Edited by Thomas J. Wren, 454–555. New York: Free Press, 1995. Kindle file.

Guder, Darrell L., ed. *Missional Church: A Vision for the Sending of the Church in North America*. The Gospel and Our Culture Series. Grand Rapids, MI: Eerdmans, 1998.

Haruna, Peter Fuseini. "Revising the Leadership Paradigm in Sub-Saharan Africa." *A Study of Community-Based Leadership, Public Administration Review* (Sept/Oct 2009): 940–950.

Healthy Alliances: WEA International Leadership Meeting Documents. Nairobi: WEA, 2007.

Hendrix, Olan. *Management That Leads*. Leadership Resource Group, Inc. Columbus, n.d. 1–2.

Houston, Paul D., and Stephen L. Sokolow. *The Spiritual Dimension of Leadership: 8 Key Principles to Leading More Effectively*. Thousand Oaks, CA: Corwin, 2006.

HRB's 10 Must Reads: On Leadership. Boston, MA: Harvard Business School, 2011.

Hughes, Richard L., Robert C. Ginnett, and Gordon J. Curphy. *Leadership: Enhancing the Lessons of Experience*. Boston, MA: McGraw, 2012.

Hyatt, L., and Peter E. Williams. "21st Century Competencies for Doctoral Leadership Faculty." *Innovative Higher Education* 36, no. 1 (Feb 2011): 53–66.

Link.springer.com. Link Springer, 2011. Accessed 30 July 2010. Web.

"Introduction." *Worldea.org*. World Evangelical Alliance, n.d. Accessed 19 August 2013. Web.

Janneh, Abdoulie. *Statement by Under-Secretary General and Executive Secretary, United Nations Economic Commission for Africa, 45th Session the Commission on Population and Development*. United Nations, New York. 23–27 April 2012.

Karlström, Mikael. "On the Aesthetics and Dialogics of Power in the Postcolony." *Journal of the International African Institute* 73, no. 1 (2003): 57–76.

Kamaleson, Samuel. "Discovering Our Gifts and Mutual Interdependence in the Body of Christ." Cassidy and Verlinden 84–91.

Kato, Byang H. "Biblical Christianity in Africa." In *Theological Task of the Church in Africa*. Edited by Tite Tienou, 11–49. Achimota, Ghana: Africa Christian Press, 1985.

———. *Theological Pitfalls in Africa*. Kisumu, Kenya: Evangel, 1975.

Kim, Sang Bok David, Yung Han Kim, and Richard Howell. "The Triune God: Creation, Church and Consummation." *Asiaevangelicals.org*. Asia Evangelical Association, 30 August 2013. Accessed 18 April 2015. Web.

Kollman, Paul. "Classifying African Christianities: Past, Present, and Future: Part One." *Journal of Religion in Africa* 40 (2010): 3–32.

Kosse, Kuzuli. "Unity of Believers." *Africa Bible Commentary*. Edited by Tokunboh Adeyemo, 1314. Nairobi: World Alive, 2006.

Kotter, John P. "What Leaders Really Do." *HRB's 10 Must Reads* 37–55.

The Lausanne Movement, *The Cape Town Commitment*. Parow, RSA: AcadSA, 2011.

Lowell, Stanley C. *The Ecumenical Mirage*. Grand Rapids, MI: Baker, 1969.

Maxwell, John C. *Twenty-One Irrefutable Laws of Leadership*. Nashville, TN: Nelson, 1998.

Mbiti, John S. *African Religions and Philosophy*. Nairobi: Heinemann, 1989.

Meyer, Birgit. "Christianity in Africa: From African Independent to Pentecostal-Charismatic Churches." *Annual Review of Anthropology* 33 (2004): 447–474.

Miller, Larry, and Olav F. Tveit. *GCF Committee Meeting, 9–11 September 2014: Document 9.1.1—WCC and GCF Memorandum*. Geneva: GCF, 2013.

Moore, Lori L. "Leadership in the Cooperative Extension System: An Examination of Leadership Styles and Skills of State Directors and Administrators." Dissertation University of Florida, 2003.

Mugambi, J. N. K. "Religions in East Africa in the Context of Globalization." In *Religions in Eastern Africa under Globalization.* Edited by J. N. K. Mugambi and Mary Getui, 3–28. Nairobi, Kenya: Acton, 2004.

Mwaniki, Lydia. "Ethnicity and the December 2007 Post-Election Violence in Kenya: A Postcolonial Examination and Theological Response." In *Our Burning Issues: A Pan African Response.* Edited by Edison M. Kalengyyo, James N. Amanze, and Isaac Deji Ayegboyin, 185–201. Limuru: Zapf Chancery, 2013.

Ngewa, Samuel. "What Is the Church?" *Africa Bible Commentary.* Edited by Tokunboh Adeyemo, 1457. Nairobi, Kenya: World Alive, 2006.

Northouse, Peter G. *Leadership: Theory and Practice.* 5th ed. Thousand Oaks, CA: Sage, 2010.

Oden, Thomas C. *The Living God.* Systematic Theology Vol 1. Norfolk, VA: Prince, 2001.

Okesson, Gregg A. "Are Pastors Human? Sociological and Theological Reflections on Ministerial Identity in Contemporary Africa." *African Journal of Evangelical Theology* 27, no. 2 (2008): 109–135.

———. *Re-Imaging Modernity: A Contextualized Theological Study of Power and Humanity within Akamba Christianity in Kenya.* American Society of Missiology Monograph Series no. 16. Eugene, OR: Pickwick, 2012.

———. "Sacred and Secular Currents for Theological Education in Africa." *Africa Journal of Evangelical Theology* 26, no. 1 (2007): 39–64.

Okullu, Henry. "The African Context and Its Issues." Cassidy and Verlinden 30–33.

"Organization." *Businessdictionary.com.* Business Dictionary.com, n.d. Accessed 10 February 2014. Web.

Osei-Mensah, Gottfried. "Why PACLA." Cassidy and Verlinden 19–23.

Palau, Luis. "Foreword." *People of the Mandate: The Story of the World Evangelical Fellowship.* By W. Harold Fuller. Grand Rapids, MI: Baker, 1996. xi-xiii.

Patterson, Paige, ed. "Baptists and Unity." *Southwestern Journal of Theology* 51 (Fall 2008): 1–5.

Pearson, John W. *Association Leadership Training Module: 9 Competencies for Building and Sustaining Your National Evangelical Alliance.* San Clemente, CA: Pearson, 2010.

———. *Mastering the Management Buckets: 20 Critical Competencies for Leading Your Business or Non-Profit.* Ventura, CA: Regal, 2008.

Pernick, R. "Creating a Leadership Development Program: Nine Essential Tasks." *Public Personnel Management* 30, no. 4 (2001): 429–444.

Plante, Thomas G., and Marcus T. Boccaccini. "A Proposed Psychological Assessment Protocol for Applicants to Religious Life in the Roman Catholic Church." *Pastoral Pschology Journal* 46, no. 5 (1998): 363–372.

"Proficiency." *Merriam-webster.com*. Merriam-Webster, n.d. Accessed 14 February 2014. Web.

Rowland-Jones, Sarah. "The Global Christian Forum – A Narrative History." In *Revisioning Christian Unity: The Global Christian Forum*. Edited by Huibert van Beek, 3–36. Oxford: Regum, 2009.

Rynkiewich, Michael. *Soul, Self, and Society: A Postmodern Anthropology for Mission in a Postcolonial World*. Eugene, OR: Cascade, 2011.

Scarborough, Lee Rutland. "What We Have to Expect from Our Seminaries: Editorial in Watchman-Examiner." *Southwestern Journal of Theology: Baptist Unity* 51, no. 1 (Fall 2008): 6–22.

Seamands, Stephen. *Ministry in the Image of God: The Trinitarian Shape of Christian Service*. Downers Grove, IL: InterVarsity, 2005.

Seidman, I. E. *Interviewing as Qualitative Research: A Guide for Researchers in Education and the Social Sciences*. New York: Teachers College Press, 1991.

Sensing, Tim. *Qualitative Research: A Multi-Methods Approach to Projects for Doctor of Ministry Theses*. Eugene, OR: Wipf and Stock, 2011.

"Separatism." *Merriam-Webster online*. Merriam-Webster, n.d. Accessed 14 February 2014. Web.

Showell-Rogers, Gordon. "Towards a Healthy Regional Alliance." *Working Paper for Meeting of the World Evangelical Alliance International Leadership Forum*, Vancouver. WEA. 1–4. 2012.

Stevens, J. Paul. *The Other Six Days: Vocation, Work and Ministry in Biblical Perspective*. Grand Rapids, MI: Eerdmans, 1999.

Stott, John. *Basic Christian Leadership: Biblical Models of Church, Gospel and Ministry*. Downers Grove: InterVarsity, 2002.

Tanner, Norman. "The African Church and the First Five Ecumenical Councils." *African Ecclesial Review* 33, no. 2–3 (1991): 201–213.

"Task." *Merriam-Webster online*. Merriam-Webster, n.d. Accessed 20 October 2014. Web.

Tennent, Timothy. *Theology in the Context of World Christianity*. Grand Rapids, MI: Zondervan, 2007.

Traub, M. "Community: Its Meaning and Expression in Africa Today." Cassidy and Verlinden, 103–109.

"WEA Welcomes Dr. Joel Hunter to the North American Council." *Worldea.org*. World Evangelical Association, 26 May 2006. Accessed 18 April 2015. Web.

Tunnicliffe, Geoff. "WEA International Director Report for International Council." Nairobi, November 2007.

Turaki, Yusufu. "Ephesians." *Africa Bible Commentary*. Edited by Tokunboh Adeyemo. Nairobi: WorldAlive, 2006. 1425–1438.

van Beek, Huibert. *Revisioning Christian Unity: The Global Christian Forum*. Oxford: Regnum, 2009.

Wallace, Jim. "Imam Omar Kobine Layama, Archbishop Dieudonné Nzapalainga and the Rev. Nicolas Guérékoyame-Gbangou." *Time*. Time Magazine, 23 April 2014. Accessed 26 November 2014. Web.

Warren, Rick. *The Purpose Driven Church*. Grand Rapids, MI: Zondervan, 1995.

"WEALI." *Worldea.org*. World Evangelical Alliance, n.d. Accessed 21 September 2013. Web.

Williamson, Christine, Gary Colvin, and Amy McDonald. *Human Resource Management*. Edited by Rachel Blackman. ROOTS Resources. Teddington: Tearfund, 2008.

Wright, Christopher. *The Mission of God: Unlocking the Bible's Grand Narrative*. Downers Grove, IL: InterVarsity, 2006.

Zizioulas, John D. *Being as Communion: Studies in Personhood and the Church*. Crestwood, NY: St. Vladimir's, 2002.

Langham Literature and its imprints are a ministry of Langham Partnership.

Langham Partnership is a global fellowship working in pursuit of the vision God entrusted to its founder John Stott –

> *to facilitate the growth of the church in maturity and Christ-likeness through raising the standards of biblical preaching and teaching.*

Our vision is to see churches in the majority world equipped for mission and growing to maturity in Christ through the ministry of pastors and leaders who believe, teach and live by the Word of God.

Our mission is to strengthen the ministry of the Word of God through:
- nurturing national movements for biblical preaching
- fostering the creation and distribution of evangelical literature
- enhancing evangelical theological education

especially in countries where churches are under-resourced.

Our ministry

Langham Preaching partners with national leaders to nurture indigenous biblical preaching movements for pastors and lay preachers all around the world. With the support of a team of trainers from many countries, a multi-level programme of seminars provides practical training, and is followed by a programme for training local facilitators. Local preachers' groups and national and regional networks ensure continuity and ongoing development, seeking to build vigorous movements committed to Bible exposition.

Langham Literature provides majority world preachers, scholars and seminary libraries with evangelical books and electronic resources through publishing and distribution, grants and discounts. The programme also fosters the creation of indigenous evangelical books in many languages, through writer's grants, strengthening local evangelical publishing houses, and investment in major regional literature projects, such as one volume Bible commentaries like *The Africa Bible Commentary* and *The South Asia Bible Commentary*.

Langham Scholars provides financial support for evangelical doctoral students from the majority world so that, when they return home, they may train pastors and other Christian leaders with sound, biblical and theological teaching. This programme equips those who equip others. Langham Scholars also works in partnership with majority world seminaries in strengthening evangelical theological education. A growing number of Langham Scholars study in high quality doctoral programmes in the majority world itself. As well as teaching the next generation of pastors, graduated Langham Scholars exercise significant influence through their writing and leadership.

To learn more about Langham Partnership and the work we do visit **langham.org**

www.ingramcontent.com/pod-product-compliance
Lightning Source LLC
Chambersburg PA
CBHW051539230426
43669CB00015B/2652

I am delighted to recommend this important book! While many good books on leadership exist, there is almost nothing dealing with leadership of associations. With keen insight, compelling research, and lucid writing, the author tills new ground. Not only will this book help establish a new research into associational leadership, but its contextual importance for Africa is as compelling as it is insightful. This is a critical read for anyone involved in leadership within associations, or who wants to probe deeper into leadership and power within the African context!

Gregg A. Okesson, PhD
Dean, E. Stanley Jones School of World Mission and Evangelism,
Professor of Leadership and Development,
Asbury Theological Seminary, Kentucky, USA

In a world of selfish ambition, in which materialism, tribalism and corruption have, sadly, also been all-too-visible among church leaders, this research project has revealed some very encouraging insights into the leadership attributes most valued by church associations in Africa. In a world desperate for "strong" leaders, Foday-Khabenje's research reveals surprising, but very biblical, African definitions of the strengths most needed in Africa and, arguably, globally. Foday-Khabenje's leadership of both a national Evangelical Alliance and the Association of Evangelicals in Africa uniquely qualifies him for this work.

But my own conviction is that the competencies valued by leaders of Evangelical Alliances in Africa are so thoroughly biblical that, with a little thought, they are transferable to any organization of any kind anywhere in the world. I warmly endorse this very helpful book.

Gordon Showell-Rogers
Former Associate Secretary General, World Evangelical Alliance

Foday-Khabenje has a strong passion for evangelical ecumenicity and the place of national evangelical alliances in the mission of the church, in making disciples for Christ in the nations. His emphasis on sound biblical foundation and leadership development in the national alliances in Africa is also demonstrated in his academic endeavours. With an entrepreneurial approach to his doctoral research, he contributes an important legacy for leading national evangelical fellowships, not only for the constituents of the Association of Evangelicals in Africa but also for the global church. The competencies identified for leading evangelical associations will be of value to all leadership. This work is heartily recommended for all in the business of leadership development in Africa.

Rev Mario Li Hing, PhD
Regional President for the Indian Ocean Islands
Movement for African National Initiatives
Chairman of the Executive Board, Association of Evangelicals in Africa

Competencies for Leading in Diversity is a masterpiece in the area of organizational leadership, especially church-related organizations. This piece of work is critical in understanding the difference between the competencies required by pastors who lead congregations and competencies required for Christian leaders who lead organizations. Rev Foday-Khabenje carefully draws the line between the competencies of a pastor whose role requires contact with people from all walks of life, and the role of a Christian organization leader who along with the characteristics of a pastor, has the role of presentation of the voice and image of the church to the society, which requires additional competencies above those of a pastor. I highly recommend this work for people interested in understanding organizational leadership competencies.

Sammy Linge, PhD
Director, Africa Leadership and Reconciliation Ministries (ALARM), Kenya